WORLD PREHISTORY

A NEW OUTLINE

Ivory carving of the head of an Advanced Palaeolithic
woman from Brassempouy, France

WORLD PREHISTORY

A NEW OUTLINE

BEING THE SECOND EDITION OF 'WORLD PREHISTORY'

BY

GRAHAME CLARK

*Fellow of Peterhouse and Disney Professor of Archaeology
in the University of Cambridge*

CAMBRIDGE
AT THE UNIVERSITY PRESS
1969

Published by the Syndics of the Cambridge University Press
Bentley House, 200 Euston Road, London N.W.1
American Branch: 32 East 57th Street, New York, N.Y. 10022

Library of Congress Catalogue Card Number: 69–19374
Standard Book Numbers:
521 07334 0 clothbound
521 09564 6 paperback

First edition 1961
Reprinted 1962 (twice) 1965
Second edition 1969
Reprinted 1969

Printed in Great Britain
at the University Printing House, Cambridge
(Brooke Crutchley, University Printer)

IN MEMORIAM

V. G. CHILDE
O. G. S. CRAWFORD

CONTENTS

vii

CONTENTS

CONTENTS

PLATES

MAPS

PREFACE

It was only possible in the course of the four reprintings of the original edition of this book to insert minor changes and corrections. In preparing this new edition I have taken the opportunity to effect a radical overhaul, taking account of the progress of archaeological publication and of my own opportunities for travel and reflection during the period since 1961. Although the same basic plan has been preserved, the result, apart from the two chapters concerned with Europe, is virtually a new book.

A new Introduction has been written and the Retrospect scrapped. Chapters 1–3 cover much the same ground as previously but have been rewritten. A new chapter 4 has been inserted to take account of radical advances in our understanding of the transition from hunting and gathering to settled husbandry. Chapter 5, which covers much of the ground previously dealt with in chapter 4, has been substantially rewritten. For the present edition chapters 6 and 7 have been left mainly unchanged. Chapter 8, concerned with the later prehistory of Africa and the rise of Dynastic Egypt, has been substantially revised and rewritten and moved forward in the book to accord with the radiocarbon evidence for the priority of husbandry in south-east Europe. The old chapter 8 has been replaced by two chapters (9 and 10) devoted respectively to India and the Far East. The chapters on Australia and the Pacific (11) and the New World (12) have been substantially revised and rewritten and reversed in sequence to accord with the findings of radiocarbon chronology. Room has also been found for a number of new maps and half-tone plates, as well as for a revised and enlarged list of works for further reading.

In a work which ranges over the whole world, chronology plays a vital part and full advantage has been taken of the very greatly increased volume of radiocarbon determinations that has been made available since my first edition. In view of the use I have made of these a few comments are in order. The first point I would make is that no great reliance can be placed on individual determinations: the potential sources of error due to contamination, faulty collection, mistakes in labelling and defective processing are in themselves enough to induce caution; and the random factor inherent in radiocarbon analysis has implications that are not always given adequate weight. It is not individual dates but the general pattern that emerges from a number of these that counts. For this reason lists of key determinations are appended to chapters 2–4, 6 and 8–12. Each determination is quoted with its laboratory reference number, so that full details can be looked up in the series of *Radiocarbon Supplements* and other publications listed under Further Reading (p. 303).

The second point I would make is that, until the effect of variations in the intensity of the earth's magnetic field has been determined sufficiently accurately to allow of definitive correction of radiocarbon dates, it is best to regard these as relative rather than as absolute in years. Where radiocarbon dates are quoted they are quoted as radiocarbon and not as exact dates in solar years.

Thirdly, and following on this, it seems important to quote all radiocarbon dates in common terms. I have quoted all dates in terms of the Christian era and I have followed the recommendations of the Cambridge Conference and the practice of *Radiocarbon* in basing these on the half-life of 5568 ± 30 years.

Once again I would like to acknowledge the interest and care bestowed by the staff of the University Press.

GRAHAME CLARK

Peterhouse, Cambridge
30 December 1967

INTRODUCTION

The days are long past when prehistory—or for that matter history itself—could any longer be equated with the experience of European nations at home or overseas or with their immediate predecessors. As I shall try to emphasize in this book, Western civilization as we know it is only one of many adventures in literate communal life, each one of which stems comparatively recently from a prehistoric experience of immense antiquity. This by no means lessens the importance of Western civilization, but rather enhances it. It has after all been one of the glories of Europe to have developed the industrial processes that have transformed the way of life of all civilizations and most cultures and so to have speeded up communications as to create an entity of the whole world. Even more to the point has been the European contribution to the conceptual framework of mankind. Speculative philosophy, the formulation of theoretical laws governing the universe which we call natural science and the concept of history by which man has broken free from the limitations of present time, all these are fields to which other civilizations and indeed primitive man himself have in some measure contributed; they are nevertheless ones in which the European contribution has from the time of the Classical Greeks been outstanding.

During the last hundred years the world at large has come of age. It is not merely that the lead in science and its applications in technology have come to be shared and in some fields appropriated by what were once the North American and Russian outposts of Western society: of still greater portent for the future are the achievements of the heirs of ancient civilizations left temporarily behind by the course of historical change; and, looking still further ahead, those of peoples until very recently prehistoric. Wide recognition has for example been accorded to the achievements of the Japanese and Chinese in many 'Western' fields of accomplishment ranging from nuclear physics to the production of optical apparatus, motor-cars and super-rapid rail transport and the successful pursuit of prehistoric archaeology. Again, granted the immense difficulties they encountered on achieving independence, the achievements of many of the new African countries are hardly less remarkable: several of the States forming the United Nations comprise peoples who were still prehistoric when first colonized by Europeans.

The widely varying degrees of cultural attainment presented by the peoples of the world to an observer in London or Paris only a hundred years ago must have appeared to many at the time as in some sense an inevitable outcome of the process of evolution. In his *Prehistoric Times* first published in 1865 Sir John Lubbock argued that peoples of simpler culture were backward in relation to the civilization prevailing in western Europe at the height of the Victorian era because they represented survivals from more primitive stages of social evolution. He explicitly pursued the analogy with palaeontology. 'Many mammalia [he wrote] which are extinct in Europe have representatives still living in other countries. Much light is thrown on our fossil pachyderms, for instance, by the species which still inhabit some parts of Asia and Africa; the secondary marsupials are illustrated by their existing representatives in Australia and South America; and in the same manner, if we wish clearly to understand the antiquities of Europe, we must compare them with the rude implements and weapons still, or until lately, used by the savage races in other parts of the world. In fact, the Van Diemaner and South American are to the antiquary what the opossum and the sloth are to the geologist.'

Some forty years later this point of view was expressed still more dogmatically by General Pitt-Rivers at a time when professional anthropologists had already begun to recognize as a result of intensive field-work the unique value and integrity of the culture of even the most primitive peoples surviving in the modern world. As lately as 1906 Pitt-Rivers could declare that 'the existing races, in their respective stages of progression, may be taken as the *bona fide* representatives of the races of antiquity...They thus afford us living illustrations of the social customs...which belong to the ancient races from which they remotely sprang.' Although there is no reason for thinking that Pitt-Rivers was using the term 'race' in this context in its strict biological connotation, there is no doubt that in popular estimation material backwardness has been linked with the possession of physical characteristics like skin colour or hair form distinct from those of the civilized peoples of western Europe. If this point of view is still expressed today it is recognized as a mere pretext for racial privilege. Archaeology has made it plain for those whose eyes are not obscured by prejudice that differences in cultural attainment are the product not of biology but of history.

Prehistory is not merely something that human beings passed through a long time ago: it is something which properly apprehended allows us to view our contemporary situation in a perspective more valid than that encouraged by the study of our own parochial histories. From the perspective of the last few million years all men, whatever their level of literary or technical accomplishment, are on much the same level. Categories like savage, barbarian or civilized, so beloved of our Victorian forebears, pale into insignificance in relation to the potential difference between men and any other kind of animal. The process of hominization, the attainment of humanity, are immensely older and more fundamental than the practice of husbandry or the ability to read or write. To be surprised that men can emerge in a few generations from prehistory on to the stage of world history is to be unaware of what prehistory means. The capacity of the cultural apparatus to absorb, combine and transmit experiences and values and the growing efficiency of modern means of communication are among the most promising omens for the future.

3

The possibility of reviewing and appreciating the achievements of the human race and not merely of those peoples able to transmit their histories in writing is something made possible by archaeology and modern science. In such a volume as this no more can be offered than an outline of what has already been discovered. Vast areas remain untouched, many problems remain unsolved and much work remains to be done in the field and in the laboratory before prehistorians can relax by the fireside.

CHAPTER I

MAN'S PLACE IN NATURE

A major paradox to be faced when we consider our own origins is that man, who through the power of his mind and imagination has come near to complete mastery over the forces of external nature as they confront him on this planet, and who is even now engaged in extending his dominion into outer space, is himself an animal. He forms part of the nexus of living things and individually is subject to the same processes of growth, maturity and death. Like other animals he lives within the framework of a physical environment. If therefore we are to understand the material traces of his culture, the apparatus developed by man to a unique degree, it is essential to take account of the evolution of his geographical setting, the setting to which human societies adjust by means of their traditional culture. Equally man owes his ability to acquire and develop his culture, by means of which he has achieved biological dominance, in the first instance to the physical and mental endowment acquired in the course of biological evolution; it is therefore no less vital to consider, however briefly, the zoological context of the hominids and the emergence of the several forms leading up to the species to which we belong.

THE EVOLUTION OF MAN

Although for a thorough-going evolutionist there can be no logical point at which to begin human prehistory, this book will in fact be limited to chronicling the achievements of a particular group of primates, namely the hominids. Yet before we consider in briefest outline the zoological context of the hominids within the Primate Order, it is worth reflecting on what Charles Darwin and his forerunners and successors have demonstrated in scientific terms and for that matter on what primitive man has always known and some of the higher religions have explicitly taught, namely that human beings are only part, albeit the most conscious part of the web of life. It is not merely that all varieties of men can be classified and incorporated within an all-embracing zoological system. Still more important is the fact that human behaviour is only a particular form of animal behaviour and can only fully be understood as such.

The Primates

Of the two sub-orders, into which the Primates are conventionally divided, we may confine ourselves to the appropriately named *Anthropoidea*, leaving on one side for inspection in the zoo our exceedingly remote relatives the miniature and engaging *Prosimii*. Similarly, we are entitled to pass by the cages containing the super-families of monkeys (*Ceboidea* and *Cercopithecoides*) and concentrate on that labelled *Hominoidea*, comprehending apes (*Pongidae*) and hominids (*Hominidae*).

The physical similarities between men and anthropoid apes have long been realized. They are indeed so close as to leave no reasonable doubt about their near affinity in the classification of zoological forms. Similarities appear whether one considers the general structure of the skeleton, the muscular anatomy or the disposition of the visceral organs, the evidence of serological reactions and metabolic processes, or even the structure of the brain itself. Even so, no zoologist would have difficulty in distinguishing parts of the skeleton of man or ape and not even the layman can remain unimpressed by significant differences in dentition and limb-proportions or by the notably larger size of the brain in relation to body-weight on the part of man. This makes it easy to understand that, to judge from the still desperately incomplete palaeontological record, the hominids appear to have diverged from the apes extremely far back, perhaps as long as fifteen, twenty or even more million years ago.

From an evolutionary point of view one of the most significant steps in the emergence of the hominids seems to have been the assumption of an erect posture. It was this which released the hands from locomotion, making them available for tool-making and the securing and preparation of food, and in due time allowing the head to be balanced on top of the spinal column rather than suspended by heavy muscular attachments from its upper extremity. No doubt also the growing facility of the forelimbs relieved the teeth of many functions and helped to bring about characteristic changes in dentition. At the same time the reduction in the size and role of the teeth and of the musculature needed to support the head affected the architecture of the skull, among other things reducing the need for strong brow-ridges. Although it was by means of his brain that man was to rise to biological dominance, it seems that our remote hominid ancestors had begun to stand upright before their brains had notably exceeded in volume those of the great apes. A likely explanation of the divergence of the hominids is that they adopted an upright posture to meet the conditions met with in open country, whereas the great apes remained more closely linked with forests in which they specialized to a brachiating way of moving, that is one in which they relied to a considerable extent on the use of their arms.

The Australopithecines

The Australopithecines, one of the two genera into which the hominids are now generally divided, owe a major part of their interest precisely to the fact that although their brains hardly exceeded in absolute capacity those of the great apes they nevertheless held themselves upright and walked on two legs. The great majority of the fossils belonging to this genus have been found in East or South Africa and a number of these come from deposits of Lower Pleistocene age. At the present time only one has come from south-east Asia, the so-called *Palaeojavanensis* (cf. *Meganthropus*) from the Djetis beds at Sangiran in Java, and it may be

7

significant that these deposits are now generally dated to an early phase of the Middle Pleistocene. On the face of it this argues for the predominating importance of Africa as the scene of early hominid evolution, but it has to be remembered that, especially during recent years, far more research has been devoted to certain parts of this continent than to south-east Asia and in particular to Indonesia.

Turning now to the morphology of the Australopithecines, the most striking fact about them, apart from their small size, indications of upright posture and small brains, is the number of detailed features which they share with other hominids. Among others may be noted the height of the skull above the orbits, the contour of the forehead and upper facial area and the conformation of the mastoid process. Their dentition also shows a number of points of agreement. The teeth are relatively small and arranged in the form of an evenly curved parabolic arcade, the canines are spatulate and there are no diastemic gaps on either side. Although the Australopithecines share these characteristics they do so in varying degrees. During the early phase of discovery some investigators were a little too free in bestowing distinctive names on their fossils. For present purposes and pending the discovery and description of a much larger and more complete volume of material it will be enough to mention three or four distinctive groups. From Lower Pleistocene deposits there are two main species: from the South African localities of Makapan, Sterkfontein and Taungs we have the relatively small-toothed *Australopithecus africanus;* and from an early lacustrine deposit at Olduvai in Tanzania the remains of *A. boisei* (formerly *Zinjanthropus*). Middle Pleistocene beds at Kromdraai and Swartkrans in South Africa have yielded a third species *A. robustus* (formerly *Paranthropus*).

Another hominid discovery that deserves mention at this point is comprised by fragments obtained from bed I in the Olduvai sequence belonging to a form having smaller teeth and a larger

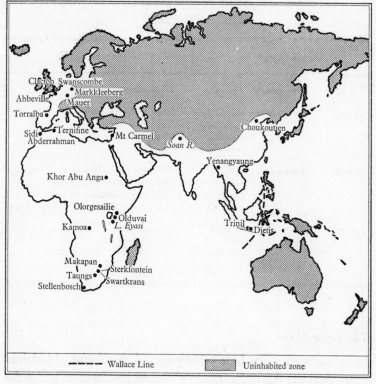

Clacton Swanscombe
Abbeville · Markkleeberg
Torralba · Mauer
Sidi · Ternifine
Abderrahman · Mt Carmel
Choukoutien
Soan R.
Yenangyaung
Khor Abu Anga ·
Olorgesailie
Olduvai
Kamoa · L. Eyasi
Trinil · Djetis
Makapan
Taungs · Sterkfontein
Stellenbosch · Swartkrans

– – – – Wallace Line   //// Uninhabited zone

1. The prehistoric world to the end of the Middle Pleistocene

brain than any Australopithecine yet known to us. Some palaeontologists prefer nevertheless to classify the fossils as belonging to an extreme form of the species *A. africanus*. Others have argued for recognizing it as belonging to a new species and one to be classified as a man under the designation *Homo habilis*, a being not only larger-brained than an Australopithecine, but provided with hands capable of exerting a power grip of the kind needed for shaping effective pebble tools. The mere fact of this divergence of view only serves to emphasize the close relationship existing between the two genera, *Australopithecus* and *Homo*.

Present and former designation of the main groups of fossil hominids

	Modern designation		Former designation
Pleistocene	*Homo sapiens*	*sapiens*	*Homo sapiens*
Upper	*Homo sapiens*	*neanderthalensis* *rhodesiensis* *soloensis* *steinheimensis*	*Homo neanderthalensis* *Homo rhodesiensis* *Homo soloensis*
Middle	*Homo erectus*	*africanus* *heidelbergensis* *javanensis* *pekinensis*	*Pithecanthropus africanus* or *Atlanthropus* *Pithecanthropus heidelbergensis* *Pithecanthropus erectus* or *javanensis* *Pithecanthropus pekinensis* or *Sinanthropus*
Lower	*Australopithecus*	*robustus* *boisei* *africanus*	*Paranthropus* *Zinjanthropus*
	Homo habilis?		

The genus Homo

In recent years it has been widely agreed that forms of hominid other than the Australopithecines should be classified under the single genus *Homo*. This means that the numerous fossils from localities in Africa, Europe, North China and Indonesia formerly grouped within the genus '*Pithecanthropus*' or even accorded separate generic status have now been transferred to form a new species of man, *Homo erectus*. Another concept to be discarded is that Neanderthal and other more or less closely related forms showing characteristics that mark them off from the living races of men qualify as a distinct species. The modern view is rather that they form sub-specific varieties of *Homo sapiens*, such as *Homo sapiens neanderthalensis* or *soloensis*, and that modern man *Homo sapiens sapiens* is merely the sub-species that happens to have been living during the last thirty thousand years or so.

Homo erectus

Since fossils of what was then known as *Pithecanthropus erectus* were first found in the Trinil beds in Java, the island has yielded further specimens and there can be no doubt that the species was living there during the Middle Pleistocene. The largest assemblage of fossils is undoubtedly that from Middle Pleistocene beds filling the rock-fissures at Choukoutien near Pekin, a discovery all the more important because traces of fire, together with stone implements and utilized animal bones came from the same deposits. More recently traces of the same species (needlessly termed *Atlanthropus mauritanicus*) have come to light in Pleistocene deposits exposed in a sand-pit at Ternifine near Palikao, Algeria. The northern margin of the range is completed by the old find of a mandible from Mauer near Heidelberg, also of Middle Pleistocene age. Morphologically these fossils show as a group a notable increase in the size of the brain: the mean of three crania from Java gave a capacity of 860 cubic centimetres and that of four from Choukoutien 1075 cubic centimetres, placing the group more or less intermediate between *Australopithecus* and *Homo sapiens*. On the other hand they show a number of characteristics that mark them off decisively from *Homo sapiens*. Thus the skull (A.I) has a low vault and frontal flattening, a marked ridge at the junction of the two main side bones, and thick walls; the mastoid process is smaller; the palate is enormous and there is marked alveolar prognathism, the lower part of the face projecting noticeably; the mandible is massive and, in the case of the Java fossils, the teeth, though human in general arrangement, show tendencies for the upper canines to overlap the lower ones and for a diastemic gap to appear between the incisors and canines; and the weight of the mandible is matched by a correspondingly massive development of the supra-orbital and occipital brow-ridges, which, together with the flattened forehead, would probably strike us most forcibly were we to meet an individual in the flesh.

Homo sapiens

Homo sapiens can be presumed to have developed from the old *Homo erectus* stock. One of the few fossils of *Homo sapiens* type known for certain to date from the Middle Pleistocene is the incomplete cranium from Swanscombe in the Lower Thames basin. It is particularly unfortunate that the frontal part is absent, but since the surviving portion agrees more or less closely with a more complete cranium from Steinheim dating from an inter-stadial of the Riss glaciation, it is on the whole likely that it shared the massive brow-ridges of the German fossil, a feature that usually goes with large teeth and heavy jaws.

Much the most numerous fossils belonging to this stage in human evolution are those named after the original discovery at Neanderthal in the Rhineland. It is important, if a false impression is not to be formed of the characteristics of this group, that it should be realized that the descriptions found in the early litera-ture are based on what now appears to be an aberrant form, that represented by the early French finds at La Ferrassie and La Chapelle-aux-Saints. This classic west European form, which dates from the first onset of the Würm glaciation, is now com-monly regarded as a genetic variation in a territory marginal to and to some extent isolated by ice-sheets; and, indeed, in indivi-dual cases pathological deformation has to be taken into account. The leading features of this form of the Neanderthal sub-species include, as is well known, a short stocky build, a flat-vaulted head with pronounced brow-ridges set rather forward on the vertical column, and massive chinless jaws set with large teeth. The Neanderthaloid fossils from more remote territories like those from North Africa, the Levant, Iraq and Uzbekistan and those from such European localities as Ehringsdorf in Germany and Saccopastore in Italy that date from the interglacial preceding the Würm glaciation share these characteristics but to a less pro-nounced degree.

Although they show a clear continuity of development from the preceding stage, this whole early *sapiens* group, including the aberrant Westerners, exhibit an outstanding advance in respect of size of brain; the cranial capacity of the Neanderthalers was well up to that of the average for modern man. There can hardly be any question, if we leave aside the aberrant form, that this group of fossils marks a significant stage in human evolution. A point which will no doubt be further underlined as discovery proceeds is that this evolution was not by any means confined to Europe or contiguous parts of Africa and Asia. The occurrence of analogous forms as far afield as Broken Hill in Rhodesia and Ngandong on the River Solo in Java has already made this plain.

Homo sapiens sapiens

Men of modern type must have emerged from the *sapiens* stock just described, though hardly from the aberrant Chapelle-aux-Saints form. There is no need to assume that this development took place at any particular locality within the wide range occupied by the Neanderthaloids. What can be said is that the earliest men of *Homo sapiens sapiens* type appeared in the context of Advanced Palaeolithic culture, which itself occupied a territory extending from western Europe along either side of the Mediterranean to the Iranian plateau. In general the Cromagnon type, to use the name of a well-known find from an Advanced Palaeolithic context in the Dordogne, was characterized by a relatively slight build, and a fully upright posture; the skull lacked signs of strong muscular attachments; the forehead was steep and well-rounded; brow-ridges were only developed to a moderate degree and were never continuous; the teeth were relatively small; and the chin prominent. According to the overwhelming consensus of professional opinion the existing races of men belong to this same species that first emerged probably around forty thousand years ago.

The modern races of man

When and where did the various races of man diverge? The first question is particularly difficult to answer, because so many of the leading criteria by which racial differences are distinguished, such as pigmentation and hair form, are such as can hardly be studied from skeletal material. Attempts have been made to read racial characteristics into some Advanced Palaeolithic remains—for instance the type first recognized from the Grimaldi Caves near Mentone has been variously interpreted as Negroid or primitive Mediterranean and that from the rock-shelter of Chancelade in the Dordogne has even been held to be Eskimo in type—but the dangers of drawing conclusions from such limited evidence are obviously very great and it is wisest to admit that we do not yet know when the races of *Homo sapiens sapiens* came into being. What seems most likely is that they arose as a result of gradual genetic diversification following on the widespread migrations and colonization of new territories that occurred some time during the final major glacial cycle. The degree to which the distribution of certain well-defined pigmentation types fits in with that of specific environments, after due allowance is made for the effect of migration since the period of characterization, is sufficiently close to suggest that differences of pigmentation must have been to some degree adaptive: thus in the Old World blonde fair-skinned people tend to go with a cool, cloudy habitat; brunettes with the strong sunlight and bright skies of climates like that of the Mediterranean area; the darkest skinned with the hottest, non-forested regions (for example, the savannah of Africa); and those with yellowish skin and crinkly hair with the tropical rain-forests of Africa and south-east Asia. Again, there are sound reasons for linking width of nasal aperture with climate, since it is a function of the nose to mitigate the temperature of the air before it is drawn into the lungs: it is therefore not at all surprising to observe the narrow nostrils of the Eskimo or even the North

European, the medium ones of the Mediterranean or the broad ones of the Negro. Yet it would be quite wrong to suppose that all geographical variations were necessarily adaptive, since the isolation which must have increased as man extended his geographical range could well in itself have been sufficient to promote genetic variations.

A last point to make is that it was only during the final stages of the Pleistocene that man spread over the greater part of the earth. The early types of men were confined to the warmer parts of the Old World: their remains are found widely over Africa from Algeria to the Cape; in Europe as far north as lowland England and central Germany; in western Asia up to the mountains of northern Iran; in India, south-east Asia and Indonesia; and as far east as the Makassar Strait, coinciding with the great biological divide first recognized by Darwin's collaborator, A. R. Wallace. It was not until some time after he had emerged in his modern form that *Homo sapiens* occupied northern Eurasia and spread on the one hand into the New World and on the other into Australia and Tasmania and across Polynesia to New Zealand. The extension of human settlement over progressively wider territories is one of the major themes of the prehistory of Late-glacial and Neothermal times to be treated in later chapters of this book: it was made possible by the relatively unspecialized character of *Homo sapiens* as a biological species, but above all by the possession of culture, by means of which man has been able to adapt himself to the widest range of environments.

ENVIRONMENTAL CHANGE

For human beings the Pleistocene or Quaternary epoch has the supreme interest that it spanned the crucial stage in their evolution as organisms and at the same time witnessed the astonishing growth in their culture that was to lead them in due course to literacy and some awareness of their own fate and destiny. If we include within it the last ten or twelve thousand years constituting the Recent or Holocene, the Pleistocene was the most recent epoch in geology. Equally and with the same proviso, it was by far the briefest, whether we allow half a million or a million and a half or even two million years for its duration. Even so it was a period of profound and often repeated climatic change, change which can hardly have done other than affect more or less markedly the physical and cultural evolution of mankind.

The major divisions of the Pleistocene have been distinguished on a basis of palaeontology. Deposits dating from the Lower Pleistocene are consistently marked by a faunal assemblage of the kind first recognized at Villefranche-sur-Mer, including such well-defined forms as *Dinotherium*, *Stylohipparion*, *Sivatherium* and *Elephas (Archidiskodon) meridionalis*. By the Middle Pleistocene these archaic forms had disappeared and new ones had arrived including a new genus of elephant, *Elephas (Palaeoloxodon) antiquus*. The emergence of a developed form of *Elephas (Mammuthus) primigenius* was one of the distinguishing marks of the Upper Pleistocene. On the other hand the Recent or Holocene epoch, during which the environment as a whole assumed its present character, witnessed the disappearance of this as of other species now extinct. If we accept the findings of potassium/argon analysis, the transition from the Lower to the Middle Pleistocene occurred some four or five hundred thousand years ago. What seems to be generally agreed is that the Lower Pleistocene, about which least is known and in the course of which vital steps must have been taken in the process of hominization, lasted substantially longer, most probably at least three and possibly even four or five times longer than the rest of the epoch. Precisely when the Upper Pleistocene began has not yet been determined, but protoactinium/thorium analysis indicates an age of around 108,000 years for the peak of the glaciation that introduced it. Radiocarbon dates are only available for the last fifty or sixty thousand years and only for the last thirty do they fall within an acceptable range of probability. Nevertheless it seems likely that the last major glaciation (Weichsel/Würm of Europe) began within a few thousand years of 65,000 before the present and that within this glaciation the first major interstadial (Laufen/Göttweig) fell within the period 40/50,000 years ago.

Subdivisions of the Ice Age

When we apostrophize the Pleistocene as the Ice Age, we no longer imply that the expansion of ice-sheets was a once-and-for-all phenomenon. On the contrary the Pleistocene witnessed a whole series of glaciations interrupted by interglacial periods during which temperatures rose above those prevailing in recent times. In the present temperate zone and at higher altitudes even in the tropics, there were, if we may judge from the evidence obtained from cores taken from ocean beds, some fifteen major phases of increased glaciation during the Quaternary period. It is this recurrence of glacial and interglacial episodes that offers the best possibilities of subdividing the main chapters of the Pleistocene. Once again, it is important to emphasize that so far as the Lower Pleistocene is concerned the geological record is woefully incomplete on dry land where alone it can be related directly to the archaeological record. This is understandable when we consider the destructive effect of the repeated glaciations of which geological traces survive. Even so there are reasons for thinking that in areas as well studied as Europe the main outlines of the story are reasonably complete at least for the Middle and Upper Pleistocene.

If it is true that the explanation for glacial fluctuations is of a cosmic order, linked with changes in solar radiation, it follows that they should be more or less synchronous wherever they occur. This is still very much in the realm of hypothesis but it is at least encouraging that radiocarbon checks have already demonstrated the contemporaneity of certain episodes in the later stages of the Upper Pleistocene. There is a real hope that more intensive

Main Pleistocene sequences in Europe

	Glacial and *interglacial* stages: North-west Europe	Alps	Marine transgressions: Mediterranean
Pleistocene Upper	South Pomeranian (Weichsel III) Brandenburg/ Frankfurt-Posen (Weichsel II)	Main Würm III Main Würm II	
		Laufen/ Göttweig Early Würm I	*Late Monastirian* (*Tyrrhenian III*)
	Stettin (Weichsel I) *Eemian/Ipswichian*	*Riss/Würm*	*Main Monastirian* (*Tyrrhenian II*)
	Warthe Saale	Riss II Riss I	
Middle	*Hoxnian* Elster	*Mindel/Riss* Mindel II Mindel I	*Tyrrhenian I* *Sicilian II*
	Cromerian	*Günz/Mindel*	*Sicilian I*
Lower	Weybourne *Tiglian* Red Crag	Günz *Donau-Günz* Donau	*Calabrian*

quaternary research in widely scattered parts of the world may before too long make it possible to establish a reliable geochronology for prehistory as a whole.

The question of pluvial periods

In the tropical and equatorial regions remote from glaciation, except at the highest altitudes, there are indications of periods of increased rainfall during the Pleistocene; and much discussion has centred on how so-called pluvial periods could be synchronized with the glacial sequence. Recent research on the other hand has called into question the status of pluvial periods as chronological markers on anything approaching even a continental scale. Evidence for variations in rainfall certainly exists in strand-lines around lakes, fossil-springs and the nature of certain widespread deposits like laterite. This means that they offer possibilities for establishing local sequences. When more of these have been worked out, when radiocarbon and other methods of dating have been applied to them and above all when greater understanding has been reached about the explanation of their causes it may be possible to incorporate them in a world-wide framework of geochronology. What is beyond cavil is that in so far as major changes in precipitation occurred in these regions they must have affected more or less profoundly the circumstances of life for prehistoric communities.

Geographical and biological changes in the Ice Age

The fluctuations of climate dramatically symbolized by the expansion and contraction of ice-sheets transformed the setting of early man across its whole range. For instance, the alternate locking-up and release of vast quantities of water as ice-sheets all over the world alternately expanded and contracted—and one has to remember that the largest ice-sheets might be thousands of feet thick—affected ocean-levels, not merely in glaciated areas but over the whole world. Periods of glaciation were in general marked by the eustatic lowering of ocean-levels and interglacials by their corresponding rise. Although in regions central to the formation of major ice-sheets this might be offset or even surpassed by local isostatic depression of the land under the weight of ice and its alternate recovery, the effect over the world as a whole was to alter, sometimes quite drastically, the shape of land-masses. For instance during glacial phases in areas immediately outside isostatic depressions continents were more extensive: most of Indonesia was joined to south-east Asia by the Sunda shelf; New Guinea and Tasmania were both attached to Australia; north-east Siberia was linked by a broad land-bridge to Alaska; and to mention an example on a smaller scale Britain was joined on a wide front to the European continent. It goes without saying that if climatic change was sufficiently pronounced during the

Pleistocene to alter the basic geography of the world it can also be expected to have had the most profound influence on living things, on man himself and on the animals and plants on which directly or indirectly he sustained life.

The fluctuations of climate implied by the succession of glacial and interglacial episodes involved corresponding shifts in vegetational and faunal distributions. For example, when ice-sheets and periglacial conditions encroached on formerly temperate zones, as must have happened with every glacial advance, this meant that forests had to give place to open vegetation and that in the animal world sylvan species were replaced by ones adapted to steppe or tundra; and, conversely, during interglacial or interstadial phases, as well as during the Recent period following the last retreat of the ice, the situation was reversed. Further, it need hardly be emphasized that ecological displacement was by no means confined to territories immediately adjacent to the ice-sheets. During glacial periods it was not merely the temperate zones that were displaced, but to some degree the sub-tropical arid zones shifted nearer the equator. At such times also the equatorial rain forests must in turn have undergone some contraction. Conversely during interglacial and interstadial periods, not forgetting the Recent period, the equatorial rain-forest expanded, the sub-tropical arid zone moved further away and the forest spread again over territory formerly occupied by open vegetation.

The impact of such changes on early man can only be fully imagined when it is remembered how closely his life was linked with that of the animals and plants on which he depended for subsistence. Men, no less than other species, must needs live in ecosystems. They have to establish some kind of relationship to the habitat (soil and climate) and biome (vegetation and animal life) in which they exist and being men they have to evolve definite transmissible patterns by which these relations are structured. The cultural apparatus of which archaeologists study the surviving traces embodies the patterns developed by particular communities for coping with particular ecological situations. It follows that any drastic change, whether this occurs in the sphere of the habitat or biome or for that matter in the sphere of culture, must have involved readjustment, either through migration or cultural innovation, as the only alternative to decline and ultimate extinction; for natural selection in however roundabout a way applies no less to human societies than to any other societies of living organisms.

Until a much more complete picture of ecological change has been built up in different parts of the world it follows that our understanding of the underlying causes of the movements and cultural changes of which prehistory is composed must remain imperfect.

Neothermal climate

The Neothermal era, in the course of which the environment acquired its present character and men first achieved a more secure basis for subsistence by developing a farming economy and from there went on to create distinctive urban civilizations, did not begin until between ten and twelve thousand years ago. In the northern hemisphere, where it was marked by Post-glacial conditions, it is commonly defined by the moment at which the Pleistocene ice-sheets began their final retreat. In the case of the Scandinavian ice-sheet it has been established by counting the varved sediments laid down in melt-water that the retreat from the Fenno-scandian moraine began *c.* 8300 B.C., a date confirmed by the radiocarbon age of the transition from Late-glacial to Post-glacial vegetation (zones III and IV of Table, p. 23). On the other hand in territories comparatively remote from the centres of glaciation it looks as if the final and quite brief pause in the contraction of the ice-sheets, corresponding with the Younger Dryas of the European sequence, may not have registered in the Quaternary sequence. In these territories, which include those where the decisive steps were taken in the emergence of civilization, Neothermal conditions evidently began about the same time as the abortive onset of temperate conditions in the north known as the Allerød oscillation (zone II of Table, p. 23).

The establishment of temperate conditions in territories formerly glaciated or subject to the influence of ice-sheets was both a gradual and an uneven process. To begin with there was a slow but gradual rise of temperature. This Anathermal period was followed by an Altithermal one when temperatures rose to a maximum some $2\frac{1}{2}$°C. higher than those prevailing today in the same latitudes. Finally came the Medithermal period in the course of which conditions prevailing at the present day were established. For a finer division of Neothermal time there remains the possibility of zoning the sequence of vegetation by means of pollen-analysis. The most complete results obtained so far are those gained from analyses of samples taken from successive sediments formed in the beds of lakes since the withdrawal of the ice-sheets (Table, p. 23). From the earliest sediments it is possible to see the effect of the final oscillations of climate during the Late-glacial period when the ice-sheets were beginning to contract. The Allerød oscillation for example was sufficiently pronounced for trees—birch and even in some localities pine—to colonize the landscape previously occupied by Dryas vegetation, a vegetation without precise parallels today but which combined with predominantly tundra species others of Alpine and even steppe habit. During the Anathermal, when a Boreal type of climate with colder winters and brief summers that became progressively warmer as time went on prevailed in what is now temperate Europe, the forests which established themselves in what had formerly been an open landscape were at first composed exclusively of trees like birch, willow and pine that could tolerate cold conditions; only gradually was it possible for the warmth-demanding deciduous trees and the shrub hazel to establish themselves. By contrast, during the Altithermal when an Atlantic type of climate with higher temperatures and a diminished contrast between summer

*Periodization of the Late-glacial and
Post-glacial in north-west Europe*

Radiocarbon dates B.C.	Pollen zones	Climate	
Post-glacial			
500–	VIII	Subatlantic	
3000– 5500	VII*b*	Sub-boreal	
5500– 3000	VII*a*	Atlantic	⎰ Climatic
7000– 5500	VI	Late Boreal	⎱ optimum
7700– 7000	V	Early Boreal	
8300– 7700	IV	Preboreal	
Late-glacial			
8800– 8300	III	Younger Dryas	
10000– 8800	II	Allerød oscillation	
10500–10000	I*c*	Older Dryas	
11500–10500	I*b*	Bølling oscillation	
15000–11500	I*a*	Oldest Dryas	

and winter prevailed the deciduous trees rose to a dominance from which they have since to some degree declined.

Pollen-analysis has already been applied to many parts of the world and an important beginning has been made in the territory between the East Mediterranean and the Iranian plateau. Indications already exist from many districts, mainly in the form of changes in the composition of fauna from human settlements, but also including changes in vegetation inferred from pollen-analysis, that there was a marked increase of dryness early in the Neothermal phase. It is only when quaternary research has succeeded in reconstructing the history of micro-changes in the environment throughout the Neothermal period in this key area that we shall be able to judge the conditions under which the decisive changes were made in subsistence and social life.

CHAPTER 2

LOWER AND MIDDLE PALAEOLITHIC HUNTERS

Tool-making as a criterion of man

Although most palaeontologists agree that the assumption of an upright posture was sufficiently important to justify separating the hominids from the great apes, few would maintain that it is possible to distinguish on purely zoological grounds between those hominids that remained prehuman and those that had attained the status of man. To qualify as human, a hominid has, so to say, to justify himself by works: the criteria are no longer biological so much as cultural. Yet it remains true that a close interrelationship must exist between cultural achievement and biological endowment. The adoption of an erect posture, which may well have been a response to the thinning of forest and the consequent need to cross open country between one area of woodland and another, in itself facilitated the acquisition of culture; the freeing of the hands from locomotion made them available for tool-using and ultimately for tool-making; and these activities stimulated the development of the brain. At the same time they facilitated it by modifying the architecture of the skull: the diminishing role of the teeth for eating and manipulating had the effect of reducing their size, the weight of the jaw and the strength of the brow-ridges and muscular attachments. On the other hand the two-footed stance had its dangers, and ultimately only those hominids survived who made an intelligent use of tools and weapons. Indeed the ability to acquire culture was evidently of adaptive value in the sense that the strains most capable of doing so were those whose genotypes were propagated most abundantly in the course of natural selection. This may well explain why the increase in the size of the brain that permitted ever greater advances in culture developed so rapidly in the course of Pleistocene times. Even the biological evolution of the most advanced hominids was thus in large measure an outcome of developments in culture.

In many ways the most striking of these, and certainly the one most likely to find reflection in the archaeological record, is the ability to make tools. Here the distinction between tool-using and tool-making is one that needs stressing: it may be true that one has grown out of the other, but it is important to emphasize that it is as a fabricator that man stands out from his fellow primates. By the use of a tool is meant the active manipulation by an organism for the furtherance of its aims of some object taken from the external environment: thus, to quote Dr W. H. Thorpe's example, a Californian sea-otter bringing boulders up from the sea-bottom to crack molluscs is using a tool, whereas a gull dropping a mollusc on a rock to break it is not doing so. Tool-using in the true sense can be traced far back among quite lowly forms of life, but it does not of itself imply intelligence or insight. Even the great apes, though showing some dexterity in the manipulation of sticks and strings and in the stacking of boxes, reveal grave limitations in their behaviour. For instance, they show little understanding of statics, and in the handling of boxes rely almost entirely on blind improvisation rather than insight. Again—and this is even more significant—their activities are directed exclusively to securing visible objectives, so that even when some preparation is involved, such as sharpening the end of one stick to fit into a socket, the element of foresight and planning is really very slight. By contrast, tool-making and the building of structures, even among the most primitive human societies, are based on a precise knowledge of raw materials and, within the limits of the technology prevailing, of how most effectively to handle them. Moreover, it is characteristic of human beings that they have a much greater appreciation of the factor of time than the other primates: in their oral (and in due course literary) traditions they draw on memories of the past, which serve them as a kind of cultural capital; and by taking account of the future they gain the impetus needed to undertake operations which may in themselves be long-drawn out, and to meet contingencies not always precisely foreseeable.

Even so it is worth reflecting that the distinction between natural objects and artifacts is not always sharply defined. All tools made under primitive conditions were after all fabricated from natural objects and even the forms found in nature had often to be broken or in some degree modified before they could be conveniently handled. We therefore have to make an arbitrary distinction. When we ask ourselves what degree of modification material objects have to exhibit before we can accept them as the artifacts of man, a useful reply might be: 'when they belong to a class or assemblage of objects modified according to a standard pattern'. The odd piece of bone or stone modified or improved to suit a passing need need not of itself imply humanity. It is when we can detect the systematic shaping of materials in accordance with some arbitrary design that we feel ourselves confronted by the work of men conditioned by a cultural pattern, a pattern acquired by belonging to a society rather than to a biological species. Even this may not be as simple as it sounds and we do well to reflect that on the evolutionary hypothesis the manufacture of tools must have emerged without any clear break from the utilization of natural forms.

While it may not be the case that the earliest standardized tools were fabricated from flint or other kinds of stone, artifacts made from these have an overriding interest to the prehistorian. This arises mainly from their hardness and durability. They were the dominant elements in the technology of early man in the sense that they were not only supremely effective in their own right but were also of vital importance for shaping the softer materials used for a wide range of equipment. At the same time they were the main and all too frequently the only element to survive from remote ages. One of their few disadvantages is that they were as capable under certain conditions of being shaped by purely natural as by human forces. Critical study has demonstrated again and again that some of the flints and stones on which early prehistorians relied as evidence for the first tools were in fact the product of quite other forces. Thus, the so-called 'Cromerian' industry is now regarded as the product of wave action on the coast of Norfolk in eastern England; many of the 'eoliths' of southern England and France are interpreted as the outcome of soil-creep or alternatively of pressure and movement set up by the solution of underlying strata; and it now seems that the 'Kafuan' industry of Zambia was made by rapids and waterfalls in steep gorges. This has led prehistorians to pay special regard to lithic material obtained from actual living-floors of early hominids, like those exposed in bed I in Olduvai Gorge in Tanzania.

When fossils of *Australopithecus boisei* (originally known as *Zinjanthropus*) were found in this bed it was at first assumed by some prehistorians that this form of hominid was responsible for fabricating the stone implements with which it was associated. As soon, however, as traces of a hominid anatomically closer to man came to light in the same bed the more economical hypothesis was favoured, namely that the more advanced type of hominid was responsible both for shaping the implements and for killing *A. boisei* along with the other food animals represented on the floor. The conclusions to be drawn from this are complicated by the failure of human palaeontologists to agree whether the new hominid should be regarded merely as a variant of *A. africanus* or classified as a new species of man, *Homo habilis*. If for the sake of argument it is admitted that on morphological grounds the fossils might with equal plausibility be assigned to the genus *Australopithecus* or *Homo*—a possibility not so remarkable if evolution is true—the question arises whether the issue might not be decided by taking account of behavioural factors. The practice of making stone industries to socially determined patterns might well be held to be an index of behaviour of great diagnostic value. The mere fact that *H. habilis* was responsible for the chopper and flake industry of bed I at Olduvai might from this point of view be taken as evidence that *H. habilis* is well named, since there is no evidence that any of the primates unequivocally classified under the genus *Australopithecus* made flint or stone implements to purposive and therefore recognizable patterns. Fossils of Australopithecines are frequently found in deposits from which no stone tools have been claimed and contrariwise when they do occur with these they either accompany traces of more man-like Primates or belong to the Middle Pleistocene when such were plentiful. If the view is taken that the more man-like fossils from bed 1 at Olduvai ought nevertheless to be included in the genus *Australopithecus*, this does not greatly alter the picture. It would merely mean that stone tool-making to purposive patterns was achieved at a stage of hominid evolution immediately antecedent to the emergence of the earliest men.

It is generally accepted by primatologists that not merely the Australopithecines and man, but also gibbons, monkeys and the great apes were anatomically adapted to a certain level of implemental activity; and such activity has in fact been observed among non-human primates in the wild. It may well be that natural objects of wood or other organic materials were systematically shaped to conventional patterns by Australopithecines, but if so no evidence for this is available. What we do have is a strong suggestion that *A. africanus* made use of selected animal bones. Analysis of the animal bones recovered from the cave of Makapansgat in South Africa in association with fossils of this primate suggests that these formed a far from random sample. On the contrary they show evident signs of having been selected with a definite preference for forms that might have been particularly useful as tools or weapons. It was claimed long ago that Peking man did precisely this, although in the latter case of course a recognizable stone industry was also being produced. Yet it needs to be emphasized that there is no suggestion that *A. africanus* did more than break the bones he selected with a view to making them easier to use: there is no sign that the bones were shaped by working to purposive and standardized patterns. As a matter of fact facility in shaping bone tools was a comparatively late development in prehistoric technology.

The evolution of flint- and stone-working

By far the greater bulk of the evidence relating to the culture of Palaeolithic man comprises the artifacts of flint and stone upon which his way of life ultimately depended. These and the technology of which they are the products and expression provide the only thread that runs all through the early prehistory of man. Fortunately evolutionary forces were as active in the sphere of technology as they were in that of biology. The mere fact that technology was concerned with sustaining and facilitating the process of living ensures that it was subject in the long run to selection in the same way as organisms: by and large techniques which provided a more effective form of livelihood were likely to replace those which were less effective. The trend was for obsolete technology to drop out in favour of innovations acquired by the transmitting generation. Progress was thus built into the system. Yet, as prehistory shows, it proceeded slowly enough even in regions most productive of innovation since it was inevitably opposed by the conservative forces whose essential role was to ensure transmission of the cultural heritage which alone distinguished men from the other animals. It is hardly surprising that these forces were strongest where the social inheritance was most exiguous. That is why progress was so extremely slow during the earlier phases of prehistory.

Yet it is possible to observe a clear progression during the Palaeolithic Age in the technology of working flint and stone. As is only to be expected of the product of an evolutionary process, the discernible stages are rarely clear-cut. It is not so much that one form of technology gave place to another as that technical possibilities were enlarged by the adoption of new processes. The degree of overlap argues that the changes on which prehistorians rely for periodization were as a rule brought about by the spread of ideas rather than as a result of actual movements of people. Again, more often than not particular industries are seen to combine techniques from more than one stage of development. Among the factors that caused peoples living on the same time-plane to retain or discard old forms while adopting new ones were of course variations in the environment to which they had to adapt. Before listing the major stages in lithic technology during the Old Stone Age it needs to be emphasized with some vigour that, although they formed a homotaxial sequence in the sense that however incomplete the succession the order was invariably the same, they were only on rare occasions and as it were by chance synchronous in different territories. In the table that follows the succession of stone technologies is equated broadly with the major phases of the older Stone Age as these are commonly conceived of in Europe and contiguous parts of Africa and Asia.

A point that needs emphasis is that although these modes were homotaxial they were by no means universal. For one thing the territories occupied by early man tended to increase in the course of prehistory as cultures were adapted to an ever-widening range of environments. For another the competition, which in the long run ensured technological advance, only applied to regions accessible to the spread of new ideas. In territories relatively remote from those in which innovations first appeared old forms of technology might survive from the mere fact that they remained without challenge. Industries in mode 1, which must have been practised over an immensely long period of time, are found over the whole territory occupied by early man. Mode 2 industries on the other hand failed to reach south-east Asia or China.

Dominant lithic technologies	Conventional divisions of the older Stone Age
Mode 5: microlithic components of composite artifacts	Mesolithic
Mode 4: punch-struck blades with steep retouch	Advanced Palaeolithic
Mode 3: flake tools from prepared cores	Middle Palaeolithic
Mode 2: bifacially flaked hand-axes ⎱ Mode 1: chopper-tools and flakes ⎰	Lower Palaeolithic

[handwritten margin note: Techno. stages based on stone tools alone maybe gross Hmm?]

Mode 3 industries still did not penetrate these regions in the Far East, but on the other hand extended northwards into European Russia and Inner Asia. This makes it less of a surprise that when for example men first spread into Australia by way of Indonesia they should have carried with them a lithic tradition in Mode 1. When men first spread into more northerly parts of Europe and Eurasia they brought with them industries of modes 4 or 5 and these were carried successively into the New World.

Physical evolution and cultural progress

Seeing that tool-making made exceptional calls on the accurate correlation of hands, eyes and brain, it would be surprising if no broad degree of correlation existed between the appearance of successive advances in the manufacture of flint and stone tools and the emergence of progressively more advanced types of men. Yet there was no precise link between the two. For instance *H. erectus* continued for some time to develop the chopper-tool tradition that was apparently inaugurated by *H. habilis*, but he went on to evolve the hand-axe. Again, the hand-axe tradition was carried forward to its peak of development by early forms of *H. sapiens*, but it was *H. sapiens* in his broadly Neanderthaloid phase of development who was responsible for the prepared core tradition. It might therefore be wrong to read too much into the fact that the final stages in Palaeolithic lithic technology, along with highly significant break-throughs in the sphere of human awareness, were associated with the appearance of modern man (*H. sapiens sapiens*). The biological and cultural evolution of man both after all unfolded in the same temporal medium. As we have seen there was in general no close linkage between the successive types of men and particular stages of technical achievement. There is no justification for the idea that people who for one reason or another were left temporarily behind at a technical level, as the inhabitants of east Asia apparently were during much of the Middle and Upper Pleistocene, must have continued in an earlier stage of physical evolution. Nothing is more certain than that even the simplest and apparently most primitive cultures of modern times were borne by people whose claim to the status of *H. sapiens sapiens* was just as valid as that of the anthropologists who discovered them. The physical characteristics of men including their present racial characteristics are one thing. Their cultural characteristics which can be transmitted quite rapidly through social contacts are quite another.

Some basic elements of Palaeolithic economy

If the systematic manufacture of implements as an aid to manipulating the environment was a characteristic of the earliest men, so also was the form of their economy. To judge from the biological materials recovered from his settlements in different parts of Europe, Africa and Asia Palaeolithic man enjoyed even from the remotest periods a diet far more nearly omnivorous than that of any of the surviving non-human primates. In particular early man was a meat-eater. Whereas the great apes, though not averse to an occasional taste of animal food, are predominantly vegetarian, the earliest men whose food debris is known to us were evidently able to secure a wide range of animal meat. If *H. habilis* was mainly restricted to comparatively small game, this by no means applies to *H. erectus*, whose ability as a hunter stands in striking contrast with the poverty of his material aids. There seems no doubt that man found himself and emerged as a dominant species first and foremost as a hunter. One result of enlarging the range of his diet was in the long run to make it possible for him to explore a much wider range of environment, something in which he was greatly helped as time went on by the development of his material equipment. Another was to initiate the sub-division of labour that was to prove one of the mainsprings of human progress: whereas men pursued game and when necessary fought one another, their mates concentrated on nurturing the family and gathering plants and small items of animal foods such as eggs and insects. It was the economic partnership of the sexes that more than anything else underlay the human family, an institution which grew in importance with every increase in the scope and range of the culture which each generation had to acquire in infancy. The importance of nurture is reflected in the growing importance of the home base. Palaeolithic man remained predatory: he bred no animals and grew no plants but depended on what he could catch or collect from wild nature. It follows that he needed extensive areas for his support. This meant that he had to live in small widely dispersed groups, comprising at most enough adults to man the hunt. Even so it would generally be necessary for him to move, sometimes over extensive territories, in the course of the year exploiting natural sources of food as these ripened and matured. Yet the most primitive man needed a home-base far more permanent and substantial than the nightly nests of chimpanzees. The longer the young needed for protection and education the more equipment was needed in daily life, the more important cooking became, the more vital it was to secure a base close to game and water and congenial for living where the tasks essential for human living could be performed.

Articulate speech and self-awareness

It can be assumed, even if the surviving evidence is necessarily slight, that early man must have owed his domination of the animal world to qualities much less tangible than his technology or mode of subsistence. In particular he must have owed much to his ability to understand his environment, accumulate and pass on his experience and ensure the proper functioning of the artificially defined societies in which he lived. One of the principal ways in which he classified his surroundings, pooled and transmitted his experiences and developed traditional modes of behaviour was of course articulate speech.

Students of the great apes are agreed that one of their greatest drawbacks is the lack of speech, which alone is sufficient to prevent them acquiring the elements of culture. It is true that chimpanzees have a wider 'register of emotional expression' than most humans and that they are able to communicate to one another not only their emotional states but also definite desires and urges; yet, as Köhler has emphasized, 'their gamut of phonetics is entirely "subjective", and can only express emotions, never designate or describe objects'. In this connection it is interesting that in their famous enterprise of bringing up the chimpanzee Viki from the age of three days to three years, Dr and Mrs Hayes found it possible to train her to certain commands, but failed after eighteen months of intensive tuition to get her 'to identify her nose, eyes, hands and feet'. Until hominids had developed words as symbols, the possibility of transmitting, and so accumulating, culture hardly existed. Again, as Thorpe has remarked, man's prelinguistic counting ability is only of about the same order as that of birds or squirrels: serious mathematics, with all the immense advances in control of the environment that it portends, first became possible with the development of symbols. Speech, involving the use of symbols, must have been one of the first indications of humanity. Its only drawback as a criterion for the prehistorian is that there is no hope of being able to verify its existence directly for the remotest ages of man. Despite suggestions to the contrary, the best palaeontological opinion is against the notion that articulate speech can be inferred either from the conformation of the mandible or from study of casts taken of the inner surfaces of skulls. Probably the best clue is the appearance of tools of standardized and recognizable form, since it is hard to see how these can have been popularized and transmitted without the use of verbal symbols.

Palpable evidence of increasing self-awareness first appears from a comparatively late stage of prehistory. It is not until the Upper Pleistocene that we get the first evidence for systematic burial of the dead by Middle Palaeolithic man. And it is only towards the end, at a time of rapid technical innovation, that we first encounter evidence for self-adornment and the practice of art, in each case in the context of *H. sapiens sapiens*.

Chopper-tool (mode 1) industries

Chopper-tools, which in most regions could most conveniently be made by striking a few flakes from the side of a pebble in one or two directions, formed the most important element, along with their associated flakes, in the material equipment not only of *H. habilis* but also of the various forms of *H. erectus* to flourish in different parts of Africa, Asia and Europe during the opening phases of the Middle Pleistocene. Moreover, in those parts of eastern Asia that never adopted the hand-axe the tradition persisted in some degree down to the end of the Pleistocene; and it looks as though the industrial tradition taken by the earliest colonists into Australia at an advanced stage of the Upper Pleistocene was also basically of mode 1.

Geographically this industrial tradition was broadly co-extensive with the areas occupied by the earliest men. Their presence in East Africa has already been remarked. In North Africa they have been particularly well studied in Morocco where they first appeared in the context of a Villefranchian fauna and continued to develop through several stages of the Middle Pleistocene. Recent discoveries have indicated that in the west they occupied territories as far north as central Europe, where for example well-defined chopper and flake tools made from pebbles of chert and quartzite have been recovered with animal bones of Middle Pleistocene age in a travertine quarry at Vértesszöllös in Hungary. Indeed, if we accept the flint industries named after Clacton as belonging to the same tradition, we can say that they extended as far as the western part of the North European Plain. To the east their range also extends from the Tropics to the Temperate zone. The Soan industries from Middle Pleistocene deposits in the north-west of the Indian sub-continent were among the first of their kind to be recognized, outside those of the North China Plain. South-east Asia has shown a variety of industries made from differing and sometimes intractable material, but conforming to the same basic pattern, notably the Anyathian of Burma, the Tampanian of Malaya and the Pajitanian of Indonesia.

In many cases it is unhappily the case that the stone implements themselves and the geological deposits in which they are found provide us with the only source of information about the people who made them. Sometimes we get remains of the makers themselves and quite often traces of the animals on which they lived. To judge from what has been recovered from bed I at Olduvai *H. habilis* had already gone some way to adopting the omnivorous diet characteristic of man; he not only caught fish, birds and small game, but certainly managed to secure the carcasses of large animals. The men of Vértesszöllös had a pronounced meat diet and it seems evident from the charring of some of the discarded meat bones that they had the use of fire. The same applies and with more certainty to the early men (*H. erectus pekinensis*) of the North China Plain.

Little is known yet in detail about the Lower Pleistocene finds from Chanchiawo in Shensi. On the other hand a wealth of information exists about the finds from Choukoutien. The earliest deposits at locus 13, dating from early in the Middle Pleistocene, yielded a typical chopping tool made by alternate flaking from a chert pebble, giving a sinuous working-edge. The main fissure (locus 1), dating from rather later in the Middle Pleistocene and the source of remains of upwards of forty representatives of Peking man, has produced a wealth of stone artifacts made from intractable materials like green-stone, coarse chert and quartz. It must be admitted that many of these were so crudely fashioned that they would hardly have been recognized as human if recovered from an ordinary geological deposit. Nevertheless the industry, much of the material of which was brought to the site and which was intimately associated with traces of fire and other human activity, has certain well-defined characteristics: there are no tools comparable to the hand-axes of Africa and parts of Europe and south-west Asia; pebbles and flakes were employed as materials for tools and the flakes had sometimes been formed by crushing nodules between two boulders, resulting in signs of percussion at either end; secondary retouch was scarce and irregular; and the leading tools were intended for chopping and scraping, the former generally made from pebbles, from which a few flakes had been struck to form irregular working-edges, and the latter by trimming lumps or flakes to form smooth edges. With this rudimentary stone equipment, supplemented by such tools as he was able to shape by its aid, Peking man succeeded in living largely on the flesh of his competitors in the animal world.

To judge from the animal remains associated with him, Peking man depended largely on venison, since two-thirds of them belong to two species of deer, namely *Euryceros pachyosteus* and *Pseudaxis grayi*. Yet he by no means restricted himself to this meat and his victims seem to have included elephants, two kinds of rhinoceros, bison, water-buffaloes, horses, camels, wild boars, roebucks, antelopes and sheep, not to mention such carnivores as sabre-toothed tigers, leopards, cave bears and a huge hyena. How he managed to secure this varied selection of game we can only speculate. No specialized projectile-heads have survived in the archaeological record, but to judge from evidence from elsewhere he would have had available wooden spears with the tip hardened in fire and it seems likely in view of the character of

37

some of his victims that he would have used primitive pit-traps. The meagreness of his material equipment only emphasizes the important part that team-work, based on articulate speech and on a conscious network of social relations, must have played even at this early stage of development, when groups were so small and so sparsely scattered. Equally we should recognize the immense courage of these primitive men, who in the face of powerful and largely unknown forces made their way—and our way—in the final resort by their prowess as hunters, by confronting and vanquishing animals larger, faster and stronger than themselves.

One of their most important aids was fire and it was in layers discoloured by burning and mixed with ash and charcoal that most of their discarded refuse was found. Fire would have been of value for keeping wild beasts at bay, for warming the cave, for hardening wooden weapons and of course for roasting meat. In addition to meat, wild animals provided skins and, in their bones, teeth and antlers, potential raw materials for making tools and weapons. There seems no doubt that Peking man utilized certain of these, though not to the extent that has sometimes been claimed. Deer antlers were certainly detached from their frontlets, the beams were sometimes cut into sections and the tines removed, no doubt for use. Again, flakes from the long bones of various animals have the appearance of having been used and even trimmed by flaking. On the other hand there is no sign that Peking man fabricated well-made artifacts from these materials.

Both the way in which the bones of Peking man himself occurred and their condition throw light on other aspects of his behaviour. There can have been no question of burial, since the remains were distributed in the cultural deposit in just the same way as animal bones. This, indeed, taken together with his primitive appearance, was enough to suggest to at least one eminent authority that Peking man was himself the victim of some more advanced human type. The fact remains that, despite the most careful search of thousands of cubic metres of deposit and the recovery of an impressive body of material relating to Peking man, no single trace of his supposed overlord has ever been found. If it be accepted that Peking man was himself the hunter—and this view is now unquestioned by leading authorities—then the condition of his bones argues strongly that he was a cannibal as well as an avid consumer of animal flesh: his long bones are normally split exactly as were those of wild animals to facilitate the extraction of marrow, and the aperture at the base of the skull has habitually been enlarged in just the same way as among the Melanesians of recent times who favoured human brain as a delicacy.

Hand-axe (mode 2) industries

The most striking technical innovation to appear during the Middle Pleistocene was the hand-axe, a tool flaked over part or the whole of both faces in such a way as to produce a working-edge round the greater part of its perimeter and apparently intended to be gripped in the hand. There seems no doubt in the face of stratigraphical sequences like those studied in Morocco or Tanzania that the earliest and most primitive hand-axes, resembling those from the French locality of Abbeville in the Somme Valley, developed from evolved forms of pebble-tool having two-way flaking. All that was involved was the extension of secondary flaking from the edge to the surface of the tool. As time went on the knappers learned to remove shallower flakes and turn out hand-axes which, like those from St-Acheul in France, were thinner, had a more regular working-edge, were easier to handle with precision and needed a smaller quantity of raw material. Evolution thus proceeded in the direction of greater effectiveness and lower requirement of material. It was adaptive in the sense that whoever made or adopted such improvements benefited in relation to those who failed to do so. This may also help to explain the remarkable degree of uniformity to be observed in the production of hand-axes whatever sources of raw material happened to be available in particular localities. To ask where the hand-axe was invented and what regions witnessed the first appearance of different stages in its evolution is not particularly meaningful; nor would it be sensible to interpret the growth of technical innovation over long periods of time with the movements of particular groups of people. One is faced, not with a series of events to be accounted for in terms of human immigration, but rather with processes which transformed lithic technology by insensible gradations over extensive territories.

Although hand-axes are the most noteworthy elements of the stone industries in which they occur, they are by no means the only ones. The point has first to be made that chopper-tools, although for some purposes rendered out of date, had not suddenly lost all utility; indeed in territories as far removed from one another as central India and Morocco it has been remarked that they continued to be made throughout the period during which hand-axes were in use. Again, the mere production of hand-axes must have yielded numerous flakes and there is evidence, where this has been observed with care, that some of these were shaped, or if not in all cases shaped at least used as implements on their own account. Furthermore, and more particularly during the more evolved stages of cultures of Acheulian type, the tool-kit was further enriched by narrow pick-like forms, steep core-scrapers and cleavers, the broad, sharp working-edges of which were formed by the intersection of two or more flake-scars.

Geographically the hand-axe industries in mode 2 never extended over the whole territory of those in mode 1. They prevailed extensively over Africa and southern Europe, but in Asia only in restricted areas of the south-west. From Egypt the hand-axe territory extended into the Levant and Mesopotamia and thence to the Indian sub-continent southward from the Narmada basin. Further east over much of China and south-east Asia stone industries continued in the old mode 1 tradition. Within their own territory the makers of hand-axe industries were by no means undiscriminating in their choice of hunting-ground. In Africa where their distribution has been closely studied in relation to palaeoecology it seems plain that they preferred savannah country and at least to begin with eschewed the dense forest.

Like their predecessors, the makers were adept at big-game hunting. For this reason it is no surprise to find that they concentrated in the valleys of rivers like the Thames and the Somme, the Nile, the Vaal, the Zambezi or the Narmada or, again, at Olorgesailie in East Africa, at Karar in Algeria, Torralba in Spain or Hoxne in England. The animal bones recovered from their sites show plainly enough their interest in meat. The Olorgesailie people for example killed and ate giant baboon, giant pig and large kinds of horse and hippopotamus; at Karar remains were found of elephant, rhinoceros, hippopotamus, buffalo, zebra, giraffe, warthog and gazelle; and at Torralba straight-tusked elephant, rhinoceros, wild ox, stag and horse. Although, as with the hunters of Choukoutien, their methods of hunting must remain to a large extent a matter of conjecture, we have at least one piece of evidence that they used wooden spears hardened in the fire, namely a broken but more or less complete specimen of yew wood nearly 2·5 metres long found among the rib-bones of a straight-tusked elephant, at Lehringen, near Verden in Lower Saxony, Germany, and dating from the Riss-Würm interglacial. In this connection it is interesting to note that the pygmies of the Cameroons have been accustomed to stalk elephant with a wooden spear not much more than six feet long, which they thrust into the animal's body with both hands; as the animal tries to escape the spear works in more deeply and the trail of blood allows the hunters to keep on his track. When a kill of a large beast is made among such people it is customary for folk to collect from far and near to feast off the meat. During the Stone Age, when implements were easily made and expendable, it is likely that these would often be worn out and discarded at the site of a kill and it seems easiest to explain in this way finds like that at site HK in bed IV at Olduvai, which yielded no less than 459 hand-axes and cleavers blunted by use and lying amid the disarticulated skeleton of a hippopotamus.

Prepared core and flake (mode 3) industries

As we have already noted, the production of flakes was an inevitable concomitant of the manufacture both of chopper-tools and of hand-axes; and there are indications that their use for making ancillary tools was well understood. What indicates a new stage in technology is when the flint- or stone-worker appears to aim first and foremost at producing flake tools, and to this end goes to particular trouble to prepare cores from which they could be struck in a finished state. One of the prehistorian's difficulties is that the intention of the prehistoric knapper may not always be apparent. It may well be indeed that at an early stage a certain ambivalency may have existed. The controversy between those who interpret the large lumps from Clactonian industries in south-east England as cores and those who see them as chopper-tools may well be unreal.

The position is much clearer during the early part of the Upper Pleistocene when we have industries like that first recognized at Levallois, a suburb of Paris, in which flake tools are found together with the tortoise-shaped cores from which they were struck. Here there can be no doubt that the primary object of the knapper was to produce flake tools, the form of which was accurately determined by preparatory work on the core. The technique was one that was developed on the northern margins of the hand-axe province, though as we shall see it also interpenetrated this. Middle Palaeolithic industries based primarily on the Levallois technique are found in relatively pure form round the southern and eastern shores of the Mediterranean from North Africa to the Levant, penetrating by way of Iraq and Iran into western Asia. Further north the culture named after the rockshelter of Le Moustier in the Dordogne also made prominent use of flake tools, though these were commonly made from smaller disc-like cores and were often trimmed into points or side-scrapers by a special technique that led to step or resolved flaking. Many variations exist in the Mousterian industries which extend from the Atlantic seaboard to the area north of the Black Sea and Inner Asia. In western Europe for example Middle Palaeolithic industries normally included elements in mode 2, including hand-axes of small triangular or heart-shaped forms, whereas further south these declined greatly in importance. Over much of this territory from the south of France and Italy to central Europe, the Crimea, the Don–Donetz region and the coastal zone of the west Caucasus the loss or minor importance of the hand-axe was compensated by a great variety of flake tools, which then included hand-awls and steeply flaked ribbon-flakes; again, and especially in the east from Greece to South Russia, the inventory included points having shallow flaking on either face and either leaf-shaped or sub-triangular in form with concave base.

Although the notion of concentrating on implements struck at one blow from carefully prepared cores is one that seems to have been developed in the northern part of the Lower Palaeolithic world and to have characterized in particular the Middle Palaeolithic Levalloiso-Mousterian province, the crucial technique certainly spread further afield. For instance flakes struck from prepared cores form a significant component alongside hand-axes and cleavers of the Fauresmith culture adapted to the savannah and high grasslands of South Africa, Kenya, South Abyssinia and the Horn. In the complementary Sangoan that flourished to begin with on the fringes of the equatorial rain-forest the flake struck from a prepared core did not become obtrusive until the late or Lupemban stage when for the first time man began effective penetration of the rain-forest. Even so the leading artifacts of the Sangoan continued to be bifacial, including core-axes, picks and narrow lanceolate forms.

Owing to their habit of occupying caves, we have reasonably

full information about the animals on which the Neanderthal and Neanderthaloid peoples mainly depended for food, about the use they made of bone and related materials and the way in which they disposed of their dead. As hunters these people show no sign of having been in any way more advanced than their immediate predecessors. Where, as in certain of the Mount Carmel caves in Palestine, Levalloiso-Mousterian levels overlie ones dating from early stages of the Palaeolithic, there is no indication that an extended range of animals was hunted. Equally, there is no sign of any marked improvement in the methods of hunting; reliance evidently continued to be placed on proved methods like wooden spears, stone balls (probably used as bolas stones) and presumably on primitive pit-traps; and there is a notable absence of specialized projectile-heads. Again, exceedingly limited use was made of bone and related materials which, as we know from later practice by Stone Age hunters, were capable of providing a variety of spear-, harpoon- and arrowheads, as well as fish-hooks and pointed fish-gorges, a variety of tools and many kinds of personal ornament: pieces of dense bone, including phalanges, or toe-bones, were used as anvils for working flint, but there is no evidence that bone or antler was worked to make well-defined implements or weapons of any description. Another and possibly more significant limitation is the absence of any indication of a developed aesthetic sense: Middle Palaeolithic man was capable of producing a limited range of tools with an astonishing economy of effort, and the perfection of form and degree of standardization that they achieved, often over great areas and despite wide variations in the qualities of the raw materials used, bear witness to firmness of intention and a definite sense of style; but as far as we know he practised no art—no sign of carving or engraving for example has been found among all the wealth of bone and antler from Mousterian and kindred sites; nor is there evidence of even so much as a single bored tooth to suggest that he fabricated ornaments to adorn his person.

In two significant ways however Neanderthal man made important advances. For one thing he extended the range of settlement well to the north of the frost-free zone to which earlier men had confined themselves and this at a time of glacial intensity. Precisely how far he reached has still to be settled in detail, but there are indications that he colonized parts of Siberia for the first time, though probably not as early as Würm I times, and even reached as far as China. The presence of well-made flint scrapers as an important element in his standard equipment suggests that he found it necessary in his northerly habitat to wear animal skins, at least out of doors. It was probably the cold conditions of Würm I times, also, that caused the Mousterian and Levalloiso-Mousterian people to occupy caves where these were available.

The other marked advance shown by Neanderthal man was in his treatment of the dead. Certain discoveries from the closing phase of the last Interglacial seem indeed to indicate the continuance of cannibalism, notably the Neanderthal skull from Monte Circeo, Italy, with the base broken open for the extraction of the brain, and the mass find at Krapina in Yugoslavia, where remains of upwards of a dozen individuals, male and female, young and old, were discovered mixed up in the cultural deposit with wild animal bones and treated in the same way, having been broken up for the extraction of marrow, partly burnt in the fire and so on. On the other hand the Mousterian deposit at La Chapelle-aux-Saints was found to overlie a grave, cut into the rock floor and containing the crouched skeleton of a Neanderthal man; similar burials have been found at La Ferrassie, likewise in the Dordogne, and also at Kiik-Koba in the Crimea. Even more significant evidence was uncovered at the Mugharet es-Skhūl, Mount Carmel, in the form of a veritable cemetery of ten graves with remains ranging from a girl of three and a boy of four to a man over fifty years of age. As at La Chapelle-aux-Saints the graves were only just big enough to accommodate bodies with

Table of radiocarbon determinations for the
Mousterian and allied cultures

EUROPE

			B.C.
1	Les Cottés, Vienne, France	⎰GrN 4334 ⎱GrN 4421	30,350± 400 35,650± 700
2	Grotte du Renne, Arcy-sur-Cure, Yonne, France	GrN 4217	32,650± 850
3	La Quina, Charente, France	⎰GrN 4494 ⎱GrN 2526	32,150± 700 33,300± 530
4	Radošiná, Czechoslovakia	GrN 2438	36,450 +2800 −2100
5	Nietoperzowa, Poland	GrN 2181	36,550±1240
6	Broion Cave, nr. Vicenza, Italy	GrN 4638	38,650±1200
7	Érd, Hungary	⎰GrN 4711 ⎱GrN 4444	37,400± 830 42,350±1400
8	Regourdou, Dordogne, France	GrN 4308	43,550±1800
9	La Cotte de St. Brelade, Jersey	GrN 2649	45,050±1500
10	Gibraltar (Gorham's Cave G)	GrN 1473	45,750±1500
11	Lebenstedt, Germany	GrN 2083	53,290±1010
12	Mussolini Canal, Italy	GrN 2572	55,950± 500

NORTH AFRICA

13	Haua Fteah, Cyrenaica (level xxviii)	GrN 2564	41,450±1300
14	Haua Fteah, Cyrenaica (level xxxiii)	GrN 2023	45,050±3200

SOUTH-WEST ASIA

15	Tabun B, Israel	GrN 2534	37,750± 800
16	el Kebarah, Israel	GrN 2561	39,050±1000
17	Geulah Cave A, Israel	GrN 4121	40,050±1700
18	Jerf Ajla, Syria	NZ 76	41,050±2000
19	Ksâr 'Akil, Lebanon	GrN 2579	41,800±1500
20	Shanidar, Iraq (level D, top)	⎰GrN 2527 ⎱GrN 1495	44,950±1500 48,650±3000
21	Ras el-Kelb, Lebanon	GrN 2556	>52,000
22	Al Ghab, Syria	GrN 2640	>53,000

NOTE. It is likely that these cultures first appeared at a period beyond the present useful range of radiocarbon determination.

the arms and legs flexed. No red ochre or personal ornaments were found, but the jaw-bones of a large wild boar were seen to be clasped in the arms of the old man. A more recent discovery of exceptional interest is that of a Neanderthaloid child in the cave

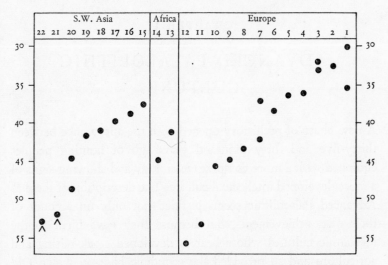

Chart of radiocarbon determinations (millennia B.C.) for the
Mousterian and allied cultures.

of Teshik-Tash, Uzbekistan, the head surrounded by six pairs of
horns of the Siberian mountain goat, which had evidently been
stood upright in a circle while still attached to the frontal bones.
Quite clearly men of the Neanderthaloid type had developed
concepts well beyond what one might have expected from their
lowly material culture.

CHAPTER 3

ADVANCED PALAEOLITHIC
CULTURE

A new phase of prehistory opened with the appearance between thirty-five and forty thousand years ago of hunting peoples equipped with a more complex technology and showing signs of a more developed intellectual culture. The description of these as Advanced Palaeolithic seems justified not only on account of their own achievements, but because they gave birth to the Mesolithic cultures whose bearers developed stock-raising and agriculture and so provided the economic base on which Old World civilizations in due course developed. With the benefit of hindsight it is not difficult to see that the Advanced Palaeolithic peoples of Europe, western Asia and Mediterranean Africa stood on the main line of progress and marked a palpable advance over the cultural stages described in our last chapter.

General characteristics

The most widespread element of Advanced Palaeolithic culture comprises flint industries of mode 4, that is industries based first and foremost on relatively narrow flint blades having more or less parallel flake-scars. The ability to make flint blades was discovered very much earlier: flint industries featuring these have indeed been recovered in stratified caves at levels antedating mode 3 industries of Levalloiso-Mousterian character both in the Levant and in Cyrenaica. Yet it was not until much later that punch-struck blades became important and indeed replaced the flake industries over by far the greater part of their extent. Why did this time-lag occur? The answer must surely be that the punch-struck blade was not further developed until the need for it

48

was sufficiently strong. It was because the blade was better adapted than the mere flake to serve as a blank for the multifarious flint forms needed for a more advanced form of technology that it ultimately came into the ascendant.

Advanced Palaeolithic cultures were distinguished from what went before by their more dynamic character. They changed comparatively rapidly and more especially in their later phase showed a rich regional diversification. Nevertheless certain traits characterized them collectively. In the field of technology they displayed a notable facility for devising artifacts suited for specialized functions. Although used on their own account, flint blades formed convenient blanks for a considerable variety of implement. Thus, whereas the Levalloiso-Mousterians made do with comparatively few forms of scrapers made by trimming the edges of fairly broad flakes, the Advanced Palaeolithic knappers made a variety of convex scrapers on the ends of blades of varying lengths as well as concave ones made by flaking hollows or notches from the edges of blades. Very great importance was paid to tools made by applying a steep, almost vertical retouch (*à dos rabattu*) to one edge of a blade or to parts of both edges in such a way as to produce well-defined forms, each combining a sharp edge or edges with the strength that came from the thickest part of the blades. Objects made in this way included knife-blades and the points of projectiles. Another artifact made from blades was the graving-tool or burin, a tool having a sharp chisel-like working-edge of great strength, suitable in its various forms for delicate engraving or for dismembering and shaping antler or bone. The vital edge was formed by striking one or more blows into the main axis of the blade. The character and potentialities of individual burins and classes of burin depended on whether blows were struck from one or two directions; whether they were aimed obliquely or at right-angles to the blade; whether the blade was intact or had been snapped across or trimmed by secondary working to give a straight, convex or concave prepared edge; or, again, whether the flint-worker had in fact chosen a blade or a core for conversion into a burin. The technique of detaching secondary flakes so as to form a sharp but strong working-edge was after all an old one. It is for instance sometimes present on the working extremity of some Lower Palaeolithic hand-axes. On the other hand it was not developed on any scale to produce flint burins until a powerful need had developed for these implements, as it appears to have done in the context of Advanced Palaeolithic culture.

Much remains to be learned from microscopic studies of wear on burins before we can be sure what they were used for, but iron tools of similar form have quite recently provided effective in Eskimo hands for working antler and bone and experiments with flint ones have confirmed their value for this purpose. It could well be, though it has not yet been proved, that there was a functional relationship between the adoption of burins and a much more ambitious utilization of antler and bone. In view of the central importance of hunting in the life of Palaeolithic man it is not surprising that animal skeletons should from early times have provided a significant source of material for tools. Yet a sophisticated use of these materials was comparatively late, first appearing in the context of Advanced Palaeolithic culture alongside the specialized flint tools needed to cut them into convenient shapes and convert them into a variety of forms. These included different kinds of working tools, such as spatulae, scraping-tools, awls and needles, projectile-points and personal ornaments. The preparation of such things as beads, pendants and arm-rings is an important innovation because it indicates a notable advance in personal self-awareness. No less striking in this respect was the appearance for the first time in the archaeological record of musical instruments and manifestations of graphic or sculptural art in the execution of some of which burins may also have been used.

Advanced Palaeolithic cultures were first explored in detail in western Europe and above all in the region of south-west France centred on the Dordogne. This at first led prehistorians to suppose that France was the birthplace of Advanced Palaeolithic culture and that the succession of industries found there could be accepted as a standard. Neither of these ideas can any longer be sustained. Archaeological exploration of central and eastern Europe, of the Soviet Union to the Urals and beyond into Siberia and Japan, of Italy and Greece, of Cyrenaica and of western Asia from the Levant to the Zagros and Afghanistan has shown that south-western Europe was not central but marginal to the Advanced Palaeolithic world; moreover at any particular period there was a veritable mosaic of variegated cultures over this extensive territory. Again, although radiocarbon dating has still been very unevenly applied it is already apparent that cultures of this character appeared both in Cyrenaica and in parts of western Asia before they did in the Dordogne.

The earliest Advanced Palaeolithic cultures

Until far more radiocarbon determinations have been made at different points in the Advanced Palaeolithic world it will not be possible to be sure where the new technology first developed. Although in many regions the transition from Middle to Advanced Palaeolithic appears to have been a sharp one, indications are multiplying that acculturation occurred, a fact hardly surprising when it is remembered that the new technology sprang up within the territory of the Middle Palaeolithic flake cultures. It is already evident as sequences are established in different areas that these were largely the product of indigenous development modified from time to time by fashions and devices that spread far and wide. The earliest manifestations of Advanced Palaeolithic culture, although all simple, are distinguished from one another by various details. Thus, the Dabban which immediately overlay the Levalloiso-Mousterian in the great cave of Haua Fteah in Cyrenaica was already distinguished before the end of its initial phase by the appearance of chamfered blades terminated by oblique burin-like blows. In the Levant the initial culture of the Advanced Palaeolithic sequence, the Emiran, resembled in many respects the Dabban, but the ensuing Antelian, Atlitian and Kebaran were all local to the region. Further east the Baradostian of the Zagros region was distinguished by the presence, alongside polyhedric burins, rods and backed blades, of the Arjeneh point, a refined version of a Mousterian form; in its later stages, apparently terminated around 25/26000 B.C. by the onset of glacial conditions, the Baradostian was marked by a progressive diminution in the size of backed blades and scrapers.

The French Sequence

The sequence in the French caves which, because of its priority in the history of research, its diversity and cultural wealth must still claim special attention, began several thousand years later than in parts of south-west Asia and probably also in Cyrenaica. The Châtelperronian with which the French sequence opened is clearly distinguished by a large and presumably hand-held knife-blade having a convex back with steep blunting retouch. In existing collections Châtelperronian assemblages often include Mousterian forms, but this could well be due to admixture with material from underlying deposits before excavators had gained their present skills : if in fact the two elements do belong to the same industry the question might arise whether to interpret them as indicating a local evolution for the Châtelperronian or as the result of the impact of an intrusive blade and burin tradition on an indigenous Middle Palaeolithic tradition.

The ensuing stage, named after the cave of Aurignac, was markedly different. Many scrapers and burins were made on cores rather than blades and were characterized by parallel fluting; and end—and hollow—scrapers and points were made on substantial blades with a heavy retouch. In addition the Aurignacian disposed of very distinctive tapered bone points having the base split to allow for the insertion of a wooden shaft. Flint industries resembling the Aurignacian occur in central Europe and the Balkans, in the Levant (in the local form of the Antelian) and as far afield as Karar Kamar in Afghanistan. Even the split-base bone point extends as far as Bulgaria. A point of particular interest is that identical points occur in the context of the Szeletian culture of Hungary, from all appearances the product of acculturation between Aurignacian and Mousterian.

The next stage in the French sequence, the Gravettian, is marked by a strongly contrasted tradition of flint-work, characterized above all by backed blades and bladelets, including narrow rods and more or less symmetrical points with convex blunted back, some of them so small that they must have been hafted in composite equipment. Although some French prehistorians have sought to derive the Gravettian from the highly localized Châtelperronian, uniting them in a 'Perigordian' tradition that ran in part alongside the Aurignacian, it seems more likely in view of the extremely wide spread of Gravettian-like industries in south and central Europe and over much of European Russia that it represents an intrusive tradition.

Before returning to industries of Gravettoid type from regions outside France, a word must be said about two traditions which overlaid the Gravettian in France and contiguous areas. The first of these, the Solutrean named after the rock-shelter of La Solutré, was confined in its earliest stages to south-western France, though spreading in its later ones into several parts of Iberia. In France it has every appearance of having been an indigenous development. For one thing the production of cave art appears to have continued without interruption from the Gravettian through the Solutrean to reach its climax in the context of the overlying Magdalenian culture; and for another the laurel-leaf points with flat flaking on either face, often taken as a symbol of the Solutrean, apparently developed from points with shallow flaking on one face only of a kind that appeared in the Early Solutrean. It is worth recalling that laurel-leaf points, which can hardly be connected directly with those of the Middle Solutrean, appeared in the Szeletian of Hungary and in several of the Advanced Palaeolithic industries of south Russia, in both cases stemming from Middle Palaeolithic traditions of flint-work.

The final stage of the Solutrean was marked in eastern Spain by what appear to be barbed or tanged arrowheads and in France by backed bladelets and eyed needles of types also present in an early phase of the ensuing Magdalenian. In its Early and Middle phase, the latter marked by antler spear-throwers carved in the form of ibex and other animals, the Magdalenian was confined to the Franco-Cantabric region. The Late Magdalenian, marked by barbed harpoon-heads with basal swelling, spread further east into Switzerland and south Germany and its influence was felt as far afield as Poland and Czechoslovakia. To the north numerous reindeer-hunting groups have been identified from the Late-glacial period, including notably the bearers of the Hamburgian, Ahrensburgian and Swiderian cultures that extended across the North European Plain and in the latter case along the northern and eastern slopes of the Carpathians. All these groups, like those dating from the same period in North Africa, the Levant and parts of south-west Asia, were distinctive cultures of relatively local distribution. On the other hand over much of southern Europe from Iberia to Greece a relatively homogeneous Gravettian culture of eastern origin prevailed down to the end of Pleistocene and into Neothermal times.

Eastern Gravettian

In parts of central Europe, notably on the loess of Czechoslovakia and again along the great rivers of South Russia, archaeology has brought to light a rich material resembling in several significant respects that first identified at the French site of La Gravette. The fact that the Gravettian tradition began markedly earlier in the east and the general pattern of its diffusion, well brought out in the distribution of the so-called Venus figurines (map 2), combine to suggest that its appearance in France was a mere episode of quite marginal significance.

For a number of reasons the East Gravettian area merits separate treatment on its own account. For one thing there is a notable difference in the nature of the sites occupied by the Advanced Palaeolithic inhabitants. In western and southern Europe these were predominantly caves or rock-shelters. Such sites provided natural, ready-made homes—though there is increasing evidence that even within such shelters early man sometimes found it necessary to build screens to protect himself and his fireplaces. To prehistorians they have been particularly valuable because they were often settled successively over long periods of time by people of markedly differing cultural traditions. In the great river basins of south Russia, however, such natural shelters did not exist. This explains why knowledge about Advanced Palaeolithic settlement in this territory for long remained so exiguous and also why even now it is proving a laborious task to establish a detailed succession. On the other hand improvements in archae-ological technique have recently made it possible to detect and recover traces of settlement on open sites. It is now plain that the Advanced Palaeolithic inhabitants of south Russia—and for that matter their Mousterian predecessors—constructed artificial dwellings from which it is possible to learn something of their social structure. One reason why it has been possible to detect them is that the floors were often scooped out of the subsoil, possibly to reduce the draughts caused by winds which during much of the glacial period would have blown over substantially open landscapes. Both in south Russia and on the loess of Moravia individual dwellings were curvilinear and often irregular in plan. This makes it most unlikely that their superstructures were built on the principle of a timber framework. A likely suggestion is that they were sometimes covered by joined animal skins sup-ported by movable poles and weighted down around the peri-meter by mammoth bones and tusks like those found at Gagarino.

Such a structure recalls those of the Eskimo, who used stone boulders to hold down the tent and support the poles needed to hold it up, an arrangement which to judge from the boulder settings found at sites like Borneck and Poggenwisch in Schleswig-Holstein was apparently favoured by the reindeer hunters of the Late-glacial period in that part of the world. Tent-like structures had the obvious advantage that they could fairly easily be dismantled and transported. On the other hand there are indications at the Moravian site of Dolní Věstonice that huts were sometimes built with low mud walls and provided with pitched roofs supported by posts. Whatever remains to be learned about methods of construction, it is already evident that the Eastern Gravettians lived in settlements comprising a number of primary families, a fact which reminds us of the need for group activity among people who depended to any extent on hunting big game. In some cases settlements were made up of a number of discrete dwellings, but in others individual units seem to have coalesced either longitudinally or in a cluster. Whatever the arrangement it seems that each living unit had its own hearth, and it is a fair assumption that it was members of primary family groups who warmed themselves and cooked by these individual fireplaces.

Three main phases have so far been distinguished in the Don basin, phases which at Kostienki I in particular have been found stratified on the same site. The first consists of sites from the base of a loessiform clay, including level V at Kostienki I and levels II–IV at Telmanskaia. The second comprises those incorporated in the loess of the second terrace, including levels II–III at Kostienki I and level I at Telmanskaia. The third and last phase which, to judge from its duration and the wide range of cultural variation, stands in need of further subdivision, includes sites in the loess loam of the first flood-plain terrace, such as level I at Kostienki I, Alexandrovka (Kostienki IV) and Kostienki III. As to chronology it is suggestive that pollen from the first phase argues for a relatively mild climate, and suggests that it may have begun during the interstadial whose close seems to have accompanied the onset of Advanced Palaeolithic culture in many widely spread territories. It is suggestive that the lowest level (level V) at Kostienki I yielded triangular points with shallow bifacial flaking remarkably similar to those from the Caucasian Mousterian site of Ilskaya. In this connection bifacial flaking techniques were applied sporadically during each stage of the Don sequence up to Alexandrovka. This has nothing directly to do with the French Solutrean. It merely reminds us that, as we have already seen in the case of the Szeletian of Hungary, fruitful contact existed outside western Europe between Advanced Palaeolithic and Mousterian cultural traditions. That the south Russian sequence began early is suggested by the fact that level VII at Molodova V on the Dniester, dated by radiocarbon to c. 21,000 B.C., correlates on archaeological grounds with an early part of the third phase of the Don sequence.

A feature of the Advanced Palaeolithic cultures of south Russia is the varied use made of the materials derived from the skeletons of animals hunted for food. This is especially true of the third stage of the Don sequence and of contemporary sites in the Dniester (Molodova level VII and upwards) and Desna (Avdeevo and Mezine) basins. Certain forms, though distinguished by nuances of style, were common between the later Advanced Palaeolithic cultures of western Europe and those of south Russia, for instance perforated needles and shaft-straighteners, awls, reindeer-antler clubs, and in the final stage barbed harpoon-heads. Others, notably a range of handled scoops and heavy chisel-like forms made of mammoth ivory, seem to have been peculiar to the east. Personal ornaments, another feature of Advanced Palaeolithic culture in general, abounded and included fine flat bracelets from Mezine, a form particularly feasible for hunters with a ready supply of mammoth ivory.

Advanced Palaeolithic art

A point to be emphasized about the Gravettians, both of eastern and western Europe, is their achievement in the field of art. Allusion has already been made to the so-called Venus figurines which extend from south Russia to central Europe and thence to south Germany, north Italy and France (map 2). These figurines, only a few inches long, were carved from ivory or stone or occasionally were made of baked clay. The heads as a rule are represented by mere knobs: hair is rarely and features still more rarely indicated (Frontispiece). The figure is shown with full breasts and buttocks and is commonly pregnant; apart from a girdle at the back of one of those from Kostienki and a fringe at the rear of that from Lespugue, the figurines are unclothed. The arms are generally puny and may be folded across the breast, and the legs taper from well-filled thighs, the feet, where these have not been broken off, being suggested rather than shown in detail. In two cases at least the figurines were coloured with red paint. The selective emphasis with which these figurines have been shaped suggests that they were connected in some way with a cult or at least with a body of ideas centring on fertility, and the fact that all those with a definite provenance came from settlements, whether from caves or artificial dwellings, argues for their domestic rather than public or ceremonial significance. In addition to the Venus figurines, the Gravettians carved and modelled figures of various animals in a more or less naturalistic style. Thus at Kostienki I, one of the most famous of the south Russian stations, figures of mammoth were cut rather crudely from the same chalk material as two of the Venus figures, together with the heads of many kinds of animal including lion, bear, and wolf, some with partly human features. The Gravettians of Czechoslovakia were similarly fond of carving animals, and in addition modelled a considerable variety—mammoth, rhinoceros, cave bear, reindeer, bison, horse, lion or tiger, wolf and lynx—from clay which they hardened on the fire like pottery.

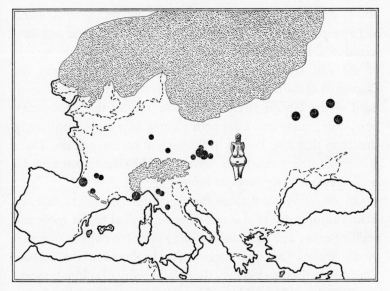

2. Europe in the last Ice Age: glaciated areas shown by stipple,
'Venus' figurines by dots (large dots indicate three or more)

The eastern Gravettians also decorated movable objects by
engraving and occasionally, as in the case of the mammoth jaws
from Mezine on the Desna, by painting. Some of the simpler
geometric patterns used by them were also common to western
Europe. Others like the meander patterns applied to bracelets and
conventionalized human figures are not found in the western
repertoire. Conversely the delight in the representation of
animals by engraving so clearly displayed in the western art does
not seem to have been expressed in the east. Yet the east Gravettians were not averse to representing animals as such. As we have
just seen they carved and modelled mammoths and other animals.
Even more to the point they painted them on cave walls.

Cave art can indeed no longer be regarded as a monopoly of the
Franco-Cantabric province where it was first recognized. A distinctive province of cave art has been recognized in the Mediterranean territory of the Gravettians, notably in Italy, where it

occurs near Rome, Otranto and Palermo and on the small island of Levanzo at present off the coast of Sicily though at one time joined to it. Even more noteworthy is the discovery on the far side of the east Gravettian province some 2,500 miles from the Dordogne of the frieze deep in the Kapova Cave near the southern bend of the Bielaya River in the South Urals that shows cave bear, deer, horse and mammoth painted in a style surprisingly similar to that long known in France and northern Spain. There is indeed a strong case for believing that the Gravettians played a leading role in the genesis of Palaeolithic art.

On the other hand there can equally be no doubt that the richest effloresence of this art, whether applied to the roofs and walls of caves and rock-shelters or to movable objects, occurred in the Franco-Cantabric region. The liveliness of the Franco-Cantabric artists, no less than the rich diversity of cultural expression found in other fields in this region, reminds us that during the Late-glacial period the territory was exceptionally favourable for grazing animals and therefore for the advanced hunters who preyed upon them. Details of the art displayed on movable pieces cannot be given here, but it is worthy of note that in the Magdalenian phase when it reached its peak it was displayed most notably on articles connected directly with the chase, for example on spearthrowers, shaft-straighteners and projectile-heads.

As to the cave art proper, most prehistorians now accept the view that this underwent a single cycle of development in the Franco-Cantabric region. With the most important exception of certain symbolic signs and a few tentative representations little is found before the appearance of Gravettian culture. From this time forward there was a continuous development in the cave art, one which apparently ignored the changes in the forms and techniques of production of implements and weapons used by archaeologists to define one 'culture' from another. A notable advance was made during the life of the Gravettian and Solutrean cultures in the Dordogne, a period that witnessed lively engravings like those of Pair-non-Pair in which special emphasis was laid on the back-lines of the animals depicted. During the time of the late Solutrean and Early Magdalenian the artists ceased to engrave limbs as though they were hanging from the back and particularly notable advances were made in painting, as one can see at Lascaux. This third phase also witnessed the first appearance of sculptures carved in relief on the limestone walls as at Le Roc de Sers where the bison was shown in a forceful but still archaic style. The climax of the cave art was reached during the last four or five thousand years of the Pleistocene during the middle and late phases of the Magdalenian. Engravings and also relief sculptures, well seen at Cap Blanc, show a greater degree of naturalism in the representation of animals. Outstanding advances were made in painting, which at Font de Gaume, Altamira and other contemporary sites shows a more developed sense of modelling. The final phase of the Magdalenian displayed at sites like Limeuil, Le Portel and Isturitz an even more notable degree of naturalism in the representation in line and paint of individual animals. It was during this last stage, also, that the carving and engraving of small movable objects reached its climax. The impression given by the products of Late Magdalenian culture is of a population living primarily by hunting reindeer under highly favourable ecological conditions. This impression is reinforced by the sudden disappearance of the art at the very time when Late-glacial gave way to Neothermal climate at the close of the Pleistocene about two-thirds of the way through the ninth millennium B.C.

Many explanations have been offered to account for the cave art; it has been explained as a way of decorating the home; as an adjunct of hunting magic; as symbolic of the complementarity of the sexes, in itself heightened in significance by the development of an advanced hunting economy; and, latterly, as a system of notation by which early man ensured that his economic activities and social round kept in step with the seasonal variations in his environment. To determine the relative importance of these would require far more extended discussion than we can enter into here. Instead, it is perhaps worth emphasizing a few of the salient implications of the art itself. As we have already suggested it has all the appearance of being the product of hunters living under exceptionally favourable environmental conditions, men who were moreover exploiting this environment with exceptional success. No one can examine the manifestations of this art without being aware of the outstanding powers of observation which it implies, powers which must powerfully have assisted success in the hunt. Again, art has important implications for the mentality of its creator. Advanced Palaeolithic man evidently had the imagination needed to depict in an increasingly life-like manner the animals on which he depended and with which he identified himself in an extraordinarily intense manner. Representational and symbolic art, like the concern with personal decoration with which it was associated, was the outcome of a marked intensification of awareness, both of self-awareness and of awareness of the environment in relation to the self and social group. It is perhaps not so surprising that agriculture and complex literate societies should have emerged for the first time within the territory of and among the immediate descendants of peoples possessed of Advanced Palaeolithic culture.

Expansion of Advanced Palaeolithic culture: Siberia and the Far East

By providing himself with artificial shelter and clothing Middle Palaeolithic man, equipped with a mode 3 lithic technology, had already extended notably the northern frontiers of human settlement in the Old World. Advanced Palaeolithic man occupied large tracts of European Russia and it was apparently during Late-glacial times that parts of Siberia were first occupied by man. Although the total extent of the territory is so vast, the area open to human settlement was in fact limited in the north by the existence of a great zone of lake and marsh south of the northern glaciated zone, between the Urals and the Yenisei and on the south by the mountain zone of inner Asia, much of the outer rim of which was glaciated. Traces of Advanced Palaeolithic settlement have so far been found in the Upper Ob and Yenisei, the Angara and Selenga basins near Lake Baikal and the Upper Lena River up to latitude 61° N. To judge from the fauna, two phases of Late-glacial settlement appear to be represented—an earlier one by Mal'ta and Buret' in the Angara Valley and a later one by Afontova Gora near Krasnoyarsk in the upper Yenisei—and these were followed by one of Neothermal age well seen at Verkholenskaia Gora. The flint industries from Mal'ta and Afontova Gora are both basically Mousterian in tradition with typical tortoise cores, points and side-scrapers. On the other hand the presence of blades, burins and, at the latter site, of microlithic points with battered backs points clearly to a contribution from the Advanced Palaeolithic blade and burin tradition, a contribution which is emphasized by the wealth of antler, bone and ivory artifacts (including eyed needles, slotted bone handles, perforated batons, and objects of personal adornment such as plaques and pendants decorated with pits as well as tubular and disc beads); and still more by the presence of female figurines. The easiest way to account for this apparent mixture is to suppose that Gravettians moving east from the south Russian Plain came in contact with descendants of the Mousterians spreading northward from Uzbekistan. The wealth of ornaments found with the ceremonial burial of a child at Mal'ta suggests that the early settlers of the Baikal region had come to satisfactory terms with their environment, which to judge from the fauna shared certain characteristics of steppe and tundra. One way in which they managed to survive the cold winters was to build semi-subterranean houses with entrance passages, a type which in its basic character still survives in the circumpolar zone. Another, testified by the fine-eyed needles and by a figurine from Buret' on the Angara River, carved from a mammoth tusk and apparently clothed in furs, was the use of sewed skin clothing, for which there is also good evidence at the other end of the Advanced Palaeolithic world in the Magdalenian of western Europe.

One of the main interests of these early Siberian industries is that they provide an obvious source for those earliest intruders into North America who laid a basis for the prehistory of the New World as a whole. In this connection especial significance attaches to the presence already at Mal'ta of bifacially flaked points of a kind that emerged from similar antecedents in many parts of the Old World. Up to the present it is true that no sites of Late-glacial age have been encountered north of latitude 61°, but research in this remote part of the Soviet Union is still in its early days and it should not be overlooked that much of the low-lying plain to the north of the inhospitable mountainous interior of easternmost Siberia, a plain that once linked Alaska with the Lower Lena Valley, has been submerged by the rise of sea-levels during the Neothermal period.

It must also have been by way of Siberia that Advanced Palaeolithic influences penetrated North China and ultimately Japan. Sometimes, as in the upper cave at Choukoutien, there appeared as enrichments, for instance in the form of perforated beads and needles, of a basically archaic tool-kit. Alternatively, we find, in the cave of Hsiao-nan-Lai in Honan a well-defined Advanced Palaeolithic lithic assemblage, including backed blades and microliths, associated with a Late Pleistocene fauna including *Rhinoceros tichorinus*. In the same way blades, burins, vertical retouch and flat-flaking all occur in variants of the early lithic industries found in Japan. The influence of Advanced Palaeolithic culture evidently made itself felt all the way from the Atlantic to the Pacific, not to mention its impact on the New World.

African survivals

Lithic assemblages of mode 4, characterized by blades, burins and a variety of forms made by a vertical retouch, a mode commonly associated with a relatively sophisticated use of antler, bone and ivory as materials for artifacts and over extensive territories associated with the use of personal ornaments and the practice of art, were confined to the northern parts of Africa including Cyrenaica, Nubia and the northern zone of the Horn. Over the rest of the continent industries of mode 3 based primarily on flakes struck from prepared cores persisted down to the close of the Pleistocene.

North of the Sahara and centred on Algeria and Tunisia a local outgrowth of the Levalloiso-Mousterian, known after the Tunisian site of Bir-el-Ater as the Aterian, was marked by tanged points, which to judge from their size could well have been used as arrow-tips. Discussion of the relationship between these points and those found in the Solutrean of Parpalló in eastern Spain has sometimes centred on the question whether the eastern Spanish Solutrean was due to an Aterian incursion or *vice versa*. Since the context of the two sets of points is quite different, one occurring as a component of a mode 3, the other of a mode 4 lithic technology, the question of an intrusion from one region to the other need not be discussed further. What cannot be excluded is some kind of contact leading to the appropriation of a well-defined cultural trait over a major technological boundary.

South of the Sahara one enters the territory of the African Middle Stone Age (*c.* 10,000–35,000 years ago). Although all sharing a basically mode 3 technology, the cultures found in sub-Saharan Africa exhibit certain differences that appear to relate to the varying ecological endowments of the territories in which they are found. The savannah and grassland territories of both South and East Africa supported the Still Bay culture, a leading diagnostic feature of which was the bifacially flaked leaf-shaped point. On the other hand the Congo forests were occupied by an outgrowth of the Sangoan in the form of the Lupemban culture, as seen for example in the upper level at Kalambo Falls. In this culture a significant element of heavy axe-like tools (mode 2)

Table of radiocarbon determinations for Advanced Palaeolithic sites in western Europe with two early ones from south west Asia

WESTERN EUROPE

Magdalenian

			B.C.
1	Grotte de la Vache, Ariège (level II)	L 336c	9700± 200
		GrN 2025	10,590± 105
2	Grotte de la Vache, Ariège (level IV)	GrN 2026	10,900± 60
3	Schussenquelle, Swabia, Germany	GrN 2090	11,140± 110
4	Angles-sur-l'Anglin, Vienne, France	GrN 1913	12,210± 80
5	Cueva del Juyo, Spain	M 830	13,350± 700
6	Altamira, Santander, Spain	M 829	13,550± 700
		C 406	13,566± 900
7	Lascaux, Dordogne, France	Sa 102	14,150± 500
		GrN 1632	15,240± 140

Solutrean

8	Laugerie-Haute, Dordogne, France (top)	GrN 4605	17,920± 190
9	Laugerie-Haute Dordogne, France (base)	GrN 4573	18,800± 150
10	Laugerie-Haute (E.), Dordogne, France	GrN 1888	18,940± 300

Gravettian

11	Abri Pataud, Dordogne, France (level III)	GrN 4506	20,830± 140
		GrN 4721	21,060± 170
12	Abri Pataud, Dordogne, France (level IV)	GrN 4280	25,110± 370
13	Abri Pataud, Dordogne, France (level V)	GrN 4477	24,650± 200
		GrN 4634	26,200± 225

Aurignacian

14	Grotte du Renne, Yonne, France	GrN 1717	28,850± 250
15	La Quina, Charente, France	GrN 1493	29,450± 350
		GrN 4296	29,050± 320
16	Les Cottés, Vienne, France	GrN 4509	29,250± 410
		GrN 4258	30,800± 500
17	Abri Pataud, Dordogne, France (level VII)	GrN 3117	30,850± 450
18	Abri Pataud, Dordogne, France (level XII)	GrN 4719	31,310± 425
19	Abri Pataud, Dordogne, France (level XIV)	GrN 4720	31,380± 410
		GrN 4507	32,300± 675

Châtelperronian

20	Les Cottés, Vienne, France	GrN 4333	31,350± 500
		GrN 4510	29,950± 430
21	Grotte du Renne, Yonne, France	GrN 1742	31,910± 250

SOUTH-WEST ASIA

| 22 | Kara Kamar, Afghanistan | W 224 | 32,050±3000 |
| 23 | Shanidar, Iraq (level C, base: Baradostian) | GrN 250 | 33,130± 520 |

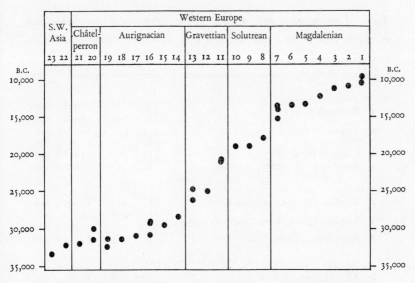

Chart of radiocarbon determination (B.C.) for Advanced Palaeolithic
sites in western Europe with two early ones from south-west Asia.

occurred as well as more elegant bifacial points. Among this latter
group it is interesting to note tanged forms that may indicate the
passage of influences from the Aterian during the period of higher
rainfall and cooler temperature that prevailed in the Sahara during
the last two thousand years or so of the Pleistocene.

That the Middle Stone Age industries of sub-Saharan Africa
served their makers in gaining a living from the various territories
they occupied requires no argument: they would not have continued to exist if they had not done so; and the mere fact that they
varied in accord with ecological differences only confirms the
truism that early man extracted what he could from his environment by means of whatever technology he had at his disposal by
adapting this to local conditions. This does not alter the fact that
sub-Saharan Africa remained a cultural backwater at a time when
changes of the utmost moment to the history of mankind were
under way in the Mediterranean and further east. It is surely no

Table of radiocarbon determinations for Advanced Palaeolithic sites in south, central and east Europe with two early ones from south-west Asia

	ITALY			B.C.
1	Romanelli (level A)	R	58	9,850± 600
		R	56	9,980± 520
2	Fucino			10,670± 410
3	Palidoro	R	83	11,050± 700
4	Grotta La Punta	Pi	152	12,538± 800
5	Romito III (level xxxiv)	R	297	16,800± 350
	GREECE			
6	Kastritsa, Epirus, Greece (hearth-1m.)	I	1960	11,450± 210
7	Kastritsa, Epirus, Greece (hearth in beach)	I	2468	18,250± 480
		I	2466	18,850± 810
8	Asprochaliko, Epirus, Greece	I	1965	24,150± 900
	CENTRAL AND EASTERN EUROPE			
9	Arka, Hungary	GrN 4218		11,280± 85
10	Ságvar, Hungary	GrN 1959		15,810± 150
		GrN 1783		16,950± 100
11	Nitra-Čermǎň, Czechoslovakia	GrN 2449		21,050± 330
12	Molodova V, Middle Dniester, USSR (level 7)	Mo. 11		21,050± 800
13	Pavlov, Czechoslovakia	GrN 1325		23,070± 150
		GrN 1272		24,780± 250
14	Aggsbach, Austria	GrN 2513		24,850± 200
15	Krems-Wachtberg, Austria	GrN 3011		25,450± 300
16	Nemšova, Czechoslovakia	GrN 2470		26,620±1300
17	Dolní Vestonice, Czechoslovakia	GrN 2902		26,390± 390
18	Istállösko, Hungty	GrN 2598		27,170± 312
19	Istállösko, Hungary	GrN 1935		28,950± 600
		GrN 1501		29,590± 600
20	Willendorf, Austria (level I)	GrN 1287		28,580± 250
21	Willendorf, Austria (level IV)	GrN 1273		30,110± 250
22	Willendorf, Austria (level V)	H 246/231		32,000±3000
	SOUTH-WEST ASIA			
23	Karar Kamar, Afghanistan	W 224		32,050±3000
24	Shanidar, Iraq (level C, base: Baradostian)	GrN 250		33,130± 520

NOTE. There is evidence for the appearance of the Advanced Palaeolithic in Cyrenaica at an early date in the guise of the Dabban culture. From a relatively late phase we have a determination of 31,150 B.C. ±400 for level XX in the Haua Fteah. An estimated age for the beginning of the Dabban is 38,000 B.C.

accident that the decisive shift from hunting and food-gathering to food-production was accomplished within the sphere of a mode 4 and indeed mode 5 rather than a mode 3 technology.

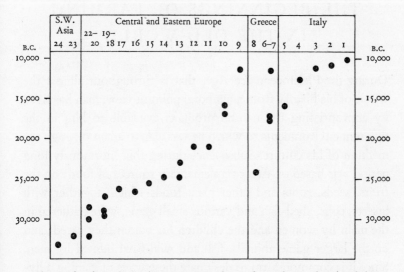

Chart of radiocarbon, determinations (B.C.) for Advanced Palaeolithic sites in south, central and east Europe with two early ones for south-west Asia.

CHAPTER 4

THE BEGINNINGS OF FARMING
IN THE OLD WORLD

During the Pleistocene Ice Age, that is throughout almost the whole of his history from a temporal point of view, man has lived by appropriating the natural products available to him in the different environments to which he was able to adapt through the medium of his culture. Subsistence during this enormously long period was based on two complementary sources of food: on the fruits, seeds, roots and other plant foods which, together with insects, eggs, shell-fish and various small game, were gathered in the main by women and the children for whom they cared; and on the larger game animals, fish and wild-fowl hunted by men. Since it is common form to designate these ways of gaining a living as parasitic and by implication inferior to those centred on the production of food by means of various types of farming or manufacture, it is perhaps worth emphasizing that their successful pursuit in the wide range of environments into which men had penetrated by the end of the Pleistocene implied a detailed knowledge of the whereabouts and habits of a much greater variety of animal and plant species than farmers had to concern themselves with; moreover, as the cave art so well illustrates, under favourable ecological conditions, hunting was capable of sustaining an interesting, exciting and in some measure leisured life. The Garden of Eden had its own, very definite attractions.

The implications of farming

All the same it has to be admitted that, except for those who were able to work their way out of it, the hunter-fisher way of life was essentially a dead-end. Individual groups like the Late-glacial reindeer hunters of Europe or the recent salmon-catching Indians of the north-west Pacific coast of North America were able, because of particularly favourable circumstances, to enjoy a certain leisure and indulge in a number of activities beyond those narrowly tied to subsistence. Yet no community whose livelihood was based exclusively on hunting, fishing or gathering has been able to share in the historical possibilities open to those whose subsistence was securely based on farming. The history of man during the last ten thousand years shows that there was something to be said for eating of the fruit of the tree of knowledge. It may be that the epoch of farming has been brief in relation to prehistory, but until men had learned to farm their historical possibilities were painfully restricted. Conversely, within a few thousand years of the sowing of the first crops, the threshold of literacy had been crossed in several distinct territories and some of the great historic traditions of mankind had been launched. What was needed above all for rapid development in the sphere of culture was an assured surplus of food: a main reason for the importance of cereal grains is precisely that they were capable of being stored for long periods without serious deterioration, and so in effect formed an important kind of capital. It was possession of this capital—and animal herds were only another kind—that made it possible for large groups of people to live together in permanent settlements, and so allowed a combination of economic specialization with large-scale organization. That is why prehistorians have come to view the attainment of farming as a phenomenon comparable in importance with the industrial and scientific revolutions which within a few thousand years it made possible.

It was no doubt because of its widespread implications over the whole range of social life that prehistorians a few years ago were so ready to accept the idea that the invention of farming constituted a veritable revolution. Yet to treat a process so long-drawn out and involving so subtle a change in the attitude of men to animals and plants in the same terms as an invention or even a series of inventions in the sphere of technology is surely to misunderstand its nature. Again, as will shortly be made clearer, the development of farming can hardly be described as 'Neolithic' since it preceded the appearance of communities practising a full-scale Neolithic technology, as this has been defined for over a hundred years. Historically it is easy to account for the hypothesis of a 'Neolithic Revolution' appearing when it did: the expansion of scientific archaeology into south-west Asia between the two world wars yielded a flood of new information from a territory which on *a priori* grounds was considered most likely to have been the earliest home of agriculture; and this information broke upon a profession brought up to accept a sharp antithesis between Palaeolithic hunters and gatherers and Neolithic farmers. Renewed exploration and excavation during the last twenty years or so has put the matter in a rather different light. It has shown that the transition from hunting and gathering to stock-raising and cultivation was a long-drawn out process that spread over several thousand years; and it has further revealed that the technology of the peoples mainly responsible for this transition conformed to the same pattern as that of the Mesolithic peoples, explored a generation previously in north-western Europe. The 'Neolithic Revolution' was neither a revolution nor was it Neolithic: it was, rather, a transformation begun by Advanced Palaeolithic and carried through by Mesolithic communities.

Before considering in more detail the history of this slow and indeed barely perceptible process it is perhaps worth trying to appreciate more clearly what was involved. Possibly the simplest way of doing so is to compare the situation of communities before and after the transformation. During the long periods during which they had to obtain their food by appropriating the natural increase of animals and plants wherever and whenever these might be available, men had normally to move over considerable distances during the course of the year and could only exist in small widely distributed groups. By contrast communities of farmers were able to concentrate on a much more restricted territory and a narrower range of animals and plants, to maintain these within close reach of permanent settlements and to select for breeding the varieties best suited to their requirements; this in turn meant that they were able to lead settled lives in communities at once larger and more closely distributed, communities in which specialization and the possibility of large-scale organization made possible the development of progressively more complex cultures.

Specialized hunting

An important step towards domestication was taken when certain groups of hunters began to concentrate on particular species of game animal instead of going for whatever was available. The risk taken by concentration—by putting almost all the eggs in one basket—was offset by the close attachment, amounting almost to symbiosis, which a group of hunters was able under certain conditions to establish with particular herds of grazing animals. Having said this it will be easy to see why this concentration is taken as a step towards domestication, a state of affairs which was ultimately to lead to complete control over certain categories of animal. This narrowing down of the range of interest in respect of animals taken for food can be noted among several hunting groups in different parts of the Advanced Palaeolithic world.

The reindeer hunters of western and northern Europe during the period between ten and fifteen thousand years ago provide a well-documented example. Analysis of the larger game animals represented in the food-refuse of the Late Magdalenians who sheltered in the south German cave of Petersfels for example shows that they obtained more than four-fifths of their meat from reindeer. An even greater concentration can be seen on the summer hunting stations of the Hamburgians and Ahrensburgians sited on the margins of glacial tunnel-valleys in Schleswig-Holstein. In this case over 99 per cent of the larger game animals were of a single species. The evidence suggests that other animals were the victims of chance encounters and that the only serious quarry was the reindeer, an animal which as is well known is highly gregarious. By attaching themselves to a herd of reindeer a group of hunters would not only possess themselves of a walking larder, comparable up to a point with a domesticated herd, but also a source of many of the most important raw materials they needed, skins for clothing and tents, antler and sinew for hunting gear. There is of course no way of determining whether, given time, the hunters would have modified their already close relationship with the reindeer herds: from the point of view of basic subsistence a highly satisfactory relationship was already in being; and when much later reindeer were domesticated in the circumpolar zone it was primarily to harness them to sledges or even to ride them. The question is in any case academic because quite suddenly, in the course of a few generations, the ecological setting changed: as Late-glacial gave place to Post-glacial climate and glaciers entered on their final retreat, forests encroached rapidly on the open grazing grounds formerly occupied by reindeer. As we shall see (pp. 79–83), the hunting peoples of the North European Plain reacted in part by reverting to the mixed hunting economy of previous ages, but in part by developing special skills in fishing and winning food from the sea-shore.

Although the evidence has not been so clearly worked out in south-west Asia there are signs that specialized hunting was carried on in some regions at the close of the Pleistocene and at the beginning of Neothermal times. For instance analysis of the animal bones from the sequence excavated in the Mugharet el-Wad, Mount Carmel, shows that gazelles and fallow deer alternated as the most important quarry during the Late Pleistocene, but that at the beginning of the Neothermal gazelles were so overwhelmingly represented that they must have been the object of highly concentrated attention on the part of the Natufian hunters occupying the coastal zone of the Levant at this time.

74

Again, there are signs that the hunters of the Zagros around the close of the Pleistocene and the beginning of the Neothermal specialized in hunting goats, significant as a possible prototype of domesticated forms.

Wild prototypes of early cultivated cereals

Recent excavations at the east Syrian site of Mureybit have shown that wild barley and two-seeded einkorn were systematically harvested by hunters of wild ox, onager and gazelle. The cereal crops principally cultivated during the seventh and eighth millennia B.C. included two-rowed barley (*Hordeum spontaneum*), emmer wheat (*Triticum dicoccoides*) and einkorn (*T. boeoticum*). Modern distributions of wild prototypes give some clue to the earliest foci of domestication, but too much reliance should not be placed on these. For one thing the climatic changes of the last ten thousand years must have caused shifts in the distribution of plants. Again, no reliance can be placed on stray occurrences since weed races must almost certainly have spread since agriculture began. Reliance is therefore placed much more on the occurrence of natural stands of wild cereals and even so it must be recognized that domestication is more likely to have occurred on the margins of these where the natural harvest was less readily available. Nevertheless it seems to be reasonably certain that wild prototypes of the early cultivated cereals were most readily available on the hilly flanks of the Fertile Crescent from the Levant through eastern Anatolia to the Zagros range of northern Iraq and western Iran. In each case the wild and cultivated forms are still so closely allied that easy crosses can be made. Where they differ is in respect of grain dispersal. Whereas each of the wild forms has a brittle rachis that disperses the seed, all the cultivated ones have tougher ones: in the case of einkorn the rachis breaks only on threshing and with barley and emmer not even then. This means that whereas wild grains disperse themselves spontaneously cultivated ones need to be intentionally sown.

So far as wild cereals are concerned significant differences have been observed in different parts of the territory where natural stands still exist. In the case of barley, which because of its relative intolerance to cold rarely grows above 1500 metres, separate races exist on different parts of the mountain flanks of the Fertile Crescent. The two most important of these are the Zagros and the Levant. In the case of einkorn the main distinction is that between the small-seeded *aegilopoides* species found in west Anatolia and the Balkans, where it occurs merely as a weed of disturbed habitats, and the large two-seeded *thaudor* species, the best stands of which occur in south-east Turkey. Emmer, which was particularly demanding in its requirements and is thus a sensitive ecological indicator, occurs in two well-separated areas, namely in Turkey, Iraq, Iran and proximate parts of the USSR, where it occurs only sporadically with einkorn and wild barley, and the Upper Jordan Valley, where a robust variety grows in massive stands. The evidence of contemporary wild cereals suggests therefore that domestication took place in more than one zone of the relatively small area that supported the earliest farming economies of the Old World. Einkorn was almost certainly cultivated first in south-east Turkey, still the main focus of the *thaudor* species, whereas emmer was most probably taken in hand first of all in the Upper Jordan Valley. In the cases of two-rowed barley there is no reason for preferring either the Zagros or the Levant and it could even be that cultivation was started independently in the two regions.

Climatic change: from Late Pleistocene to Neothermal

It might be judged improbable on *a priori* grounds that major changes in the basis of subsistence and in technology should have coincided with significant alterations in climate without there being any link between them. Indeed, if we take account of the fact that we are dealing with comparatively primitive subsistence economies, the burden of proof lies on the other side: the only reasonable assumption must be that the relationship between climatic change and cultural innovation was indeed one of cause and effect. This is not by any means to adopt a deterministic view. It is never the case that patterns of subsistence are determined in normal human societies by narrowly climatic or other environmental factors. Equally, on the other hand, it is almost invariably true under the conditions of primitive society that these patterns are adjusted to local ecological conditions. Far from derogating from the dignity of man this merely emphasizes his humanity, for as we have seen again and again man owes his superiority as much as anything else to his ability to adapt to a far wider range of environments than other mammals. He is able to do this through his possession of culture by which he fulfils his social needs in whatever context he finds himself. Whereas other animals were often unable to adjust quickly enough to environmental change, man was able to meet new stresses in his environment and even to turn new conditions to his own profit. One way in which he was able to do this was to modify his technology and alter the pattern of his subsistence.

Within the territory of the Advanced Palaeolithic peoples the end of the Ice Age, the transition from Late Pleistocene to early Neothermal, was marked by environmental changes of widely varying character. These were on the whole more drastic in territories near the borders of the old ice-sheets. Thanks to Quaternary research a good deal is already known about the course of events. In particular pollen-analysis has revealed in clear outline the history of vegetational change. The Pleistocene ice-sheets appear to have begun their final retreat rather more than ten thousand years ago. From one point of view this was favourable for human settlement because it opened up new territories for settlement, more particularly in Scandinavia and the northern parts of the British Isles. Yet the approach to temperate conditions was no unmixed blessing. Admittedly in the long run when temperatures had reached their maximum the possibility opened up of introducing farming. Yet for the first few thousand years or so conditions were worse in the sense that the herds of reindeer, on which the specialized and almost self-sufficient hunting of north-west Europe was based, were no longer able to graze a unique Late-glacial flora. Adjustments had to be made to the spread of forest trees and it was the changes involved in the sphere of subsistence and technology that gave rise to the Mesolithic cultures so well developed on the North European Plain.

Much less is known as yet about the course of environmental change in territories more remote from the former ice-sheets. Until much more detailed work has been done in the way of Quaternary research the course of climatic history in the Mediterranean basin and in the parts of south-west Asia crucial to the early history of farming must remain obscure. Yet it can be said that there is evidence from some areas that the transition was marked by a period of greater aridity. The pollen and animal remains from the Cueva dell Toll between Barcelona and the Pyrenees for instance point fairly strongly to a relatively warm, dry fluctuation at the end of the Ice Age. The rise of bovids at the Haua Fteah in Cyrenaica and of gazelle at Mount Carmel may well be the result of selective hunting, but at least they are consistent with dry conditions. Again, increasing aridity was indicated by the pollen in Shanidar Cave and there are clear, if not yet precisely dated, indications of climatic change in the sediments in Lake Zeribar in the Zagros. Over the extensive territory involved even quite minor changes of climate may well have resulted locally in changes of widely varying character. Details will have to wait on research. In the meantime it may be noted that the period around ten thousand years ago was marked by climatic adjustments that may well have posed acute problems in the sphere of subsistence. What mainly needs emphasizing is that, whereas in northern Europe environmental change ran counter to the trend towards concentrating on particular species, in south-west Asia it may well, if anything, have encouraged intensification of the food-quest.

Mesolithic hunter-fishers

It is no accident that the most clearly defined hunting groups practising a mode 5 lithic technology are those that flourished on the North European Plain in territories most severely affected by environmental change at the close of the Pleistocene. The Neo-thermal inhabitants of this region had to adapt to a landscape transformed from park-tundra into closed forest. The pastures available to herbivorous animals were now restricted to forest glades, river courses and the margins of lakes and of the sea-shore. People could no longer support themselves by hunting a single species. Instead Mesolithic man was driven to extending his quest for food to include a wide range of animals and plants. Useful information about this is preserved in the organic muds and peats filling the old lake-beds favoured for settlement.

Information is particularly rich in respect of the Maglemosians who take their name from the big bog (*magle mose*) at Mullerup where their culture was first recognized. Their hunting-grounds on the North European Plain extended in the west to eastern England and Flanders with outliers as far as Ulster, and were centred on the marshy region now covered by the North Sea, and North German Plain, and the west Baltic area including Denmark and south Sweden; in the east they occupied parts of northern Russia as far as the Ural mountains. Over the whole of this territory they were fond of camping along river banks and lake shores on the margin of the encompassing forest, a favoured resort of certain game animals, including notably elk, as well as of wild-fowl, water-plants and fish.

A useful insight into the sources of food available to the Maglemosians at the close of the birch period around the middle of the eighth millennium B.C. is given by the find at Star Carr in Yorkshire. Red deer was admittedly the preferred game, but aurochs (*Bos primigenius*) and elk were also hunted rather commonly, as were also roe deer. It is plain that already hunting had reverted to the ancient unspecialized pattern. Water-birds were also taken but there is no evidence that fishing was carried on when the camping-place was occupied, even though from later settlements of the Maglemosian tradition there is good evidence for the systematic catching of pike. Although evidence for plant food is only indirect there can hardly be any question that nuts, fruits, seeds and rhizomes of different kinds were gathered and eaten. The only trace of domestication relates to the remains of dog recovered from Star Carr itself and from certain sites in Denmark. The dogs from these Maglemosian contexts were characterized by large teeth in short jaws. They could of course be the product of local domestication from wolves. Alternatively they might have come in from centres where agriculture was already being practised, a reminder that cousins of the Mesolithic hunter-fishers of Europe were already developing a farming economy in parts of south-west Asia.

The material equipment from Maglemosian sites clearly reflects the way in which they adapted to form a comprehensive hunting and fishing economy in a forested environment. The flint industry on which their technology was ultimately based was aimed first and foremost at producing the artifacts needed for hunting game, preparing skins and cutting up the bone and antler and felling and shaping timber. Microliths made from narrow bladelets in the fashion of mode 5 were used in the main for tipping, barbing and arming the edges of projectiles and knives. Scrapers were probably used among other things for preparing skins and burins for cutting up antler and bone as they had already been in Advanced Palaeolithic cultures. A particularly noteworthy item, though one that was not of great numerical importance, was the adze-blade. This was often chipped down from a nodule, sharpened by a burin-like transverse blow and mounted in a sleeve made of wood or antler through which the wood handle was passed. The appearance of this form already during the first phase of the Maglemosian is interesting because it shows how rapidly men adapted to the new forest environment. The felled birch trees on the lake-edge at Star Carr bear witness to the effectiveness of such tools, which must have been used to shape dugout canoes like that from Pesse in Holland and probably also the paddles found at Star Carr and other sites. Long single-piece wooden bows were used for hunting. Wooden arrows were nocked and fletched at one end and either barbed and tipped with microliths or in the case of those intended for birds or small fur-bearing animals provided with flat bolt-like heads. Barbed points made of antler or bone were mounted as spearheads and used for both hunting and fishing. Equipment specifically designed for fishing included seine-nets supported by bark floats and weighted with stones, fish-hooks notable for having barbless points, and basket weels; and no doubt it was largely for fishing on inland waters that canoes and paddles were employed.

The Maglemosians found time to adorn themselves—even the Star Carr hunters wore necklaces made up of perforated deer teeth, sections of bird-bone, shale pebbles and lumps of amber—and also, more especially in the West Baltic region at the heart of their culture, to practise art. This took the form mainly of engraving objects of daily use as well as pendants or amulets and antler staves apparently of ceremonial or other social use; but amber lumps were sometimes carved in the round to the shape of animal forms. The techniques employed included line engraving, sometimes so fine as almost to escape scrutiny, and pits neatly drilled into the surface. The commonest motives were linear chevrons, hatched zones, criss-cross lines and various kinds of barbed line. Alongside these abstract designs occasional schematic representations of men and animals may be seen. As a rule these were of single individuals. Occasionally, as on a piece from Fünen, anthropomorphic designs were knit together in such a way as perhaps to suggest generations; and in the case of engravings on an aurochs bone from Ryemarksgaard we find a definite if enigmatic scene in which an animated individual with outstretched arms appears at one end of a row of four more restrained figures lacking arms and backed by three vertical chevrons. In the case of some of the geometric designs the suggestion has been made that they may perhaps relate to a system of calendrical notation of a kind particularly useful to people who had to take account of the seasons of maturation of a wide range of animals and plants.

The Maglemosians were unique among the Mesolithic groups in Europe for the vigorous and creative character of their adjustment to forest conditions. On the other hand the general form of their economy, the widespread use of the bow, the practice of a mode 5 flint technology and the generally abstract art were features general to the hunter-fisher groups of much of Europe during early Neothermal times. Although some of these, and most notably the Maglemosians, made significant innovations, the culture of all these groups stemmed from Advanced Palaeolithic sources and represented substantially the result of adjusting to Neothermal conditions. It is interesting to see how rapidly this adjustment was made in the heart of the Franco-Cantabric region where reindeer hunting gave place to the hunting of stags and other forest animals and how this was accompanied by a configuration of new forms, including harpoon-heads made from stag antler, sufficiently distinct to cause archaeologists to speak of passing from a Magdalenian to an Azilian culture, named after Mas-d'Azil in Ariège. The designs painted on selected river pebbles found in such large number at the name-site are even more abstract than the designs engraved on Maglemosian objects, but it is interesting to observe analogies between the schematic anthropomorphic representations in the two territories. To judge from the general impoverishment of material culture found in most parts of Europe in the context of Mesolithic communities of hunter-fishers, the break-up of herd-hunting and the reversion to mixed hunting and gathering reduced the possibilities open to most peoples.

One way in which Mesolithic man could compensate in the Neothermal environment of most of Europe was, as we have seen, to develop fishing. For the most part this was confined to inland waters, but on the coast maritime resources were brought in to make up for the reduction of grazing ground caused by the spread of forests. Much of the evidence for this lies submerged by the rise of ocean levels due to the continued melting of ice-sheets during the Post-glacial period. For the Scandinavian peninsula itself the position is better. Here isostatic recovery of the land as the ice-sheets melted more than offset the eustatic rise of ocean levels. As a result the old beach-lines formed during temporary periods of relative stability are available for study. This has shown that at intervals from West Sweden to Fosna on the west coast to Finnmark on the north coast of Norway settlement during the early and middle part of Neothermal times was concentrated on the sea-margin. It seems a fair assumption, though not one that can be proved owing to the lack of organic traces on the early sites, that those who settled on the coast did so to take advantage of two environments, that of the interior and that of the actual beach and of inshore waters. There is plenty of evidence for this from the middens dating from the height of the Post-glacial period in the west Baltic and around the Atlantic coasts, for instance in western Scotland, Brittany and the Tagus estuary. The mounds, themselves composed in large measure of the shells of marine molluscs, contain the bones of land mammals, side by side with those of marine fish and on occasion seals and toothed whales.

The earliest farmers in the Old World

Whereas in north-western, and for that matter in central, eastern and southern Europe peoples equipped with microlithic flint industries of mode 5 continued to depend on hunting, fishing and gathering for subsistence, other groups sharing the same basic technology laid the foundations of settled life. They did so in those parts of south-west Asia where prototypes of the earliest domesticated animals and plants existed in a wild state and where, as we have seen, the concentration on particular species as sources of food, already begun during the Late Pleistocene, was not

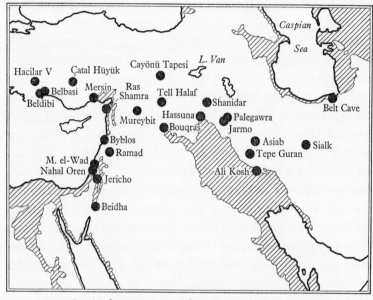

3. Key sites in the transition to farming in south-west Asia.
Land below 200 m. shown in shading.

interrupted but if anything stimulated by the ecological changes
that marked the transition to Neothermal climate. Here the transition could be effected broadly between the ninth and seventh
millennia B.C. by peoples having the same transitional or Mesolithic
character and basically the same technology as their cousins in
Europe condemned to eke out a poor existence in an environment
that from the point of view of hunters had undergone a change
for the worse at the end of the Ice Age.

Zagros

Evidence has been found both on the Iraqi and Iranian sides of the
frontier for the transitional phase in farming before pottery had
been taken into common use. To take first the Kurdish zone, the
evidence comes from both rock-shelters and open settlements.
Layer B in the cave of Shanidar is particularly instructive. In the

lower portion (B2) dating from around 10,000 B.C. a lithic industry of the type first recognized at Palegawra occurs with remains of wild goats that seem to have been hunted as a herd and
may have been systematically culled. In the upper part (B1) belonging to the early half of the ninth millennium the same lithic
tradition persisted, though now enriched by blades for slotted
reaping-knives. Bones of domestic sheep bear witness to herd-
maintenance and such traits as querns, baskets and reaping-knife
blades point to the harvesting of cereals. The same people, it
appears, also inhabited open stations at this time, notably at
Karim Shahir and Zawi Chemi Shanidar.

The most fully, though still incompletely explored village relating to this phase is that of Jarmo, which most probably dates
from the first half of the seventh millennium B.C. The settlement,
situated on a promontory in the Kurdish hills, can hardly, to
judge from the thinness of its deposits, have lasted for more than
a very few centuries. It probably consisted of about twenty-five
houses huddled together, each having an open alley or small
court on two sides. The houses themselves, which had several
small rectangular rooms each, were constructed of packed mud
built up course by course, each being allowed to dry in the sun
before the next one was added. Clay ovens and the bases for silos
were built into each house and marks on the floors showed that
these were covered by plaited mats. The villagers lived only to a
slight extent by hunting—the bones of wild animals account for
about 5 per cent of the whole—and depended mainly on mixed
farming: two-rowed barley, emmer, spelt and peas were certainly
cultivated and sheep and goats were herded and maintained. A
Palegawra-like array of microliths reflect the continuance of hunting and whole blades showing the tell-tale gloss that came from
friction with corn stalks, as well as milling-stones, confirm that
cereals were harvested, cereals which we know were now domesticated in the sense that they had been improved by breeding and
systematically sown. Since mats were made it is highly probable

that baskets were as well, but although figurines of women and animals were modelled from unfired clay there is no sign from the main part of the deposit that pottery was made, nor was there any evidence for textiles. On the other hand the fact that pottery was found in the top third of the deposit, taken in conjunction with the original radiocarbon dates, suggests that the Jarmo settlement belongs to the last phase of farming before the development of formal Neolithic culture in the region.

Recent excavation in south-western Iran has brought to light important evidence bearing on the evolution of farming in the provinces of Khuzistan and Luristan. Three classes of settlement have been recognized: permanent villages of mud-walled houses occupied by up to a hundred persons; seasonal camps without permanent structures; and caves, which like Shanidar itself were probably resorted to seasonally by herding units belonging to permanent villages. At least two phases of farming settlement antedate the appearance of the earliest pottery in this region round about 6000 B.C. The initial Bus Mordeh phase witnessed the systematic collection of seeds, including those of wild alfalfa, spring milk vetch, wild oats and other wild cereal grasses and the fruit of wild capers. Indeed, wild seeds often of very small size, of a kind that must have been shaken into a fine basket or tray, made up over nine-tenths of those recovered in carbonized form. The remaining fraction included grains of emmer wheat and two-rowed barley which can be presumed on account of their size to have been planted. The fact that seeds of the sea club-rush occurred mixed with cultivated cereal grains suggests that crops must have been grown and harvested in close proximity to marshy ground; and it may be significant in this regard that carp, water-turtle, mussel and water-birds were included in the diet. Hunting remained important, gazelle being the principal quarry along with onager, wild ox and wild boar, but livestock were also maintained. Goats were presumably introduced from the near-by mountains and were herded on a considerable scale. Sheep had hardly begun to appear in any number. The flint-work reflects the economic base of Bus Mordeh society: microliths point to hunting; and blades for insertion into reaping knives to reaping.

During the succeeding Ali Kosh phase cereal cultivation greatly increased at the expense of plant-gathering and emmer and two-rowed barley accounted for two-fifths of carbonized seeds. Goat still outnumbered sheep. Increased prosperity based on higher production of cereals was reflected in larger houses that were now built of sun-dried bricks held together by mud mortar and often plastered over with mud on either face. Mats were used on the floors and the villagers also made twined baskets some of which they apparently waterproofed with pitch. Stone bowls became more numerous and diverse in form. Personal ornaments now included a tubular bead made from cold-hammered native copper. Pottery on the other hand was not brought into use until the onset of the ensuing Mohammad Jaffar phase around *c.* 6000 B.C.

The Levant

At the opposite extremity of the crescent in Jordan and Israel a parallel sequence of development can be observed from a hunting and gathering economy to one in which farming played an increasingly important role, a development associated with quite a distinct manifestation of a mode 5 lithic industry. Early in the Neothermal period we find a well-defined culture termed Natufian after the Shouqbah Wady en-Natuf cave, where it was first recognized. This was centred on a strip within forty miles of the coast from Beirut to the Judaean desert with extensions to the south-west as far as Heluan near Cairo and northwards to Syria and even to Beldibi in south Turkey. The bearers of this culture occupied both rock-shelters and open stations, the former represented by the Mugharet el-Wad, el-Kebarah and Shouqbah and the latter by phase 3 at Naḥal Oren on the west slope of Mount Carmel as well as by the earliest occupations at Tell-es-Sultan (Jericho) and Beidha near Petra.

As we have already noted, the animal bones from Natufian sites indicate a concentration on gazelle so marked as to suggest that the hunters concentrated on herds of this animal for the bulk of their protein, but they supplemented this by fishing and more importantly by the harvesting of cereals. Their material culture reflects their needs. Microliths, the predominant form of which was the crescent with its back blunted by bipolar flaking giving a marked ridge, were presumably used to arm weapons for hunting. The rich bone work included finely barbed spearheads and barbless fish-hooks closely similar in form to those of the Maglemosian in northern Europe. The importance of harvesting is suggested by the number of blades with lustre caused by friction with stalks and by the slotted bone handles for holding these. Numerous mortars, some of them cut out of the living rock, as well as stone pestles, also point to the importance of plant food. The numbers of people found buried together in cemeteries—87 persons (64 adults) at el-Wad, c. 50 at Naḥal Oren and 45 at Shouqbah—suggests that the Natufians were able to live in sizeable groups. Other evidence of a certain prosperity lies in the wealth of personal ornaments buried with the dead who were presumably fully clothed. These included head-dresses and thigh-bands made up of *Dentalium* shells, necklaces of beads made from the perforated and carved articular ends of gazelle phalanges, bored teeth and twin-pendants of carved bone separated by *Dentalium* spacers. Again, Natufian art, although not very plentiful, occasionally, as in the case of a carved cervid from Umm ez-Zuetina, reached a degree of naturalism comparable with that of the Magdalenian. Other carved work included the ends of bone reaping-knife handles shaped into the form of animal heads and a small stone head of a human being.

The vitality of the Natufian culture is also witnessed in an even more significant way by the fact that it formed the basis for further advances towards settled life. It is significant that many of the flint artifacts made by the people who built the first massive defences of Tell-es-Sultan, comprising a rock-cut ditch 9 metres wide and 3 metres deep backed by a stone wall with bastion-like towers, were made in the same tradition as the original Natufian encampment round the spring. The original builders of the Jericho defences (stage A)—known as the hogback-brick people, from the slope of the bricks used in building their beehive-shaped huts within the defended area—are only presumed to have farmed on the grounds that they can hardly otherwise have afforded to construct defences on such a scale. Stage B at Jericho has often been referred to as the plaster-floor stage on account of the use of lime-plaster for finishing the interiors of the rectangular buildings which now came into use. At both stages some form of skull-cult seems to have been practised: the hogback-brick people packed skulls in nests very much in the same way as the Mesolithic folk of Ofnet and Kaufertsberg did in Bavaria; but the plaster-floor makers showed greater sophistication in modelling the faces of the dead in fine painted clay, marking the eyes in some cases by inset cowrie shells (Pl. III).

The humbler settlements at Naḥal Oren and Beidha in each case overlaid Natufian encampments and further agreed with Jericho in their architectural sequence. At Naḥal Oren only structures of stage A were well preserved. These comprised round huts with dry-stone walls, well-defined entrances and interior fireplaces set on a series of artificial terraces and accompanied by clusters of rounded ancillary structures. At Beidha on the other hand it is only the houses of stage B that have yet been examined, though it is known that these overlay rounded structures of stage A. The houses of the upper level were rectangular in plan and each covered around 42 centiares (30 square yards). The basement or cellar floors, which alone have yet been recovered, had very thick walls and central passages with rows of small chambers on either side. As at Jericho the rectangular buildings of stage B had been finished with white lime-plaster. The flint industry from stage B at both sites shares a number of features in common with that first recognized at Wadi Tahun, notably chipped axe- and adze-blades sharpened by transverse blows like those from Maglemosian sites in northern Europe and long barbed and tanged flake arrows, often with shallow surface flaking, of a kind widely known from Anatolia. Stage B at Beidha is particularly notable for producing the earliest precise evidence about cereal crops in the Levant. Much the commonest cereal was wild barley (*H. spontaneum*), which must either have grown in exceptionally fine natural stands or have been sown. Emmer on the other hand was certainly domesticated, even if the conspicuously wide range in grain size suggests that this had only happened very recently. Several members of the pea-family and pistachio were among other sources of plant food to be gathered. The Beidha B villagers undoubtedly obtained a very high proportion of their meat from goats and the high proportion of young represented in the kill—substantially higher than, for example, in the case of gazelle—argues that the herds may have been directly controlled and thus to some degree domesticated.

Anatolia

For several reasons, not least its position between the Zagros and the Levant, Anatolia is an area of high strategic importance, but for various reasons very little is known about this stage of its prehistory. Only one site from the critical period has yet been examined—and that incompletely—in the south-east region where einkorn was most probably domesticated, namely Çayönü Tepesi near Ergani in the country west of Lake Van. Here the inhabitants built rectangular houses with grid-like stone foundations. They made clay figurines but no pottery. Their work in flint and obsidian marks an extension of the Palegawran tradition of the Zagros and Caspian regions. They made beads from malachite and drills or reamers from native copper, but of course their technology was no more chalcolithic than that of the bearers of the Archaic culture of the eastern United States of America.

Information about western Anatolia is still scanty, but two things stand out. First there is evidence from a number of caves and rock-shelters in the Antalya region for Mesolithic levels intermediate between Advanced Palaeolithic ones and others, containing Neolithic pottery. At Beldibi and Belbasi these intermediate levels have yielded crescents with bipolar retouch that indicate clear Natufian affinities as if to balance the Palegawran affinities of Çayönü Tepesi; and from Beldibi pebbles with vaguely anthropomorphic designs in red paint remind one in a general way of paintings from Romanelli, but above all of the painted pebbles of Mas-d'Azil. Secondly, there is evidence from a later period near the end of the eighth millennium for a lithic tradition parallel in respect of its projectile points to the Tahunian of the southern Levant. Level V at Haçilar, underlying the well-known chalcolithic mound, is marked by other features paralleled in the 'B' levels in the Levant as far south as Jericho and Beidha, including the absence of pottery, the presence of rectangular houses with plastered walls and floors and evidence for a skull cult. The diet of these earliest inhabitants of Haçilar included meat from wild animals and others of ill-defined status. Plant food included einkorn, cultivated emmer and two-rowed barley as well as lentils.

That Anatolia was linked culturally with both arms of the submontane crescent that gave birth to farming has recently been emphasized by a study of obsidian. The most important sources of this volcanic glass to have been utilized during prehistoric times in south-west Asia are located respectively in the Lake Van–Kars–Erevan districts of Armenia and in the West Cappadocian districts of Ciftlik and Acigol. That obsidian from Armenia was passing south as far as 300–400 kilometres already during the Late Pleistocene is shown by its occurrence in a Baradostian level at Shanidar and in a final Advanced Palaeolithic one at Zarzi. The traffic gained markedly both in intensity and range during the period of transition between 9000 and 6000 B.C. with which we are concerned, reaching as far as Ali Kosh, about 1,000 kilometres

Some key radiocarbon dates for early farming settlements in south-west Asia and north-east Africa

			B.C.
1	Belt Cave	P 26	5840±330
		average of P 19, 19A, 19B	5330±260
2	Bus Mordeh phase	Hole and Flannery	c. 7500–6750
	Ali Kosh phase	Hole and Flannery	c. 6750–6000
	Mohammad Jaffar phase	Hole and Flannery	c. 6000–5600
3	Tepe Guran (U)	K 1006	6460±200
	(H)	K 879	5810±150
4	Tepe Sarab (S5)	P 466	6006± 98
5	Jarmo	estimated (Braidwood)	c. 6750
6	Zawi Chemi Shanidar	W 681	8920±300
7	Matarrah (middle)	W 623	5620±250
8	Çayönü Tepesi	MI 610	6620±250
		MI 609	6840±250
9	Mersin (base)	W 617	6000±250
10	Çatal Hüyük (X)	P 782	6142± 98
11	Bouqras (I)	GrN 4852	6290±100
	(III)	GrN 4820	5990± 60
12	Ras Shamra (VC)	P 459	6192±100
		P 460	6414±101
	(VB)	P 458	5736±112
13	Ramad (II)	GrN 4426	6260± 50
	(III)	GrN 4823	5930± 55
14	Jericho (Pottery)	estimated (Kenyon)	c. 5000
	(PPN/B)	average of GL 28, 38 and GR 963	c. 6310
	(PPN/A)	F 40	6775±210
	(Natufian)	F 72	7850±210
15	Beidha (IV)	BM 111	6830±200
16	Merimde	U 6	4180±110
17	Haua Fteah (VIII)	NPL 42	4420±102
18	Fayum A	C 457	4145±250
		C 550	4441±180
19	Shaheinab	C 753	3110±450
		C 754	3396±380

in a direct line. Cappadocian obsidian was being used by the Advanced Palaeolithic and Mesolithic inhabitants of the Antalya region to the west and, what is much more to our immediate point, by early farmers in the Levant as far south as Jericho and Beidha some 700–800 kilometres distant.

This traffic, already ancient before the first grain of emmer or two-rowed barley had been sown, may remind anyone forgetful

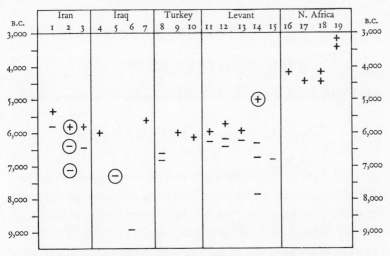

Some key radiocarbon dates (B.C.) for early farming settlements in south-west Asia and north-east Africa. + Indicates sites with pottery; − indicates aceramic sites; ○ indicates estimations.

of the situation in, say, aboriginal Australia that material objects and ideas may travel great distances among peoples not yet firmly attached to the soil. It also warns us of the essential futility of trying to identify precisely where within the vast arc of sub-montane territory over which the ecological prerequisites existed farming first developed. As has already been suggested it seems likely that particular wild cereals were taken into cultivation where they flourished best in the wild state. In this connection it is worth emphasizing that, although the earliest farmers were equipped as might only be expected with a modified Mesolithic lithic technology (mode 5), this conformed to two distinct traditions, the Palegawran extending from south-west Persia to Armenia and the Caspian and the Natufian from south Anatolia through the Levant to Sinai and even the Nile Valley. The last point to make is that it is Anatolia, the home of both sources of obsidian, that provides the largest gap in our knowledge of the prehistory of the zone of south-west Asia most crucial to our enquiry between say 20,000 and 6000 B.C.

CHAPTER 5

THE ACHIEVEMENT OF CIVILIZATION IN SOUTH-WEST ASIA

NEOLITHIC SETTLEMENT IN THE HIGHLANDS

Around 6000 B.C. the early farmers whose beginnings were considered in chapter 4 had developed their economy to the point at which they were able to settle down permanently at fixed sites in their submontane habitats. The peasant communities, whose practice of periodically rebuilding their houses of mud and sun-dried brick on the same sites gave rise to the stratified tells which incorporate the material evidence of their history, still depended for their technology on flint and stone and on the organic materials they could shape with tools made from these. The way in which they were distinguished from their predecessors was by their use of pottery for containers and cooking vessels. In some cases at least they also wove textiles even if actual fabrics have only survived exceptionally. In a word they were fully Neolithic in the sense that this has been understood for over a hundred years; and the Neolithic character of their technology is hardly affected by the use of copper for such minor things as pins and trinkets. The adoption of settled life in itself made for local differentiation and the fact that pottery was at this stage largely made on the site means that it was a vehicle for local variations of taste and fashion, rather as rugs have been in the same region down to the present day. Regional and temporal variations in the make and above all the decoration of pottery are properly subjects for specialist publications. No more will be attempted here than to bring out the broad distinction between the cultural traditions of the two main zones already recognized for the period of transition.

Kurdistan, Iran and Turkmenia

The Neolithic communities of the southern margins of Turk-menia (e.g. Djeitun), the south slopes of the Elburz facing the inner desert zone of the Iranian plateau (e.g. Sialk) and the western slope of the Zagros from Kurdistan and Kermanshah to Fars and ultimately to Baluchistan, although differing in their pottery styles, were united by the basically Palegawran nature of their flint-work. The normal dwelling was rectangular in form and built of either mud or sun-dried brick. At Djeitun it could be seen that the village was made up of a concentration of about thirty farmsteads and there is no evidence at this stage or indeed for another few thousand years of large urban settlements in this part of the world. The animal bones show that the hunting of such species as antelope and goat contributed significantly to subsistence and no doubt the continued manufacture of micro-liths and notably of trapezes was related to this. On the other hand the cultivation of cereals involved the manufacture of equipment for reaping. It is extremely interesting to see how at Djeitun and Sialk I flint-blades continued to be inset into slotted bone handles as they had been since Mesolithic times. Much of the pottery made at sites like Djeitun and Sialk was plain but some of it was painted with simple geometric designs; at the former vertical arrangements of wavy lines sometimes broken by hori-zontal straight ones were favoured, whereas at the latter it was chequer patterns and shaded triangles. Clay figurines of animals and women were a recurrent feature.

There is comparable evidence for farmers settling down and starting to make pottery containers and cooking vessels from many localities along the western slopes of the Zagros from Kermanshah to Fars and on to Baluchistan. Long sustained systematic excava-tion in Khuzistan has brought to light particularly impressive evidence for a gradual evolution of farming and the appearance around 6000 B.C. of fully formed Neolithic culture. The earliest pottery, that of the Mohammad Jaffar stage, included some red-slipped burnished vessels, but for the most part it was buff in colour, mostly plain, but sometimes painted with simple geometric designs. It is significant that alongside reaping-knife flakes and other forms related to farming the microlithic component continued down to the ensuing Sabz phase of the second half of the sixth millennium.

Anatolia, Syria and Northern Iraq

The region extending from the upper Tigris far into southern Anatolia continued to be distinguished by its basic flint technology: instead, for instance, of trapeziform microliths we find projectile-points and even dagger-blades made from heavy tanged blades retouched over the convex and often over part of the under surface by flat shallow flaking. On the other hand reaping-knife blades and polished stone axe-blades were both common elements. The earliest pottery was uniformly monochrome. At Çatal Hüyük, where it was supplemented by abundant wooden containers of varying shapes, the pots were of elementary ovoid form, though provided with lugs or sometimes with bucket-like handles. The earliest villagers at Mersin made hole-mouthed pots and ornamented them with impressions from shells which were sometimes applied with a continuous rocking motion. Shells were also used to ornament monochrome pots of simple form at the Syrian sites of Ras Shamra and Byblos. That this same cultural province included northern Iraq is shown by the flint and obsidian lanceheads from the earliest levels at Tell Hassuna as well as by the pottery. As we shall shortly see the same community of culture obtained during the ensuing period when copper came into increasing use.

The possibilities opened up by an assured supply of food are brilliantly displayed at Çatal Hüyük on the Konya Plain of southern Anatolia. The very extent of the mound covering some 13 hectares (32 acres) and the manner in which the houses are packed together in the excavated area argue for a sizeable community. Subsistence rested to a significant degree on the cultivation and harvesting of cereal crops, including bread wheat as well as einkorn, emmer and barley. Sheep and goats were kept, in addition to dogs, but hunting made a big contribution to the supply of meat. Wild ox, wild pig and red deer were the most important game. The people lived in rectangular houses built contiguously but interspersed at intervals by courtyards. The walls were built of large sun-dried bricks held together by thick layers of mortar containing ash and bones. The buildings were bungalows with flat roofs that were doubtless used during the summer for many purposes other than serving as a means of circulation. The absence of doorways indeed suggests that access to the dwellings was gained through holes in the roofs from which stepped timbers against one wall led down to the ground floor. Indoor ovens were built into the walls so as to help retain heat, but open fireplaces were set near the middle of the floors. Features of the houses were the carefully plastered benches used for sitting and sleeping and not least as receptacles for the family dead. The skeletons, up to thirty or more in a simple bench, appear to have been exposed some while before being buried, but some of them have been set at rest in fairly good anatomical order. The twelve constructional phases noted by the excavators show that houses were frequently rebuilt and the remarkable evidence for continuity of tradition in successive levels suggests that rebuilding took place at frequent intervals.

Although pottery was made from the very beginning, the good conditions of preservation encountered in some levels allow us to observe that wooden vessels and coiled baskets played an important part as containers. The fact that copper and lead were used for beads and trinkets in no wise alters the fact that technology was basically Neolithic. Flint and obsidian provided materials for lanceheads, dagger-blades and blades for setting in the slots of antler reaping-knife handles.

The blades of the axes and adzes needed for felling and shaping timber were made from hard greenstone polished to a sharp edge. Blocks of obsidian were split and polished with the utmost skill to provide mirrors for the women, who used a variety of cosmetics. Antler and bone were worked to provide a wide range of artifacts, including spoons and ladles, needles, belt-fasteners and handles of various kinds. Animal skins were prepared for garments. Woollen textiles were used both for clothing and—to judge from certain wall-paintings—for rugs or hangings. It is impressive to note the wide area from which these early Neolithic people drew their raw materials, and no less to observe the extremely high standard reached in a variety of crafts. The absence of waste materials from the dwellings so far explored argues that separate workshops existed elsewhere on the site and it would seem likely that craft specialization had gone much further than one is accustomed to expect of a Neolithic community.

Richness in material goods was more than matched in the sphere of art and cult. Reliefs and paintings were applied to the plastered walls of certain rooms so richly as to denote their use as shrines, but the number and small size of these argues for domestic family cults: public temples manned by whole-time priests were still something for the future. The iconography of the wall art, as of the numerous small plastic figurines and stone carvings, argues that worship centred round the generative forces of nature. No emphasis was laid on the organs of sex, but the figures shown on the walls were either women or animals such as bulls or rams symbolic of male potency. These last were sometimes represented only by heads and horns, as in scenes showing women giving birth to bulls. Men and boys were sometimes represented in the figurines and one stone carving shows two pairs in embrace, on one side a goddess and her partner and on the other a goddess and her son. Conversely the theme of death is symbolized by leopards, counterparts of the jaguars of Mesoamerican iconography:

opposed leopards are shown in wall reliefs and among the figurines one of a woman in childbirth supported on either side by leopards and another of a goddess holding a leopard on either arm.

Late Neolithic communities

It was not until about the middle of the sixth millennium that the fashion of painting pottery spread fairly rapidly over territories where monochrome wares had existed for some centuries. Simple multichevron designs appeared on pots from northern Iraq (Hassuna Ib, c and II: Nineveh I) to Cilicia (Mersin XX–XXIV). Further west more complex geometric designs occurred on pottery from Can Hassan and from the fifth level upwards in the mound of Haçilar.

The most brilliant manifestation of early painted pottery in south-west Asia was that named after Tell Halaf. Halafian pottery is outstanding on account of the variety of its forms and above all of its painted decoration and because of the excellence of its firing; but it was still hand-made, and there is no reason to think it was necessarily or even probably made by whole-time potters. In addition to dishes and flasks the forms included bowls with sharp-shouldered bodies and flaring necks and bowls and flasks on hollow stands. The decoration comprised geometric patterns like triangles, chevrons, lozenges, chequers, stars, Maltese crosses, quatrefoils and rosettes; stipples, including egg and dot; and stylized representations of men and animals, including designs based on the bull's head. It was applied to a buff or cream slip by glaze paint. At the climax of the industry the decoration was polychrome; red, orange, yellow and black paints being used, sometimes highlighted by white spots. The pottery was apparently fired to temperatures up to 1200°C. in great domed kilns with rectangular annexes, like those preserved at Carchemish, with walls and ceilings of clay on stone footings.

For some time Halafian technology continued to be based on

obsidian, flint and other kinds of stone tool with copper being used only for small things like beads, and the tradition continued for some time after copper metallurgy had spread from the Ubaid culture of southern Iraq. The Halafians were particularly skilled at working hard stones, which they made into button seals, beads, amulets and small vessels, and they were accustomed to draw raw materials from a considerable range of territory. At its greatest extent Halafian pottery extended as far west as the Syro-Cilician region where it occurred at Mersin (XVII–XIX) and Ras Shamra (III), as far east as Hassuna (VI–XI), as far north as Lake Van and as far south as Babylon. Over this extensive territory it displayed similarities not merely in material equipment but also in evidence of cult. As at Çatal we find on the one hand female figurines and on the other symbols of masculinity such as bulls, whose horned heads were in this case painted on pots and carved in the form of amulets. In addition double-axe amulets and representations on pottery betray the existence of a respect for thunder if not indeed for a thunder-god.

URBAN CIVILIZATION IN SUMER

Ubaid

Although settled life, as we have seen, first developed over a tract of high ground extending from the Iranian plateau to Anatolia and the Levant, it was on the alluvial lands of the great river valleys of Tigris–Euphrates, Nile and Indus that the earliest urban and literate societies emerged. Whereas the highlands provided abundant prototypes for the domestic animals and cereals on which settled life was based and at the same time were rich in the stones, minerals and timbers needed for creating the very fabric of a more advanced material culture, the river valleys were deficient in these. On the other hand they were potentially extremely rich. What they needed was the discipline to exploit the possibilities of irrigation. This discipline implied a higher degree of political integration than was yet known in the upland valleys. And the great rivers were themselves arteries capable of knitting together unified states.

The land that was to become Sumer lacked building-stone or even timber (apart from palm-stems), let alone minerals; its climate was arid and its rivers did not give rise to annual inundations like those provided by the Nile. Yet it was a land of opportunity. The soil was potentially fertile and the water was there for irrigation; given the level of technology that had already been reached over extensive tracts of south-west Asia and above all given the possibility of public works on an adequate scale, it was capable of producing food enough to support societies at increasing levels of complexity; moreover, the great rivers that gave the possibility of exercising political control also facilitated access to sources of raw materials in the distant highlands. To anyone capable of profiting from these conditions the potentialities were immense.

When the alluvial lands were first occupied is still uncertain. The first inhabitants well known to us are those named after Al Ubaid, a humble village set on a low mound or island of river silt in the Euphrates Valley. These people first appear in the archaeological record in the latter part of the fifth millennium at a time when the Halafian culture had for some centuries been flourishing in the north. The huts of the name-site were built of the most abundant raw materials of the area; some had a flat roof, the walls formed of reed mats suspended between palm-stems and plastered with mud, and others a rounded one formed by bending bundles of reed over from one side to another, creating a structure like a Nissen hut. The peasants lived by farming: cereal crops were harvested by reaping-knives or sickles set with flint teeth, like those used on the highlands and in the Syro-Cilician region, or alternatively by sickles made of baked clay; and, though no bones have survived, the use of dung as plaster and the manufacture of animal figurines confirm that domestic livestock were kept. There is some evidence also for hunting and fishing in the marshes and rivers. To judge from a clay model with upturned ends, it would appear that they were already using boats made from bundles of reeds like the modern *bellum* to navigate the rivers. Potting was still mainly done by hand during the early stage of the culture, but already the foot-rings added to certain vessels before firing were being shaped on a slow-moving wheel or tournette turned by the potter's hand. The finer wares, of a light buff colour which turned when over-fired to a greenish hue, were decorated by painting with a smooth ferruginous paint having a matt surface, generally blackish but sometimes reddish in colour. The patterns were made up predominantly of relatively simple geometrical designs, such as zigzag lines, triangles, lozenges and cross-hatching, but very occasionally animal motifs, like those used more freely in the highlands, were employed.

The picture of village life given by the exploration of Al Ubaid has been corrected by later work on a number of town sites. Excavation of Tell Shahrain (the ancient Eridu) and Ur in the south and of Tepe Gawra (XII–XIX) in the north has shown that the Ubaid people also lived in towns and erected their buildings from sun-dried bricks. Another sign of their relative advance over predecessors in Mesopotamia was that they practised metallurgy. In the south few copper objects have been recovered from Ubaid deposits, but at Tepe Gawra and Arpachiya and further afield at Tell Halaf a number of cast copper axes and other tools have been found; even at Al Ubaid the peasants made baked clay copies of copper tools, notably shaft-hole axes with expanded blades. The most striking monuments of the Ubaid people, not only on account of their physical size but even more because of what they imply in social organization, are their temples. At Abu Shahrain no less than thirteen, the two bottom ones known only from a few walls, were found in the Ubaid levels underlying structures dating from the third Dynasty of Ur. The earliest temple of which a plan could be recovered (level XVI) was a small, nearly square room with a door near one corner, two short screens suggesting a division of the inner space, an altar in a niche in the rear wall and an offering-place showing signs of burning in the middle; by level VIII, on the other hand, the tripartite plan with a central cella flanked on either side by rows of small rooms had been evolved. This latter type occurred again in the two lower-most Ubaid layers (XVIII–XIX) at Tepe Gawra and was to recur throughout the succeeding Warka and Protoliterate stages of southern Iraq. The construction and above all the frequent re-construction of temples, which might be of very substantial size, go to show that the Ubaid people had already so to speak created the characteristic form of early civilization in Mesopotamia, the sacred city whose economic, social and religious life was centred on the temple and its priests.

Warka

On the Ubaid foundation Sumerian civilization developed com-paratively rapidly in the south, where its progress can most con-veniently be followed in the sequence of deposits found in the precinct of the Eanna Temple at Warka (= Sumerian Uruk, Semitic Erech). Here the Warka stage proper is represented by the bottom six layers (XIV–IX), the succeeding six (VIII–III) being assigned to the Protoliterate stage. The Warka stage is marked by the spread of a new kind of pottery which first coexisted with evolved forms of Ubaid ware and then replaced it. Culturally this pottery is interesting because it belongs to a ware at home in Anatolia and suggests an enrichment of Mesopotamia by impulses from the north. Economically its main significance is that it was turned on a free-spinning wheel, generally a sign that its manu-facture had ceased to be a domestic craft and was in the hands of whole-time potters. No architectural remains of outstanding in-terest were found in the levels of this phase at the Eanna site, but in another part a succession of temples was erected at this time to the god Anu. The earliest of these, represented only by a ramp, may have been earlier than Eanna XIV, but those whose plans have been recovered were probably contemporary with Eanna XI–VIII. The culminating structure of the Warka phase was the White Temple, built on the traditional threefold plan and having on the central axis of the cella a rectangular pedestal with a low semicircular step bearing traces of burning, presumably in connection with offerings or incense. The White Temple measured 22·3 × 17·5 metres and it was set on a great platform 70 metres long, 66 metres broad and 13 metres high, built of rectangular mud bricks. The size of the temples erected during the Warka phase and above all, perhaps, the frequency with which they were rebuilt go to emphasize their importance in the social structure of the day. Another feature to appear at this time, destined to be of even greater importance in Sumerian society, was the cylinder seal, which first occurred between two underlying building phases most probably of Eanna X–IX age.

Protoliterate Sumer

The Protoliterate phase at Warka was marked by a renewed activity in the construction of temples. On the Anu site a true ziggurat or stepped platform was erected for the first time in Eanna VIII; on the Eanna site a tripartite temple was raised on a limestone footing during period V and above it in period IV a building with great free-standing columns; and on another part of the site a temple was built directly on the level soil, the surface being decorated by vast numbers of small cones of variously coloured stones pressed into gypsum plaster, that gave the effect of a vast mosaic covering not only the building itself but also the wall round the court. The phase further witnessed a number of innovations, including the use of vessels of copper and silver, monumental sculpture and pictographic writing. The uppermost Protoliterate level at Warka (Eanna III) yielded an almost lifesize human head of marble and a number of large sculptures of animal heads. Again, from a hole beside an altar at Tell Asmar we have a series of human figures (Pl. IV) carved from yellow limestone with the eyes inlaid by shell, figures which are thought to represent in most instances individual devotees of the god whose temple they originally helped to furnish. It is significant, in view of the central role of the temple and its priests in Protoliterate society, that the earliest traces of writing and numeration belonged to the temple accounts. Pictographic signs first appeared in Eanna IV and by Eanna III they had become notably more conventionalized. The numerical system associated with these primitive scripts combined features of the decimal and sexagesimal systems and emphasizes the way in which economic activities were controlled from the centre by the temple community. That means of transport over land as well as on rivers had been developed at this time is shown by the occurrence among the pictographic signs of representations of wheeled vehicles and of boats with upturned ends.

The Early Dynastic period

The Early Dynastic phase of Sumerian civilization, which began somewhere around 3000 B.C., was marked from a material point of view by an overall increase in wealth rather than by any notable innovations in the sphere of technology. Many of its basic traits were already present in the Ubaid culture and, as we have seen, the use of the wheel for potting and for transport, monumental sculpture, cylinder seals and pictographic writing were all added during the ensuing Protoliterate phases. Among the most potent signs of increased wealth should be mentioned the greater abundance and elaboration of metal tools, weapons, ornaments and vessels, among which forms were evolved that spread in time to Syria, Anatolia, the Aegean, the Caucasus, central Europe and vast tracts of Russia. By the end of Early Dynastic times the Sumerian smiths were riveting and soldering, as well as casting, and were making bronze with a content of from 6 to 10 per cent of tin. Quantities of gold and silver were used for ornaments and vessels, as well as a wide range of more or less hard stones. Representations on painted pottery, models and remains from tombs give us more detailed information about the wheeled transport available at this time: chariots and waggons were evidently mounted on solid wheels, made from three pieces of wood held together by cross-pieces and bound by tyres held in place by copper nails, and drawn by Asiatic asses (onagers) or oxen harnessed by collars and yokes. From this time also engravings on cylinder seals indicate that animal traction was being applied to light wooden ploughs for cultivating the soil.

The rise in material well-being was accompanied by major changes in social structure, the most notable of which was the emergence of kings or officials of comparable status, at first as temporary war leaders, but in due course as established rulers of the city states. The immediate cause of this was undoubtedly the rise of warfare as an institution and this itself was linked with the increase in wealth already noted: thus, the growing affluence of the cities only served to increase their attraction to marauding pastoralists of the highland and the desert; the citizens needed to secure raw materials in increasing variety and volume from more or less remote territories inhabited by poorer and more barbarous peoples; and, even more to the point, rivalry between the cities grew as the opportunities for enrichment increased and this occurred at a time when armament was becoming more effective and the inhabitants found themselves able to support warriors. Whatever the factors responsible there can be no doubt that war had by this time become a well-organized institution: on the so-called 'Royal Standard' of Ur we see depicted not only the royal chariot with prisoners under guard, but three distinct grades of combat troops, namely ass-drawn chariots riding men down, a phalanx of heavy troops helmeted and cloaked, and light skirmishers in contact with the enemy. Eloquent insight into the status achieved by the Sumerian rulers is given by the Royal Tombs at Ur, which show that a whole procession of grooms, guards, courtiers and women, together with the oxen drawing the funeral car, were slaughtered to accompany the royal personage to the next world.

Akkadians and Babylonians

Although the Sumerians had developed policies sufficiently effective to ensure irrigation and the acquisition of raw materials from a wide range of more or less distant sources, the level of organization was still that of city states. At least eleven of these, including Ur, Erech, Larsa, Kish and Nippur, at one time supported independent and sometimes warring dynasties. It was not until c. 2370 when Sargon and his Semitic-speaking followers founded the city of Agade only a short distance south-west of Babylon that we enter on an ampler stage of history. Although the paucity of information surviving from contemporary documents and the opaqueness of subsequent legend have between them made it difficult to establish more than dim outlines of his reign, it seems clear that Sargon and his successors exercised a hegemony not only over Sumer itself, but over the northern part of Mesopotamia later known as Assyria, as well as over Elam, and that their influence extended over north Syria and probably even into Anatolia. The extent of Akkadian influence and the fact that it lasted for several reigns suggests that it was founded on far more than mere crude military force.

When the Akkadian dynasty was nevertheless overturned by a incursion of Gurian highlanders from the Zagros, the way was open for a revival of Ur which under its Third Dynasty enjoyed what from many points of view was its most splendid period. Further waves of rough folk from without, Amorites from the west and Elamites from the east, by toppling the dynasty at Ur opened a period of some confusion, from which the land of Mesopotamia and ultimately large tracts of south-west Asia were in due course to benefit through the founding about 1990 B.C. of the First Dynasty of Babylon. The succession of Hammurabi about 1800 B.C. brought into a position of power an individual as commanding in his way as Sargon of Agade and one about whose reign more details are known. Under his leadership Babylon rose supreme not only over the riverine zone of Mesopotamia but also over the uplands of Assyria, the Zagros and Elam. The benefits of Babylonian law and commerce spread even more widely. During Hammurabi's reign the use of cuneiform writing and Akkadian speech for commerce brought extensive tracts of south-west Asia into fruitful and peaceful contact. This meant that the overthrow of the First Dynasty of Babylon by the Hittites who sacked the capital in *c.* 1595 B.C. and by the Kassites from the east, who in turn set up their own dynasty, was not so serious disaster from the point of view of civilization in general as it might have been.

CIVILIZATION IN THE HIGHLANDS

Anatolia and the Hittites

The vast upland regions from Iran to Anatolia and the Levant that gave birth to farming were at once too extensive and too broken to encourage the early growth of centralized authority or of the higher civilization which this makes possible. Innovations like writing or the use of cylinder seals that emanated in Sumer only spread later and sometimes much later to these territories. Yet the mere fact that they were endowed with traditions based on thousands of years of settled life as agriculturalists meant that the upland peoples were capable of absorbing new elements and even leaders speaking new languages without losing their own regional styles. This is nowhere truer than of Anatolia.

The antiquity of settled life in southern Anatolia has been stressed earlier in this chapter. No attempt will be made here to set out details of the cultural history of this extensive region, still less to distinguish the differences exhibited by each of its several provinces, differences which contributed richness and texture to the pattern as a whole. It will be sufficient to make a few general points. The first is that until trading posts manned with Assyrians were set up in central Anatolia there was no rapid acceleration in the tempo of cultural development. This can be seen in the length of time it took before metal tools began to take the place of stone ones. Copper, as we have noted, was used in its native form for beads and other trinkets from a very early stage in the development of farming economy. The metallurgical treatment of copper ores and the casting of metal in moulds for the production of weapons and implements did not come until the fifth millennium; and the production of standard bronze based on the addition of tin alloy did not begin until *c*. 3000 B.C. and then only in favoured localities.

The next point to observe is that some of the most striking features of Hittite civilization made their appearance already during the Early Bronze Age (*c*. 3000–2000 B.C.) and that some were even older. Evidence for the concentration of wealth and power that reached its climax under Hittite rule is to be seen first of all in the great walled fortresses at Troy II and Kültepe (the ancient Kadesh) dating from Early Bronze Age II; and it may be noted that the megaron type of public assembly hall, comprising a rectangular structure with inner hall having a central fireplace and outer porch, enclosed by these citadels also appeared in earlier and more modest surroundings at Troy I. Then, again, we have the evidence for concentrated wealth in the great treasures from the royal tombs of Alaca Hüyük (level VII) and in the so-called Priam's treasure of Troy II: it is not merely the value of the metal locked up in these that calls for remark, but still more the high standard of smithing and jewellery, and the evidence for social rank embodied in the personal ornaments, metal utensils and weapons of display. If the Early Bronze Age metal-work itself is scrutinized more closely, we find evidence of the love of polychromatic effects contrived by inlaying, overlaying and incrusting silver, electrum or even semi-precious stones on a bronze base displayed in work of the Hittite period; and conversely the pre-dilection for bulls and stags exhibited in Hittite and Early Bronze Age metal-work alike goes back to the lowermost level at Çatal Hüyük, if not in all probability beyond.

The Middle Bronze Age of Anatolia (c. 1950–1700 B.C.) was marked most significantly by the arrival of Assyrian merchants. One of their trading posts was situated in the suburbs formed round the citadel of Kadesh, by now a town covering some 50·6 hectares (125 acres). The object of these posts was to regulate traffic in raw materials to the south, notably copper and the then extremely rare and precious iron, in exchange for manufactures of which textiles were the most important. Merchandise was carried on the backs of donkeys organized in caravans and we know from business records not merely that silver in the form of rings and bars was used as a standard of value but even the equivalents in terms of silver shekels of most goods common at the time in Central Anatolia. The records themselves were written in Akkadian by an Assyrian cuneiform script on clay tablets and signed by impressing cylinder seals. In other words central Anatolia was brought within the sphere of literacy, at least so far as commerce was concerned, by virtue of direct contact with Assyria. It is significant that when the Hittite rulers wished to record their triumphs and conduct their correspondence they did so in Assyrian cuneiform script, even if their language was Indo-European.

Hittite names began to appear first in mercantile records from the closing phases of the Middle Bronze Age. Much controversy surrounds the arrival of Indo-European speakers into Anatolia and the directions from which they came, but the consensus is that some spread into the south-west by way of the Bosphorus, whereas others penetrated central Anatolia from the north-east by way of Armenia. At a stage of social development when only comparatively few people monopolized power and authority it required no mass invasion to infiltrate, seize power and establish

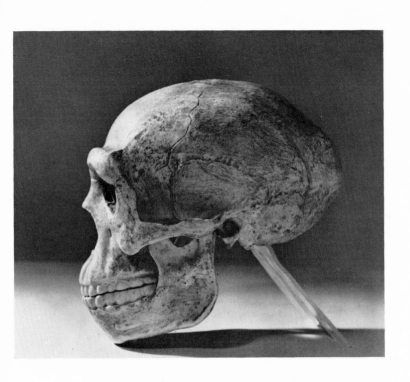

1 Reconstructed skull of Peking man (*Homo erectus*)

11   Chimpanzee extracting termites from a mound
by poking in a blade of grass

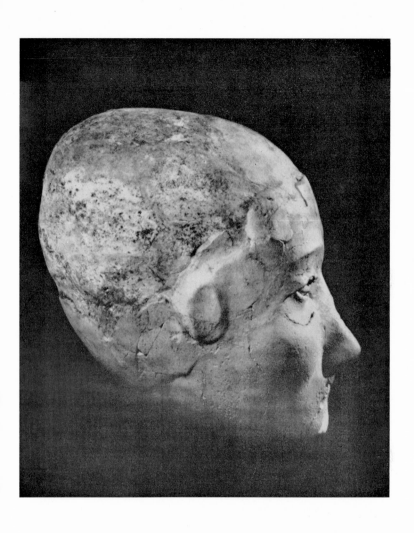

III   Skull with face modelled in clay from pre-pottery
level at Jericho

IV   Sumerian statuette of Early Dynastic times
from Tell Asmar, Mesopotamia

v Clay figurine from Early Neolithic site of Nea Nikomedeia,
West Macedonia, Greece

VI   Gold funeral mask of Agamemnon, Shaft-grave V, Mycenae

VII   Stone 'Janus' head from Roquepertuse,
Bouches-du-Rhône, France

VIII Bronze dies for embossing helmet plates, showing Teutonic
personages of the Migration Period, Torslunda, Sweden

IX   Relief carving of King Nar-mer on stone palette,
Hierakonpolis, Egypt

x   Terracotta Negroid head from Nok, Nigeria

XI   Stone carving of bearded man from Mohenjo Daro, Pakistan

XII Pottery figure of Late Jomon culture, Satohama, Honshu, Japan

XIII   Aboriginal hunter, Australia

XIV   Statue of Hoa-haka-nana-ia, Easter Island

xv   Model of Maya youth's head, Palenque, Mexico

XVI   Inca figurines of gold (male) and silver (female)

a reigning dynasty, and it is likely that the Hittites who took over were comparatively few in number. They were evidently able people and they realized the political possibilities inherent in the natural wealth of their country. Although they established themselves at the head of affairs during the seventeenth century B.C. it was not until the fourteenth century that their power had attained the imperial status symbolized in their great capital city of Boghazköy.

Despite its size—the circuit of the walls was some four miles—the powerfully defended city was founded on a long-standing tradition. The great stores of archives which now included a wide range of state documents including diplomatic correspondence have proved particularly enlightening. Although the language was by this time Indo-European, the script impressed on the clay was still cuneiform, though cylinder seals had given place to stamp ones of a more ancient tradition. The leading divinities of the Hittites comprised a weather god, whose attributes the bull and the axe both go back to the Halafian culture, and a sun goddess, a version of the great mother goddess of long-standing antiquity. Their art, hieratic in style, took a monumental form in reliefs cut on natural exposures of rock-surface or again in figures standing guard at gateways.

In history the Hittites took advantage of their situation at the head of the Fertile Crescent to keep at arm's length the two great empires into which the world at that time was divided. Although they sought as far as possible to gain their ends by diplomacy, they were effective warriors. We have already noted that it was a Hittite army that sacked Babylon and helped to topple its First Dynasty. Centuries later at the height of their power they administered a punishing defeat to Ramses II before their strong city of Kadesh. Yet early in the twelfth century B.C. the Hittite Empire crumbled in a veritable power tremor that brought down the Mycenaeans and Troy VIIA and before long the New Kingdom of Egypt. Phrygians issuing from Thrace overran

Anatolia and destroyed the centres of Hittite power. Hittite culture lived on only as the heritage of a number of small states in northern Syria set up by refugees, states which only preserved their independence precariously at the height of the Assyrian Empire. Ironically, the end of Neo-Hittite culture only came when the Assyrian Empire itself fell a victim (612–610 B.C.) to a combination of Babylonians, Scythians and Medes. Anatolia, having nourished Assyrians, Babylonians and Sumerians, as well as Hittites, on its mineral wealth, was engulfed successively in the empires of Persia, Alexander, Rome, Byzantium and the Ottoman Turks. It was indeed a rich prize. Yet in its heyday it had been able to stand up to the two great powers of the times. It is only in the light of its long prehistory that we can appreciate how this was possible. The Hittites owed much to the strength of a long cultural tradition in Anatolia, much to its mineral and agricultural wealth and much also to the ability of their Indo-European-speaking rulers.

The Levant

For much of later prehistoric times Syria shared fully in the cultural development of Cilicia and Mesopotamia. Palestine on the other hand after playing a leading role in the eighth and seventh millennia relapsed into provincial insignificance. Pottery did not appear until c. 5000 B.C. and when copper-working reached Palestine nearly a thousand years later it did so as part of a provincial version of the richer culture of northern Syria. Again, at the beginning of the Early Bronze Age Syria and Palestine profited from the cultural influences that radiated from Mesopotamia to Egypt and contributed so notably to the rise of civilization in that country immediately preceding the First Dynasty. Similarly, the change in pottery styles that marked the beginning of Early Bronze Age I in Palestine towards the end of the third millennium was inspired from Syro-Mesopotamia during the expansive Sargonid era. The country did not begin to be drawn within the sphere of literacy until around 2000 B.C. and it is significant and entirely consistent that the clay tablets from sites like Byblos and Ugarit should have been written in cuneiform script of ultimately Mesopotamian origin in the same way that the pottery tradition of Middle Bronze Age Canaan was of Syro-Mesopotamian derivation. Early Bronze Age II was marked by renewed northern influence, this time in the guise of a warrior aristocracy rendered mobile and formidable by their horse-drawn chariots and possessed also of advanced knowledge of the technique of fortification, including the use of earthen ramparts with stone revetment as a base for defensive walls. It was no doubt a prolongation of this thrust that carried the Hyksos into Egypt (*c.* 1680 B.C.) during the intermediate period that followed the Middle Kingdom. Having established themselves the Hyksos maintained their own rule there for over a century down to the time when Ahmosis I succeeded in expelling them (*c.* 1573 B.C.) and establishing the New Kingdom.

During its Late Bronze Age Palestine formed part of the Egyptian realm, and culture remained eclectic and provincial drawing elements from Syria, Egypt and the East Mediterranean without creating any well-defined image of its own. The fact that the country was subservient to Egypt prevented the rise of any central authority, and the military skills and techniques brought in by the Hyksos strengthened the hands of the rulers of individual cities. Again, it is important to remember that those who sheltered in defended cities were encompassed by semi-nomadic peoples. The tension between the two has after all been a recurrent theme in the history of the life of the region.

It is very easy when depending on archaeological evidence to over-stress the role of settled and urban peoples and under-estimate that of peoples less productive of material debris and bric-à-brac. Yet it is vital to remember that, just as the Fertile Crescent was backed and on the east flanked by mountains, so it enclosed in its wide arc a vast zone of arid land passing on the south into desert. Although this was incapable of supporting settled communities it was well adapted to nomadic or semi-nomadic life with a strong bias to pastoral economy. Yet it remained marginal over large areas even for pastoralists. When pressure on grazing exerted by variations in rainfall weighed too heavily the nomads had an obvious way out of their difficulties in pillaging, infiltrating or even dominating their richer neighbours settled on productive ground. Since the nomads were fitted by selection to withstand hardship and adapted by their economy to be mobile, it is no surprise that they were able to play a role in history disproportionate to their numbers or wealth.

In the archaeological record they made themselves felt indirectly through dislocating the ordered progress of more settled societies, whether as hill-men from the Zagros or as nomads from the Syrian desert moving east into the Euphrates basin or west and south into the Nile Valley. The most positive information about them comes from their own traditions enshrined in the Old Testament scriptures. Here we see patriarchal societies responding to famine by moving their tents into new and sometimes distant lands, pitting themselves if need be, like the modern Beduin, against the peoples settled on richer land. Correlation between the Bible stories and the evidence of archaeology and historical records is unfortunately rarely possible because the sources seldom overlap. One can only say for instance that the traditional trek of Abraham and his people from Mesopotamia to the land of Israel would fit quite well into the context of Early Bronze Age I. Again, the story of Jacob's migration to Egypt to escape famine may well accord with the movements of people that included the Hyksos' irruption into Egypt.

By the same token there is no evident reflection in the Late Bronze Age culture of Palestine of stylistic features attributable to the arrival of the Israelites, dramatized in the story of the Exodus from Egypt under the leadership of Moses. The movement did not begin until the thirteenth century B.C. and is best thought of as an infiltration by Beduin-like folk rather than as a set military invasion. It looks as though fortified cities and townships were only very gradually reduced. And early in the twelfth century B.C., before the process has been completed, the incursion of iron-using raiders from the north Mediterranean, raiders who came to be known when they settled down as Philistines, started Palestine on its Early Iron Age. From a technological point of view Palestine was in this respect several centuries in advance of Egypt, though for some time the Philistines kept the use of the metal to themselves in their coastal tract. From a material point of view the Israelites were relatively poor, but their sense of identity helped them to triumph over the Philistines under the leadership of David (1013–973 B.C.) and enter on a few brief centuries of independent nationhood. Palestine was soon overshadowed again by a great power, this time the Assyrian Empire. Kings continued to rule in Jerusalem after the Assyrian invasion of 721 B.C., but only as tributaries of Egypt, Assyria and Babylon; and in 587/6 B.C. Nebuchadnezzar destroyed the temple of Solomon and carried off the leading men of Israel into captivity at Babylon.

From a worldly point of view it was the coastal branch of the Canaanites, named Phoenicians by Mycenaean traders, who turned the difficulties of their environment to most profit. They did so by looking to the sea and earning by commerce the wealth denied them by the rich but narrow strip of fertile land between the mountains of the Jebel Libnan and the Mediterranean. Their situation between Egypt and Mesopotamia was turned to good account during the Bronze Age as we know from the wealth of cities like Byblos and Ugarit, but it was not until the fall of Mycenaean power that the Phoenicians were able to profit from trade with Cyprus and the Aegean. Local products like cedarwood and purple dye had long been staples of their commerce and from early times they had acted as middlemen in the interchange of goods manufactured at the main centres of civilization.

The opening up of the Mediterranean brought them access to the sometimes remote sources of important metals like copper and tin.

It was as an outcome of their zeal for commerce that the Phoenicians contributed most to world history. The importance of maintaining clear business records provided at least the context in which they developed an alphabetic script that had been brought to a standard form by the tenth century B.C. When Greek traders in the Levant came into contact with this script they were sufficiently impressed to improve it further by introducing letter forms for vowel sounds. Yet much of the credit for the alphabet on which the literature of the western world has ever since been based must rest with the aesthetically unattractive businessmen of Phoenicia. The other great achievement that followed as they entered upon their Mycenaean inheritance was the establishment of colonies along their trade routes, colonies sufficiently vigorous to enter into rivalry with the Classical Greeks and in respect of Carthage to engage in mortal conflict with Rome. Far beyond this the colonies in Sardinia and southern Iberia affected the course of trade and cultural influence as far afield as Brittany and south-west England, but not even the Phoenicians could in the end escape in their homeland the effects of Assyrian and finally of Babylonian power. Phoenicia passed under the same succession of empires from Babylonian to Ottoman as did the rest of Palestine.

In the end it is worth reflecting that the history of mankind was changed not by Tyre or Sidon but by Jerusalem, not by a merchant or a king so much as by the son of a carpenter in a village set in what appeared to be an insignificant province of the Roman Empire. The limitations of archaeology are pointed up again by the fact that, when the men of large parts of Asia and Africa wish to pray, they mostly turn to Mecca in an oasis of Arabia rather than to the rich cities of Egypt or Mesopotamia.

Iran and Turkmenia

Certain parts of the Iranian plateau and its neighbourhood shared as we have seen (p. 84) in the early history of farming, notably the upland valleys in the south-western Zagros, the western rim of the great inner desert zone, the Caspian shore and the southern margin of Turkmenia. Yet the natural heart of the plateau was desert, and localities favourable to early farmers were not necessarily well adapted to the early emergence of politically larger units. The most likely territory from this point of view was the low-lying region between the lower Euphrates and the Zagros which in fact provided a setting for the kingdom of Elam, the first unit of its kind to emerge in the whole region. Already in prehistoric times the site of Susa testified both to the natural wealth of the province and to the advantage that came from bordering the Mesopotamian focus of higher civilization. Throughout levels A to D the inhabitants of Susa continued to decorate their pots by painting in the manner of the Neolithic societies discussed previously. Copper metallurgy had already been adopted by Susa A and the inhabitants of Susa B had appropriated the potter's wheel. Both metallurgy and the potter's wheel spread far and wide among the makers of painted pottery, appearing for example at Sialk III and Hissar I on the western and northern fringes of the central desert zone. The appearance of cylinder seals at Susa C—the earlier inhabitants had used stamp seals—and their spread as far afield as Hissar III bear further witness to the cultural impact of Mesopotamia on Elam.

Susa and the province of which it was the capital was the earliest centre of highly integrated political authority in Iran. To begin with the Elamite kings were dominated by the Akkadians and in due course by the Third Dynasty of Ur, but around 2000 B.C. they were strong enough to attack and destroy Ur itself. For nearly a thousand years Elam was to enjoy some measure of political independence. Yet, if the development of an Elamite script and of a distinctive style of seal-engraving bear witness to a certain degree of self-expression, the fact remains that texts were frequently written in Akkadian or Sumerian; and it is significant that the earliest large-scale monument in Elam at Tchoga Zanbil took the form of a ziggurat. Even this modest degree of independence was broken when Nebuchadrezzar I invaded the country towards the close of the twelfth century B.C.

When the Assyrians were campaigning to secure their eastern frontier late in the ninth century B.C. they left the first records of the names of the Iranian peoples whose union was to destroy their own Empire, namely the Medes to the north and the Persians to the east-south-east of Elam. The arrival of Iranian-speaking peoples on the plateau is still something about which little is known. What is certain is that, as with the Hittites, another group speaking an Indo-European language, the Iranians demonstrated in a signal way what could be achieved by energy and leadership even when geographical conditions were not particularly favourable. The transformation wrought by the Achaemenid Dynasty in the ancient world as a whole was as rapid as it was sweeping. The Empire was founded on the defeat by Cyrus of Persia of his grandfather Astyages king of the Medes in c. 550 B.C. Within a single generation the Medes and the Persians engulfed Babylonia, Lydia and Egypt. Their expansion was only checked in the west by the Greeks who, by their victories on land at Marathon (490 B.C.) and Plataea (479 B.C.), and on sea at Salamis (480 B.C.), made possible the development of a distinctively European civilization.

CHAPTER 6

THE FOUNDATIONS OF EUROPEAN
CIVILIZATION *c.* 6000–1500 B.C.

Geographical setting

The European continent, so pregnant for the future of mankind, owed much to geography. Not least important is the fact that its south-eastern extremity lay adjacent to south-west Asia, the earliest home in the Old World of husbandry, metallurgy and literacy. By sea the Aegean islands, including Crete, and the Greek mainland itself lay open to contacts with Anatolia and Syria; and influences still little known may well have reached the southern Balkans by way of Thrace or even the west coast of the Black Sea. In due time, improved navigation and the economic needs of the Aegean world, including notably the need for tin, made of the Mediterranean a potent means for the transmission of ideas, which passing through the Straits of Gibraltar and traversing southern France by way of the Carcassonne gap and the Gironde were borne along the Atlantic sea-routes as far as the west Baltic. It is hardly less important to remember that the parts of Europe where settled life and civilization first developed were open to impulses from a broad arc of territory from Scandinavia to the Caspian and beyond: the Pontic steppes formed a broad corridor linking eastern and central Europe to Caucasia and Turkmenia; and northern Europe formed a reservoir of peoples whose vigour more than compensated in the end for their cultural retardation. Then, again, the Atlantic sea-board, which in pre-history transmitted cultural influences of ultimately Mediterranean inspiration, provided during the historic period a base for the expansion overseas of European power and influence, an expansion that was ultimately to create a world market and a single nexus of scientific and historical awareness.

If civilization in the guise of literate, urban and politically integrated communities first appeared in any part of Europe a thousand years later than on the Nile or Euphrates, five hundred years later than in the Indus Valley and very little earlier than it did in North China, radiocarbon dating shows that the farming economy on which urban life rested was established in south-east Europe long before it was in Egypt, let alone India or the Far East. If the Middle Minoan palace-civilization of Crete or the Mycenaean civilization of the Greek mainland did not appear respectively until early in and at the middle of the second millennium B.C., at least they grew up in lands with four millennia or so of peasant life behind them. The early farmers of the south Balkans were cousins, not descendants of the formally Neolithic peoples of Anatolia, Syria, Iraq and Iran; and by the time urban, literate civilization had appeared in Sumer and Egypt, husbandry was being practised in such remote parts of Europe as Ireland or the west Baltic.

The fact that husbandry took some three thousand years to spread from Greece to Denmark is a striking reminder that Europe was far indeed from being a *tabula rasa*, a passive recipient of impulses from south-west Asia. Even in the Aegean area, where climate and vegetation were not so different from those obtaining in parts of south-west Asia, the cultures of the earliest farmers nevertheless took on an individual style; and as farming expanded into more distant zones with differing endowments so the cultures based on this took on more divergent characteristics. The differing climate and vegetation of the temperate zone was only one factor. Another was that the lands into which the new economy spread were by no means empty or devoid of indigenous cultural traditions; and this was more particularly so in the territories like Iberia, Britain or northern Europe that were most distant from south-east Europe and in which the pattern of hunter-

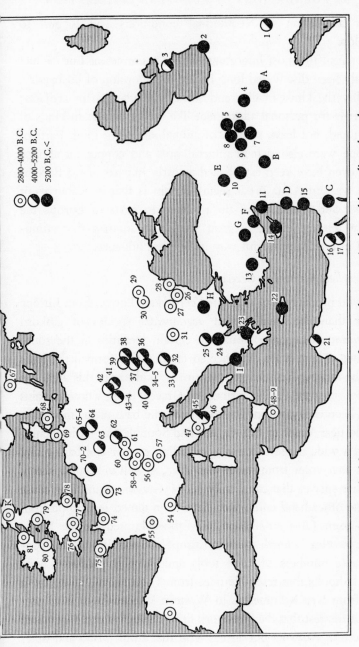

4. The spread of farming into Europe from south-west Asia charted by radiocarbon dates.

For key to dates for sites 1–81, see *Antiquity* (1965), p. 47.

For site A (Ali Kosh), B (Bouqras), C (Beidha), D (Ramad), E (Çayönü),
F (Mersin) and G (Çatal Hüyük), see table at end of chapter 4.

Site H Karanovo: Bln. 291. 5208 ± 150 B.C.

Site I Sidari: Gxo 771. 5720 ± 120 B.C.
Site J Fragoas: GrN 4925. 3110 ± 50 B.C.
Site K Pitnacree: Gak 601. 2860 ± 90 B.C.

2800–4000 B.C.
4000–5200 B.C.
5200 B.C. <

fisher adaptation to Neothermal conditions had longest to develop.

Some of the most important natural resources of Europe had already been discovered long before the adoption of husbandry, notably the kinds of flint and stone best adapted for artifacts; materials for personal adornment like amber or certain kinds of shell; and, not least, sources of animal and plant food. Parts of Europe were also rich in mineral ores and copper metallurgy may even have been established as early in parts of the Balkans as in western Asia. What seems certain is that its resources of copper and above all of tin attracted to parts of Europe the active interest of the Aegean world, an interest that stimulated in a most powerful way its cultural advance.

The earliest farmers in Greece

No wild prototypes of cultivated cereals are known from Europe other than the small-seeded *aegilopoides* species of einkorn (*Triticum monococcum*) found in certain localities in the south Balkans. There is no evidence so far that this formed the basis for the independent development of agriculture in this area. On the contrary the earliest farmers of Greece, those whose remains have been excavated in Thessaly from the base of the mound at Sesklo near Volos and at Argissa and Souphli near Larissa, cultivated a wide range of cereals, including emmer and barley that must have come from south-west Asia, as well as keeping sheep, another species that can hardly be of Greek origin. The cattle on the other hand could well have been tamed in Europe from wild oxen (*Bos primigenius*) like those hunted by the Mesolithic peoples of north-western Europe. All the sites yielded considerable numbers of bone tools and Souphli produced bone buckle-hooks that resemble ones from Çatal Hüyük in Anatolia and from Nea Nikomedeia in Western Macedonia. It is of particular interest that the flint-work differs notably from that found in western Anatolia but agrees with that from Jarmo and other sites in Iran and eastern Anatolia occupied by farmers who were not yet making pottery.

The aceramic settlement of Argissa was overlaid by a succession of deposits left behind by settled farmers whose accumulated rubble, composed very largely of the floors and walls of mud-built houses, created a mound resembling the tells of south-west Asia. Analysis of the materials found in the course of excavating a number of these in different parts of Greece has revealed a sequence of cultural development up to the Bronze Age. The Early Neolithic farmers, represented at Otzaki, Sesklo and Argissa in Thessaly and at Nea Nikomedeia in western Macedonia, lived in villages composed of houses built of timber and wattle and daub and buried their dead in a contracted attitude with no or few grave-goods within the boundaries of the settlement. Their flint-work mainly comprised blades that were probably inset into wooden handles and at Nea Nikomedeia it included a few trapezes like those from pre-pottery levels at Argissa and for that matter at Jarmo. They used polished stone for woodworking equipment, including axes, adzes and chisels, as well as occasionally for bowls and animal figurines, and for plugs and studs that may have been used for facial ornaments. They also used bone for many things including awls, chisels, heavy needles, belt-hooks and beads. Much the commonest artifacts were those of baked clay, including above all hand-made pottery. Their pots were of globular bowl or jar form with simple rims, pierced lugs and occasionally ringed feet. Much of the better pottery was slipped and burnished. To begin with it was monochrome in Thessaly, but simple geometric designs were painted on a few pots from the beginning at Nea Nikomedeia. Although vase-painting was almost certainly introduced to Greece, the designs are too elementary to point to any particular source. Clay was also used for making figurines, particularly those of women, and it is interesting that at Nea Nikomedeia they were sometimes made from several pieces—head, trunk and lower limbs—pegged together in the same way (Pl. V) as on the contemporary Zagros sites of the same period. Anthropomorphic pots, again, remind one of those from Haçilar and clay stamps recall parallels from Çatal Hüyük, both sites in Anatolia. The curious coffee-bean eyes have many parallels in south-west Asia and may ultimately recall the inset cowrie-shells of the Jericho heads.

The Middle Neolithic Sesklo people normally used mud bricks for their houses—another Asiatic trait—but their pottery was now quite distinctive. They made a wider range of shapes, including flat-bottomed dishes with flaring sides, footed bowls and mugs with flared handles. Some of these they painted either red on a pale slip or white on a red ground. The designs were geometrical: these included multiple linear chevrons, but also block-like rectangles, lozenges and triangles that may have been inspired by birch-bark vessels. No less distinctive were the Late Neolithic wares, including that named after Dimini with its bold spiral and meander designs. If farming economy and several of the basic traits in material equipment were derived from Asia, the ceramic styles of Neolithic Greece became progressively more idiosyncratic.

The Balkans, central and eastern Europe

The earliest pottery-using farmers to appear in the Balkans occupied an extensive territory over which they are named after different key localities, including the site of Starčevo near Belgrade, Yugoslavia, the River Körös in Hungary and the site of Kremikovci in west Bulgaria. It appears to have arisen from impulses, presumably brought by actual colonists, following the river valleys from the Aegean: an important route seems to have been that provided by the Varda and Morava rivers into eastern Yugoslavia and on to the Danube and Körös rivers, but western Bulgaria may have been penetrated directly by the Struma as well as by the Morava and Danube valleys. It may prove significant that the Starčevo people cultivated einkorn and millet, both of

Sequence of early peasant cultures in parts of Europe down to C. 1200 B.C.

South Britain	Denmark	Danube	Greece	South-east Balkans	Ukraine
		VI			Black burnished
Bronze Age (Wessex)	Bronze Age	V	Late Helladic (Mycenaean)	Karanovo	
Secondary Neolithic	Late Neolithic	IV	Middle Helladic (Minyan)		Tripolje
	Middle Neolithic	III			
Primary Neolithic	Early Neolithic	II	Early Helladic	Gumelniţa	
			Late Neolithic (Dimini)		Izvoare
		I (Spiral-meander ware)		Boian	
			Middle Neolithic (Sesklo)		
			Early Neolithic (Impressed; Otzaki)	Starčevo	
			Proto-Neolithic		

which have wild prototypes in the south Balkans, but it is significant that the reaping-knives by which these were harvested have close analogues in western Asia. Their pottery included footed bowls and, in the Körös Valley, lop-sided flasks with perforated lugs, probably designed for slinging on the back. Impressed decoration was common, though cardium shells were not used for this purpose as they were in parts of the Mediterranean area, and other favoured varieties included roughening of the surface and plastic relief, including representations of animals and men; and footed bowls in fine ware might be decorated by painting. The widespread use of the Aegean mussel *Spondylus gaederopus* as a material for beads and bracelets shows that contact was maintained with the south. Clay seals, apparently barbaric versions of stone stamp seals of ultimately Asiatic origin, marble vessels, bone and clay idols and four-footed pottery stands that may have served some cult purpose are among enrichments which may well have been acquired from the more settled villagers whose settlement mounds had begun to accumulate in Greece and the south Balkans.

Immediately north of the Starčevo province, over a territory which extended from south of Lake Balaton to near the estuary of the Oder—a distance of nearly six hundred miles—and laterally from the Rhine and the Maas to the Vistula and the Upper Dniester—a span of a thousand miles—the earliest peasants made pottery decorated with spiral-meander patterns and exhibited a cultural uniformity so great as only to be explained if we suppose that the whole area was colonized comparatively rapidly. From the Middle Danube region, comprising much of central Hungary, Lower Austria and Bohemia, the pioneer farmers pushed along the great rivers, east to the Vistula and the Upper Dniester; north down the Vistula, Oder and Elbe; and west by way both of the Upper Danube and overland across Saxony and Hesse to the Rhineland and the Maas. The rapidity of their spread—according to radiocarbon dating they had reached South Germany and Dutch Limburg before the end of the fifth millennium B.C.—was due in part to their use of slash and burn agriculture, in part to the discontinuous distribution of the fertile and easily worked loess on which they settled, and in part to the lack of opposition. Emmer and barley were grown, as well as einkorn, peas, beans and flax, and the common farmyard animals were kept. Material equipment remained very simple during this first phase in the settlement of the Danubian zone. There is no evidence either for weaving or for metallurgy. The pottery was made from carefully prepared clay that required neither slip nor burnish, and took the form of the standard early Neolithic shapes, round-based bowls and flasks, the latter sometimes flattened on one face, having plain rims and no handles other than lugs. Plastic ornament, like that on Starčevo ware, was used, especially in the Middle Danube area, but the most characteristic form of ornament consisted of bands defined by two or three more or less parallel incised lines and conforming to spirals or meanders; in addition designs were sometimes painted on the surface after firing. Where flint was readily available it was flaked into the form of blades which might be inserted into slots to provide cutting-edges for reaping-knives, or worked into end-scrapers and trapeziform arrowheads. The commonest stone tool, a polished stone adze-blade of D-section with a slightly hollow-ground working-edge, was probably used mainly for dressing the timbers needed for building. The peasants lived in large houses, generally of rectangular plan, but in parts of Germany and in Poland often wedge-shaped with one end markedly broader than the other. They were commonly of twenty or thirty and might be up to fifty metres in length and it is thought that they must have provided space for storage and possibly for sheltering livestock as well as for the peasant family. The Danubian I peasants seem to have lived in fair-sized villages. Although they appear to have rebuilt these fairly frequently, it looks as though after an initial phase of clearance they had learned to take advantage of the qualities of the loess soil (cf. p. 223) and settle down in more or less permanent village communities. Like the Starčevo people they continued to import *Spondylus* shells all the way from the Aegean and deposit ornaments made of these with their dead which they buried in cemeteries of single graves.

Meanwhile another group of peasants, whose culture is named after the Boian lake near the head of the Dobrudja, began to develop in eastern Roumania. The Boian pioneers cultivated the same crops and occupied rectangular houses with matting on the floor. For felling and working timber they used a variety of stone tools, including polished adze-blades of bevelled and shoe-last form. Their pottery, which included bowls with ringed feet, biconical jars and large pear-shaped storage jars, was decorated by several different methods, but most commonly by incising or excising the surface to form in the first case either spiral or other curvilinear patterns and in the second rectilinear ones, each of which were emphasized by encrusting with red or white paint. The Boians were of more than local interest because they initiated the spread of peasant economy over much of Roumania and the Ukraine as far east as the River Dnieper. The first stage in their expansion, well exemplified at the site of Izvoare in Moldavia, penetrated the Alt Valley on the west of the Carpathians and on the east extended as far as the Bug; it was only during the developed or classical phase of the culture, commonly named after Cucuteni on the Pruth or Tripolje near Kiev, that the full extent was attained. The excised technique continued to be fashionable during the Izvoare stage, but this was replaced by painting before firing, a technique already practised by the Starčevo peasants, or by U-sectioned grooves designed to hold encrustation. The spiral, a motive already exploited by the Starčevo and Danubian peasants and one that may well have been suggested originally by making coiled basketry, continued to play a leading part in decorating pottery. As regard the forms of pots, the simple rims, flat bases and absence of handles other than lugs are all persistent features. Other Balkan elements include polished stone adzes, a lithic industry based on blades, and clay stamps and female figurines made from baked clay. Like the Danubians, whom they dispossessed on the Upper Dniester, the Tripolje peasants shifted their settlements at frequent intervals as they took into cultivation fresh areas of the fertile black earth that directly overlay the loess. Likewise they lived in substantial rectangular houses, up to 30 metres in length, but they differed at least in the Ukraine in arranging these in circles or even in concentric rings, as at Kolomiisshchina or Vladimirovka. It seems likely that this circular arrangement may have been designed for security against their warlike pastoral neighbours of the steppe who decorated their pots with cord imprints.

In the Middle Danube area there is evidence for the penetration, possibly as early as the beginning of the third millennium B.C., of renewed impulses from the south-east. The pottery ascribed to the Danubian II stage of settlement in this cortical area is more sophisticated in form than that of the Danubian I stage, having flat bases and including footed bowls. It was also much more diversified and one may distinguish even in Hungary between the monochrome ware of Lengyel and the encrusted ware, painted after firing, of the Theiss Valley. Apart from the painting of pottery, southern traits include female figurines and model houses of fired clay, clay stamps reminiscent of stone seals, cubical clay block vases recalling Early Minoan ones of stone, and spiral ornaments made of copper wire.

While these innovations were making themselves felt in the Middle Danube area and spreading thence over Czechoslovakia and into Germany, the heirs of the original colonists occupying the extensive outer tracts of the Danubian I territory were undergoing a certain degree of barbarization. In default of any more intensive occupation of the loess soil, such as might be implied by the growth of settlement mounds, the peasants were driven to spread on to poorer soils and develop hunting as an accessory source of food, both processes that brought them into contact with Mesolithic hunter-fishers. Among the leading features of this time was the disappearance of the spiral and meander from the decorative motives used by potters and the substitution of horizontal lines and chevrons—designs that reproduced the webbing in which round-based pots were commonly carried; and further the incised line was replaced or at least supplemented by impressions made by toothed stamps or combs, producing the so-called stroke-ornamented ware. Other more specialized wares included that named after the cemetery of Rössen near Merseberg in Saxo-Thuringia, which spread over much of the Middle and Upper Rhineland and beyond, and was decorated by broader furrowed lines apparently made by a jabbing motion and intended to secure white incrustation. Wild animal bones show that the Rössen people went in for hunting on a considerable scale and it is significant that the arrowheads belonging to the younger phases of the Danubian were of devolved microlithic type, trapeziform and triangular and commonly with flat flaking. A final point to mention is that on the margin of their distribution in the west the Danubian peasants in their later phase began to come into contact with others of alien culture. No doubt it is this which explains why in its last period the great settlement at Köln-Lindenthal was defended and why in South Germany the Rössen people chose to occupy such a natural fortress as the Goldberg. What is certain is that Rössen pottery occurs on settlements of the earliest peasants of Switzerland, whose cultural affinities lie in the west.

The Mediterranean and western Europe

The earliest pottery from western Europe is that from the islands and shores of the Mediterranean, simple bowls and flasks with round bases and lugs, plain or decorated by impressions of cardium shells. Closely similar pottery has been recovered from western Asia, for example from the lowest levels in the tells at Mersin in Cilicia and Ras Shamra (Ugarit) in Syria. The distribution of cardial impressed ware in the Mediterranean area strongly suggests that it was transmitted by sea: it is found on the islands of Leukas and Corfu; on the coast of Yugoslavia and the Adriatic coast of Italy, including the Tremiti islands; on Malta, Sicily, Elba and Sardinia; on the coast of Liguria; in the French provinces of Languedoc and Provence; and on the east and southeast coasts of Spain and the south coast of Portugal. The impressions, which were frequently made by toothed stamps and other objects as well as by cardium shells, were most commonly arranged as horizontal or vertical lines, zigzags or hanging arcs. Most of the settlement material has come from caves or rockshelters and represents what appear to have been temporary occupations. The lithic industries of these early farmers were based on the production of blades, from sections of which trapeze and transverse arrowheads were made; hunting evidently played some part in a mainly pastoral economy. Polished stone axes and adzes testify to the felling of trees and the working of wood. Among the simple objects made from bone the most noteworthy were spatulae used, in all probablity, for eating cereal food. For personal ornamentation perforated animal teeth, shells and foot-bones of hare were used as beads, and bracelets were made from polished stone or shell.

Whether the predominantly plain, round-based wares associated with Neolithic farmers in France, parts of Iberia and beside the Swiss lakes stemmed from the same source as the impressed wares or whether they represent a distinct and to some extent parallel tradition remains uncertain. Although the pottery from the Camp de Chassey in the French department of Saône-et-Loire was frequently plain it was sometimes decorated by geometrical patterns incised before firing or scratched on afterwards, and the pots of the younger stage of the Swiss Cortaillod ware, named after the locality on Lake Neuchâtel, might be ornamented by patterns cut out of birch-bark and applied to the surface of the pot by means of resin. Plain western ware is found with flint blades, trapeziform arrowheads and polished stone axes and adzes on settlements like El Garcel in Almeria and with collective burials in southern Iberia. The Chassey culture spread extensively over France from the Mediterranean, by the valley of the Rhône and Saône to the Paris basin and west of the Massif Central to the Atlantic coast of Brittany; and it is significant that fired clay female figurines have been found as far north as Fort-Harrouard, Eure-et Loire. The makers of the Cortaillod pottery, which has a counterpart to the south of the Alps in the Lagozza culture of North Italy, occupied rectangular wooden houses resembling those made by the Rössen and other Danubian II groups from whom they may well have derived them. The lakeside locations of their settlements favoured the survival of a much greater range of material equipment than is normally available from Neolithic sites and has shown that the Cortaillod people made an extensive use of wood and bark for containers and other things, as well as making baskets, nets and a great variety of linen textiles. Yet the Alpine countryside set limits to agriculture, and the proportion of wild animal bones shows that hunting contributed in a significant way to the supply of food; moreover, stag antler played a conspicuous role as a raw material for making a wide range of objects, such as mattock-heads, holders for adze- and axe-heads, harpoon-heads and personal ornaments.

The west Baltic area

Meanwhile a distinctive culture, characterized by beakers with flaring, funnel-shaped necks, was beginning to develop on the North European Plain beyond the frontiers of the Lengyel and Rössen groups of the Danubian II tradition. In spite of many differences of detail between its various sub-groups, the Northern culture was marked by features common to its whole extent from Mecklenburg to the Vistula and from central Prussia to Denmark and south Sweden. Its distinctive character rules out the possibility that its appearance can have been due solely to the expansion of any of the Neolithic cultures previously established in territories further south; and yet, at the same time, the appearance of basic Neolithic traits, notably stock-raising, cereal-growing and the making of pottery containers, can only be attributed to impulses from the south. On geographical grounds the most likely source is the Danubian province, and indeed pottery of Danubian II–III character has commonly been found in the same graves as Northern forms in Silesia and Poland. Quite plainly the northward spread of Neolithic civilization was accomplished by means of acculturation rather than of colonization. The North European Plain supported in the Maglemosian culture and its successors the most vigorous Mesolithic settlement in Europe. The hunter-fisher populations of the region were correspondingly selective in their borrowings: thus, the coast-dwelling Ertebölle people, while adopting the arts of domestication, continued to rely substantially on hunting, fishing and the gathering of shell-fish, and, in taking over the art of potting, applied to the manufacture of their larger, coarse vessels the technique of coiling used in basketry; similarly, the stone shoe-last adze failed to penetrate in face of flint forms evolved over millennia in a territory lavishly provided with the essential raw-material, though flint celts were now for the first time in this region finished by polishing. The vigour of the indigenous 'Mesolithic' heritage is shown in other ways, for example in the lavish use of amber, but the adoption of rectangular houses as far north as the Vrå culture of middle Sweden shows the force of the intrusive impulses. In burying their dead in single graves, the Funnel-neck Beaker people conformed to the general Danubian practice, but in constructing stone monuments they were making the most of their own habitat and giving expression to their own genius. Definition of individual graves by means of the glacial boulders so widely distributed on the North European Plain was practised by the Danubian groups north of the Sudeten mountains as well as by the Funnel-neck Beaker people, but the use of thin stone slabs or large blocks of megalithic proportions to form closed cists was peculiar to the northerners. Still more was this the case with the mounds erected over the graves and frequently themselves defined by boulders: in Denmark these mounds might be circular, but over the North European Plain in general they were built like the houses of the living on the elongated plan, which in the west was generally rectangular, but in the east, again corresponding with the local house-plan, was characteristically wedge-shaped.

The primary Neolithic culture of southern and more particularly of south-western Britain drew some elements from French sources, but it is becoming increasingly evident that much of its inspiration came from the North European Plain to the east, a conclusion which in view of the common Maglemosian heritage should hardly occasion surprise. The earthen long barrows, occasionally parallel-sided, but more often wedge-shaped in plan, have been notoriously difficult to parallel in France, but find analogues as far east as the Kujavian graves of Poland, even though, apart from the Medway group, their structural elements are of timber and turf rather than stone. The causewayed camps, for which again no adequate parallel has been adduced from France, have been wrongly compared with the fortified sites of Urmitz and Mayen in the Middle Rhineland; a more significant, if rather loose, analogy lies with enclosures formed by radial settings of houses noted at Kolomiishchina and other Tripolje sites in South Russia. Again, the flint-mines, for which parallels admittedly exist in North France and the Low Countries, can be matched by the examples with vertical shafts and radiating galleries at Krzemionkach Opatowskich and other sites in Poland.

On its western margins the Northern culture came into contact with the Western province both in the Middle Rhenish and Alpine zones. From these contacts arose the Michelsberg and Pfyn cultures respectively, the former named after a hill-fort overlooking the Rhine plain a few miles north of Karlsruhe and the latter designated by the locality to which it is confined in the eastern part of Switzerland. The Michelsberg culture, typified by the tulip beaker and a series of ceramic forms, was centred on the Main, the Middle Rhine and the Neckar, whence it spread east into Bohemia, south into Alsace-Baden and north into the Koblenz area and Belgium.

Copper-working in central Europe

Meanwhile impulses emanating ultimately from the East Mediterranean had already begun to carry exotic burial rites, metallurgy and the use of metal tools over wide zones of Europe. Several central European groups of the Danubian III stage, notably the Bodrogkeresztur of north-east Hungary, the Jordansmühl of Bohemia and Silesia and the Baden of Austria and much of

Czechoslovakia, fabricated copper artifacts, including perforated axe-adzes and a variety of ornaments. The sources of the copper ores used by these early smiths are still not fully known, but it is likely that the copper ores of the eastern Alps and of central Germany were already being worked, and certain that flat axes made from copper won in the latter region were being traded to the peasants of the Northern Neolithic culture before this had emerged from its early phase. The replacement of the flint axe with pointed butt and lozenge section by one polished all over and having a thin butt and flattened sides, which took place towards the end of the Northern Early Neolithic, was almost certainly inspired by the flat copper axe that was too costly for general use. Before considering any further how the comparatively simple peasant societies of temperate Europe were affected by impulses from the East Mediterranean, it will be necessary to turn to the relatively advanced civilizations of Crete and the Greek mainland.

Minoan civilization

The island of Crete, legendary home of the Minotaur and hence of the Minoan culture, was originally colonized by immigrants from Asia Minor in a Neolithic stage of culture, but from an early period Egyptian influences made themselves felt in the central and southern regions. The Early Minoan culture grew up in eastern Crete under the impact of fresh immigration from Asia Minor, but it was on the Messara Plain in the area cross-fertilized by Egyptian contacts that the richer culture of Early Minoan II–III developed. During this time copper came into more prominent use for daggers and axes, and circular dry-stone structures up to 13 metres in diameter, having portals made from heavy stone lintels resting on monolithic jambs, were built as collective tombs to house successive generations of the dead. The Early Minoans stood at the same general level of culture as the Early Helladic people of the Greek mainland, who were likewise largely recruited from Asia Minor. On the other hand, like the Early Cycladic islanders, they were better placed to enrich themselves by maritime trade: indeed, their situation at the southern margin of the Aegean world was even more favourable, since it encouraged contact with Egypt and the eastern coasts of the Mediterranean.

It was a combination of wealth gained by trade and of inspiration derived by contact with the civilized peoples to the south and east that made possible the decisive advance that led to the development in Crete of the first distinctively European civilization. The Middle Minoan period (*c.* 2000–1580 B.C.) was marked by many of the features associated with the rise of the earlier oriental civilizations: a finer sub-division of labour made possible advances in technology reflected in the manufacture of bronze and the adoption of the potter's wheel; population increased in density and concentrated in the larger units represented by towns with two-story buildings; authority was centralized in the hands of rulers who combined religious and political authority and whose palaces were also centres of economic importance; and centralized control was assisted by improved communications in the shape of wheeled transport and roads as well as by the development of writing, primarily for purposes of accountancy. The first approach to literacy took the form of hieroglyphs engraved on seals, but by Middle Minoan III times a true linear script—linear A—was being inscribed on unbaked clay tablets.

The zenith of Minoan civilization was reached during Late Minoan I–II times (*c.* 1580–1400 B.C.) between the rebuilding of the palace of Cnossos after its second wrecking by earthquake and its final destruction, presumably at the hands of the mainland powers centred at Mycenae, that took over the hegemony of the Aegean world during Late Minoan III times. Although they owed much to Asiatic and Egyptian influences, the Minoans were unique in far more than the style of their decorative art, for they created the first European civilization and the first one anywhere to depend for its well-being on maritime contacts. Their art, as expressed most freely in palace frescoes, in engraved gems and in pottery, betrays a pleasure in the representation of natural forms, maritime as well as terrestrial, for which no parallel exists in the ancient oriental world; and by comparison with the bearers of earlier civilizations the Minoans were freer from either priestly or militaristic oppression.

Early Helladic

The Early Helladic people of the Greek mainland, like their contemporaries in Asia Minor or in Macedonia, Bulgaria and southern Roumania, occupied permanent villages or townships and these were set as a rule on the mounds of their Neolithic predecessors. Yet innovations in pottery and architecture and the rise of metallurgy itself speak, if not of ethnic movement, at least of trade or other contacts with various parts of Asia Minor, some of which may have passed through intermediate islands. The rite of collective burial in rock-cut tombs or built ossuaries on the other hand reminds us that Greece was a Mediterranean land. Another reminder is the facility with which the Early Helladic people entered upon maritime trade that extended directly or indirectly to Egypt.

Aegean trade

The vigorous civilizations that arose in the East Mediterranean early in the third millennium were the first in the ancient world to rest primarily on the basis of maritime trade. The Neolithic colonization of the larger Aegean islands and of Crete presupposes traffic over the sea, and the flowering on these islands of cultures based on metallurgy and on the utilization of raw materials from a distance indicates a close and well-maintained network of seaborne commerce. An excellent example is given by the Cycladic islands, many of which, left to themselves, would have been too barren or too small to sustain more than a handful of poor peasants on a subsistence basis. The islanders owed the possibility of developing the kind of urban life displayed by the ruins of Phylakopi on Melos to their activity as traders: indications of this are indeed provided by the distribution of raw materials narrowly localized in nature, like the copper of Paros and Siphnos, the emery of Naxos and the obsidian of Melos, or by evidence for the export of manufactured objects like marble idols and vases to Greece, Thermi, Troy, Crete and Egypt. Equally, there can be no doubt that trade relations extended as far afield as the West Mediterranean. Thus idols of local marble from Sardinia reflect Cycladic influence; one might also cite beaked pottery, flagons of Melian type, not to mention a tanged dagger of Cypriot form from the Rhône delta. Again, though it is known that Crete entered on a phase of intensified trade activity in the East Mediterranean during Middle Minoan II times, there are signs, for instance in the pottery or the bossed bone plaques, representing female forms, from the Tarxien culture of Malta and from Castelluccio in Sicily, and in the copper daggers of the Remedello culture of North Italy, that impulses may have begun to reach the Middle Mediterranean before the end of the Early Minoan period. The Aegean peoples had long been practised mariners: their boats, probably up to 20 to 30 metres long, were provided with oars and projecting keels to reduce the impact on landing; and, though incapable of tacking or sailing close to the wind, they could presumably have run fairly rapidly before it. It seems likely therefore that the coasts of Tuscany, the south of France or Iberia could each have been reached quite quickly from the East Mediterranean.

The main drive behind early exploration in the Mediterranean may well have been, as was the case with the Vikings, the comparative poverty of the homeland, but prospecting for metals may also have been a particular attraction so far as the far west is concerned. Yet, while there is no evidence that the mariners were impelled by missionary zeal, they certainly carried their religious convictions with them, and these were sufficiently strong to impress themselves in due course on many of the native peoples with whom they came into contact. Many of the elements of Aegean religion, notably the mother goddess, the sacred bull, the horns of consecration and the double-axe, stemmed directly from western Asia, but the practice of collective burial, whether in natural caves or in artificial tombs hollowed out of the rock or constructed in dry-stone masonry, seems to have been a peculiarly Mediterranean development. Collective use of natural caves for places of burial, in itself a practice of very remote antiquity, was undertaken in Crete in Early Minoan I times; by Early Minoan II the islanders were building circular dry-walled tombs above ground; and in the South Cyclades collective tombs were being provided with corbelled or cupola roofs. Again, on the southern part of the Greek mainland Early Helladic folk were burying their dead in family vaults that might be cut from the rock or built in dry-walling.

Diffusion of chamber tombs

It is hardly possible to doubt that it was from the Aegean area that the rite of collective burial, associated with belief in a mother goddess, spread widely over the Middle and West Mediterranean or that this was associated with the voyages of exploration and prospecting at which we have already hinted. The earliest collective tombs in Malta, Sicily, the Balearic islands, the south of France and southern Iberia were as a rule cut in the rock, as though they were artificial caves, but in the latter case they might be rendered in dry-walled structures at ground-level to form corbelled graves approached by passages. These rock-cut and dry-walled collective tombs emanating from the East Mediterranean were reproduced in Sicily, Sardinia and the Balearic islands by diverse structures of cyclopean masonry, and in Malta, the south of France and Iberia by megalithic chambers walled and roofed by upright and transversely laid stones. When the idea of collective burial spread widely over western and north-western

Europe it was embodied mainly in tombs of megalithic construction, though the chalk-cut grottoes of the Marne and the corbelled vaults of certain Breton, Irish and Orcadian chambers remind us in outlying regions of ultimate Mediterranean sources, as do the representations of goddesses on the grottoes and gallery-graves of the Paris basin or the more schematic ones on passage-graves in Brittany, Anglesey or Ireland. The diffusion of the idea of building megalithic chamber tombs, like that of Neolithic economy itself, was accomplished partly by primary intrusions of adventurers from without and partly through adoption by aboriginal populations with a more or less devolved culture.

The route followed by the pioneers is marked by megalithic chamber tombs approached by passages and covered by round mounds (Map 5): from Atlantic Iberia they sailed across the Bay of Biscay to the southern shore of Brittany, up the western seaways to Ireland, Anglesey, the Hebrides, northern Scotland and the Orkneys, and ultimately either down from the north or by way of the English Channel to the west Baltic area. Although noticeably concentrated in the western part of their distribution on areas rich in copper, it was only in southern Iberia that the passage-graves yielded metal objects: elsewhere it was only in the forms of lithic artifacts, like the greenstone axes of Breton tombs, that their chalcolithic background finds any reflection in their contents. The vast majority of megalithic chamber tombs were secondary to the pioneer spread: they were erected by Neolithic peasants and pastoralists, who themselves were often comparatively recent converts from a Mesolithic hunter-fisher way of life. Although they adopted the rite of collective burial, they departed more or less widely from the architectural prototypes. Over large parts of western Europe they built tombs that were clearly degenerate passage-graves, often no more than small chambers with or without some kind of portal.

An alternative to the passage-grave that was widely adopted was the gallery-grave, a long chamber, generally under a long mound which, though it might be sub-divided, had no separate entrance passages. Among the many variants of this type one might mention the gallery-graves of the Severn–Cotswold area of Britain having pairs of opposite side-chambers or transepts, prototypes of which probably came from the Biscayan area of France, and the segmented ones with concave forecourts, which with their elaborations are found in Ulster and south-west Scotland, both associated with variants of the Western Neolithic pottery. Another important group is that of the Paris basin, comprising long subterranean chambers lined and roofed with megalithic slabs, often with porthole entrances. Representations of what may be funerary goddesses were occasionally carved on slabs at the entrance to the tomb and this was more frequently the case in the tombs of the upper Marne Valley that were cut entirely from the chalk rock. The people of the Seine–Oise–Marne area, though they continued to depend to a significant degree on hunting and made crude pottery, nevertheless used daggers of honey-coloured chert from the quarries at Grand-Pressigny in Touraine that were evidently designed as substitutes for copper.

Small tombs of megalithic construction (*dysse*) were already being built in Denmark during the final phase of the local Early Neolithic, but these were only variants of cist graves intended for single burials. The idea of collective burial reached the west Baltic area from outside in two main waves. Passage-graves came in at the beginning of the northern Middle Neolithic, evidently by one or other of the western sea-routes; and gallery-graves or long cists appeared in the final stage of the northern Stone Age, the period of the flint daggers that ran parallel in time with the Early Bronze Age both in central Europe and in the Hiberno-British province. Although a few of the northern passage-graves stand fairly close to the prototype in plan, none shows signs of corbelling or traces of rock-engravings, and the great majority diverge more or less markedly: some have oval plans, but often the chamber was long and rectangular, leading with the passage to a

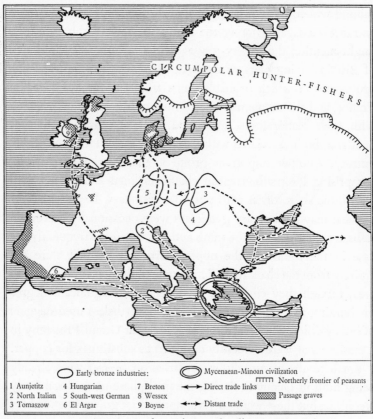

		○ Early bronze industries:	◎ Mycenaean-Minoan civilization
1 Aunjetitz	4 Hungarian	7 Breton	◄─► Direct trade links ⊓⊓⊓ Northerly frontier of peasants
2 North Italian	5 South-west German	8 Wessex	▨ Passage graves
3 Tomaszow	6 El Argar	9 Boyne	◄┄┄► Distant trade

5. Europe in the mid-second millennium B.C.

T-plan. The grave-goods were in the main indigenous; the pottery comprised a succession of styles identified from settlements and originating in different parts of the north German plain; the thick-butted flint axe was evolved locally from the thin-butted one with squared sides, itself inspired by copper prototypes; and the commonest ornaments were beads and pendants of west Baltic amber.

'Secondary Neolithic' groups

The diffusion of collective burial and of megalithic tomb-construction in the west and the rise of copper-working in central Europe and north Italy, at a time equivalent to Danubian III in central and Early Neolithic C in northern Europe, are only symbols of the influence exerted from the Aegean towards the close of its Early 'Bronze' Age on the still predominantly Neolithic peasantries of barbarian Europe. By contrast, in the more marginal territories of the temperate zone the process of acculturation, by which surviving Mesolithic groups were led to adopt elements of Neolithic culture, was still actively proceeding. Some such process must have been involved in the genesis of secondary Neolithic groups like the Tripolje, Funnel-neck Beaker and Western, in territories immediately adjacent to zones of primary Neolithic spread. Examples of what might be termed tertiary Neolithic groups include the Alpine Horgen and the Seine–Oise–Marne of the Paris basin, both of which continued to lay emphasis on hunting and the use of stag antler and made pottery of debased character. In the same way the indigenous element in the Late Neolithic of Britain, the makers of Mortlake and Fengate pottery, may well have incorporated surviving groups of hunter-fishers. Yet it has to be remembered that these people associated with Beaker intruders in developing from humbler prototypes the sacred sites of which Avebury and Stonehenge were the most prominent examples.

Battle-axe and Beaker peoples

The close of the Stone Age was marked over large parts of temperate Europe by the rapid movement of ethnic groups, which through their impact on the static peasantries and through their blazing of new routes helped to prepare the way for the spread of metallurgy. East of the Rhine warrior groups, armed with stone battle-axes, spread widely, burying their dead everywhere in single-graves. They issued from the lands between the Vistula, the Baltic and the Dnieper, from which the Funnel-neck Beaker folk had emerged in a previous period, but the custom of barrow burial, which not all of them adopted, came in all probability from the steppe region further east. There were spreads in several directions and each of the main regional groups that emerged was distinguished by differences of style both in battle-axes and pottery. To the north they spread across the Baltic to Sweden and Finland and through the East Baltic lands to the Gulf of Riga; and in the forests of the Oka–Volga watershed east of Moscow there grew up the distinctive Fatyanovo group. To the south others moved into central Europe and some few penetrated as far as Greece at the close of Early Helladic times. Another main drive was to the west: some turned north into Jutland, where they contrasted notably with the megalith-builders, who practised mixed farming on the richer soils of the drift; and others proliferated in Saxo-Thuringia and spread into the Rhineland on a broad front from the Alps to the Low Countries. In the Rhenish area they came into contact with powerfully built, broad-headed bowmen, having distinctive archer's wristguards, barbed and tanged arrowheads of flint, copper daggers, V-perforated buttons and bell-shaped beaker pottery, the latter decorated in horizontal zones by means of toothed stamps. These Bell-Beaker folk seem to have spread immediately from Iberia, following the megalithic sea-routes, but also finding their way into central Europe and in small numbers into Denmark, as well as into the Rhine Valley and thence, as well probably as from the south, to the British Isles. In thus linking Bohemia, a major source of tin, with both the Mediterranean and Denmark, the Beaker prospectors pioneered routes essential to the development of metallurgical industries in central and ultimately in northern Europe; and there is evidence that another group, this time coming ultimately from the Rhineland, first opened up the copper deposits of Ireland and so initiated the Hiberno-British industry.

Arctic hunter-fishers

The development of bronze metallurgy in Europe will be reserved for the next chapter. Meanwhile it needs to be emphasized that the spread of Neolithic farming economy in Europe was limited by ecological factors and that, beyond the northern margin of the deciduous forest, hunting, fishing, fowling and gathering provided the only or at least the principal means of subsistence. The circumpolar zone, with its great tracts of coniferous and birch forest and areas of open tundra and extending from the Atlantic coast of Norway to the Urals and far beyond, supported a type of Arctic culture which, though overlapping in south Scandinavia and the Baltic coasts with cultures based primarily on farming, rested fundamentally on a 'Mesolithic' type of economy. The emphasis laid on different aspects of the food-quest naturally varied: on the Atlantic and Arctic coasts of Norway deep-sea fishing with hook and line was particularly important; whereas the hunting of elk played a leading role in the interior of Sweden, Finland and northern Russia; and seal-hunting was a main activity on the coasts of the southern territories, in which alone mixed farming was combined with catching activities. Certain cultural elements of Neolithic origin were appropriated by the Circumpolar people, notably the making of pottery, which they built up by coils to conoid forms and decorated by sinking pits in the thickness of the walls, as well as by impressing combs or toothed stamps, commonly arranged in zigzags over the whole surface of the vessel. Although they turned out projectile-heads, knives and, in north-west Russia, some notable profiles of animals, from flint or alternative materials by means of bifacial pressure-flaking, the sub-Neolithic Arctic people were notable above all for the extent to which they utilized slate. Both the forms, and the techniques of sawing and polishing used to shape them, suggest familiarity with the working of bone. The antlers and skeletal material from game animals provided material indeed for harpoon-heads perforated near the base for securing to a line, barbed spear-heads, arrowheads, handles slotted for flint insets and fish-hooks; nearly all of these were of Mesolithic ancestry, though the hooks were now commonly barbed and sometimes made in two pieces bound together at the base. Polished adzes, frequently hollow-ground and evidently inspired by tools made from split tubular bones, were another widespread feature and presumably indicate the importance of wood-working.

The Arctic people were aided in their quest for food by various means of transport. On the sea and inland water they almost certainly used skin boats which, to judge from the north Norwegian rock-engravings, were of *umiak* type and propelled by paddles: vessels covered by seal-skin which would have been tolerably resistant to floating ice. For traversing the snow, which in Scandinavia lay for nearly half the year over most of the zone, heavy dog-drawn sledges, built up on struts set in grooves and braced to runners up to 12 feet long, were used as well as two kinds of ski, one for compact snow, having straps passing through a raised foot-rest, and the other for slushy snow with foot-thongs threaded through side flanges. Boats and devices for moving rapidly over land during the long winter made it possible to carry on trade over surprisingly long distances; thus axes and adzes of Danish flint were traded up the west Baltic coast and across Sweden to the north-west coast and adjacent islands of Norway; others roughed out of a kind of slate at Olonets in Karelia found their way over much of Finland and the East Baltic states; and amber pendants and figurines from East Prussia found their way across Scandinavia to the west coast of Norway. The existence of this trade helps to emphasize the broad homogeneity of culture over very extensive regions, a homogeneity only partly explained by an underlying ecological and economic unity.

In Finland, Norway and Sweden settlement tended to concentrate on the coast so that advantage could be taken of the resources of the sea and the shore as well as of the interior. In Russia on the other hand and in the interior of Scandinavia the shores of lakes and rivers were main foci of settlement. The hunter-fisher way of life commonly involves migration and this applies particularly to the circumpolar regions where seasonal differences are so pronounced. Thus, where they were available, as on the west and north-west coasts of Norway and on the island of Karlsö off Gotland, caves might be used during the summer for particular catches of seals or fish. As a rule, no doubt, tents or other light structures were used at this time of the year. On the other hand, during the winter, dwellers on the exposed coasts of north-west and northern Norway built rectangular semi-subterranean houses having thick walls of earth and rubble faced with dry-stone work, the roofs supported on two rows of vertical posts. Although it is difficult to be sure how many houses were occupied at once, it seems that under favourable conditions the Arctic hunter-fishers were able to live in sizeable groups. This is confirmed by the existence of cemeteries like those of Olen on Lake Onega in Russian Karelia and Västerbjers on Gotland. The first of these, though partly destroyed, yielded more than 150 graves. The dead were normally buried in an extended position wearing skin garments fringed with perforated animal teeth and accompanied by personal ornaments, weapons and tools.

The wealth of grave-goods suggests that the Arctic people practised their economy, the only one feasible at the time over most of their territory, at least as successfully as their contemporaries practising farming further south. In addition to repetitive patterns applied to pottery, which they shared with the peasant communities of Neolithic Europe, they created an impressive body of art—rock-engravings, plastic models in fired clay, carvings in amber, bone, slate, greenstone and wood, profiles chipped from flint and outlines impressed by toothed stamps on pottery—devoted primarily to representations of the animals on which they depended, above all elk, bear, reindeer, seals, small toothed whales, fish and water birds, but also including human beings and boats. In the case of the rock-engravings several distinct local styles may be recognized, but the general character of the carvings is remarkably uniform as far east as the bog of Gorbunovo in the mid-Urals.

CHAPTER 7

THE FOUNDATIONS OF EUROPEAN CIVILIZATION: FROM MYCENAE TO THE AGE OF EXPANSION

Mycenaean origins

About the same time as the Battle-axe people were swarming in central and eastern Europe, the Middle Helladic phase of Greek prehistory was ushered in by warriors who apparently spoke the Greek language and so belonged linguistically to the Indo-European family. Their wheel-made, grey 'Minyan' pottery, which included among its forms high-handled cups based on silver prototypes, belongs to a ware found widely over Asia Minor and as far afield as north-east Iran and Turkmenia, a fact consistent with a homeland on the steppes of south Russia for speakers of the pristine and undivided Indo-European language. Whether the warrior incursion reached Greece by way of Asia Minor or, as others think, from Macedonia, the event gave a decisive flavour to the Late Helladic or Mycenaean civilization that flowered in Greece during the sixteenth century B.C. Though clearly subject to strong Minoan influences, Mycenaean civilization is no longer believed to have been introduced fully formed by conquerors from Crete. The mainlanders adopted many elements of the island civilization, but the Mycenaeans and their culture were deeply rooted in mainland Greece. This is illustrated by the fact that the site of Mycenae was occupied already from Early Helladic times and that the royal shaft-graves, which yielded many of the finest objects from the beginning of the Mycenaean civilization, formed part of a cemetery of Middle Helladic origin. Again, though sharing the centralized palace organization of the Minoans, the Mycenaeans incorporated the megaron or great rectangular hall with porch and inner chamber, a plan absent from

Crete, but which existed in Troy II and in Late Neolithic Thessaly. Even more to the point, the records maintained by Mycenaean scribes in connection with the palace economy introduced from Crete are now known to have been written in the Greek language, though the script (linear B) was itself probably derived from one (linear A) widely used in Crete already by *c.* 1600 B.C. for an unknown but almost certainly non-Greek language. Many phonetic signs were common to both scripts and it could well be that the changes which did occur resulted from the need to adjust to a different tongue.

The mainland was a larger and naturally richer unit, which only needed the stimulus of the 'Minyan' incursion to realize its potentialities. No doubt it was this economic pull that drew Cretan artificers as well as Minoan manufacturers to Greece and led in due course to the introduction of the palace economy. The most vivid picture of the wealth attained in Mycenaean Greece already by the middle of the sixteenth century B.C. is to be gained from the goods placed with the dead in the shaft-graves. Vessels of gold and silver, mirrors with carved ivory handles, lavishly decorated personal ornaments and weapons and the use of exotic substances give evidence not merely of wealth, but of wealth concentrated in the hands of chieftains (Pl. VI) whose attributes and status are symbolized by light war-chariots, drawn by horses and running on spoked wheels, vehicles of a type that had first spread with the Hyksos to Palestine and Egypt and with the Hittites to Anatolia. When it came to blows with the Cretans, it was the mainlanders who won and the burning of the Cnossian palace *c.* 1400 B.C. marked the beginning of Mycenaean dominance in the east Mediterranean. It was during the following centuries that Mycenaean trade reached its peak and it was to this period that the cyclopean walls and the palaces of Mycenae and Tiryns belong, as well as many of the tholos tombs, whose great circular underground chambers approached by sloping passages are roofed with domes that might be up to 14 metres high.

Bronze metallurgy in central Europe

Until the intensified working of the east Alpine copper mines had begun to cheapen metal and so to influence technology on a broad front during the last century or two of the second millennium, the spread of tin-bronze metallurgy had only a limited effect on the peasant and pastoral societies of prehistoric Europe. The broad pattern of Neolithic cultures, as this was modified by the spread of the Beaker and Battle-axe peoples, persisted; flint, stone, bone and wood continued to be the most important materials; and few important appliances came into use at this time, unless we except the wooden ox-drawn ard or scratch-plough and the farm waggon with solid one- or three-piece wheels, of a type that was probably transmitted from south Russia through the territory of the Funnel-neck Beaker people of the north European plain. While metal was still expensive, its use was mainly confined, apart from the all-important axe, to weapons and personal ornaments. The metal-smiths themselves were either itinerant, peddling their own wares, as in the west or, as in central Europe, working at a few centres for middlemen who apparently organized the sale of their products. The conjunction of copper and tin needed for the rise of a bronze industry admittedly implied trade that might extend over long distances, but neither this nor the basic activity of mining was in itself new, since it had been developed, even among hunter-fisher peoples, for the stone axe and adze-blades needed for felling and shaping wood. On the other hand the metal trade opened up greater possibilities for the concentration of wealth and there seems little doubt also that it marked a further intensification of the prospecting activities of more advanced peoples centred on the east Mediterranean, the early stages of which have already been traced. This is confirmed by the fact that the early smiths of central Europe practised techniques invented earlier in the Near East. Among these was the use of valve moulds consisting of two pieces pegged together, which allowed the casting of objects having raised features like mid-ribs and flanges on either face, and of the *cire-perdue* process whereby wax models were encased in clay and after firing replaced by molten metal, a method which made it possible to produce a wide range of complex forms with greater ease and economy. Many of the leading metal types manufactured during the Early Bronze Age of central Europe (Danubian IV, *c.* 1800–1450 B.C.) among the Perjámos, Tószeg A, Aunjetitz and Straubing groups of the Maros, Upper Theiss and Middle Danube, Bohemia and Bavaria respectively, such as for example racket-shaped and knot-headed pins of bronze, gold wire earrings and copper torcs or neck-rings with coiled ends that served as metal ingots, were likewise of Near Eastern origin.

Mycenaean trade with barbarian societies

Although bronze metallurgy was thus established in limited parts of central Europe before the rise of Mycenaean civilization, it was the Mycenaean market (Map 5) that more than any other factor was responsible first for its spread to other centres and then for its intensification. Although copper was worked in Crete and certain Cycladic islands on a small scale and in Cyprus on a larger one, the requirements of the Minoans and later of the Mycenaeans grew with every advance in their technology. The adoption of standard bronze in Middle Minoan times accentuated the need for prospecting and trade, because the east Mediterranean area was notably deficient in tin. It was the need for metals that in the first instance attracted Mycenaean attention to central Europe and it was doubtless there that their emissaries came into contact with the Jutish amber that was already during the final phase of the Northern Neolithic being traded south. Their interest in the fossil resin with its magical 'electric' properties seems to have been aroused at first sight because Danish amber, distinguishable from that found in the Mediterranean, was already being buried in the shaft-graves of Mycenae; as it turned out it was their sustained appetite for this substance, as well as their hunger for metals, that determined in large measure the course of trade in Bronze Age Europe down to the breakdown to Mycenaean power in the twelfth century B.C. The original route by which amber travelled south from the west Jutland coast was up the Elbe to the junction with the Saale, thence by way of both rivers across the territory of the Aunjetitz culture to the Brenner pass and so by way of the Po Valley to the head of the Adriatic and down by sea to Greece. When in the second phase of the central European Bronze Age a distinctive bronze industry, associated with tumulus burial, arose among descendants of Corded-ware folk occupying the highlands of south-west Germany, a western loop was added, making first for the Middle Rhineland, passing up the Neckar, thence across to the Danube and so downstream to join the old one. The amber route formed a veritable hub around which the Early Bronze Age industry of much of Europe revolved. East of the Saale and extending as far as the Warthe another distinct centre marked by rich tumulus burials grew up which, like that in south-west Germany, was carried by descendants of the Late Neolithic Corded-ware people. Another distinctive industry developed in North Italy adjacent to the southern end of the overland route, and at its northern end the Danes, still in the final stage of their Stone Age, were importing bronze manufactures both from central and also from western Europe.

The only manufactured objects of east Mediterranean origin found in barbarian Europe and sufficiently numerous to define commercial routes are beads of faience, an artificial substance consisting of a core of fused quartz grains and a covering of glass glaze. Almost certainly the trade in these beads to the west and north-west was in the hands of Mycenaeans or their emissaries. The large numbers present in the Aunjetitz territory and in that of the adjacent Tomaszów culture of the Upper Vistula and a single find from north Jutland confirm the importance of the central European trade, but equally the distribution of the beads points to an alternative route by way of the Mediterranean and the western sea-ways. Faience beads from the cremation cemetery of Hal Tarxien, Malta, and from sites with Late Helladic III A pottery on Sicily and the Lipari islands mark the passage of traders towards the western Mediterranean. On the other hand the scarcity of finds on the coast of eastern Spain and their relative abundance in the south of France from Languedoc to Provence makes it plain that the main routes to the west no longer encircled Iberia. The El Argar culture that followed and carried forward the Almerian in the east of Spain was relatively provincial in character, and its metal-smiths had to make do with an insufficient supply of tin. Trade now flowed north of the Pyrenees, down the Garonne to Morbihan, itself a source of tin, and on across the open sea to Great Britain and Ireland, attracted no doubt by the tin of Cornwall and possibly of Wexford, by the copper of Waterford, Cork and Kerry and by the copper and gold of Wicklow.

Although two main routes can be distinguished, these were themselves interconnected; for instance the chieftains' tumulus burials in Brittany probably indicate a movement from the Saale–Warthe province, and the Hiberno-British region was linked by two-way movements both with this and with the west Baltic area. Indeed, it was the position of Wessex at the cross-roads of the two routes that made it possible for the ruling class to gain riches from Irish gold, Cornish (and possibly Irish) tin and Baltic amber. Clues to the ultimate destination of at least some of the tin are given not merely by the presence of segmented faience beads in a fair proportion of the Wessex tumulus burials, but also from the many indications that Wessex goldsmiths had learned from the more sophisticated practitioners of Mycenaean Greece.

Wessex and Stonehenge

In the wealth of their tumulus burials the Wessex chieftains have many analogues on the Continent, but in the lintelled circle and horseshoe setting of trilithons erected from sarsen blocks at

Stonehenge they can show a monument unique in barbarian Europe and one which they have autographed by means of engravings pecked on certain of the uprights. Much attention has rightly been paid to the representation of a metal dagger of a kind found in the shaft-graves at Mycenae, but it is at least as significant that more than sixty representations occur of an ordinary Wessex type of cast flanged axe. Further, while it is true that the sarsen settings stand apart in sophistication both as to form and finish, it should be remembered that they relate to a comparatively late stage in the history of the monument. Stonehenge began, as we have noted, as a circle of ritual pits surrounded by a penannular bank and ditch, and was originally constructed during the Secondary Neolithic phase. The first stone erections on the site were made from bluestones quarried on the Prescelly Mountains, and dragged and floated all the way to Salisbury Plain by the Beaker people. In view of the role of these people in opening up the copper resources of Ireland and initiating a native Hiberno-British metallurgical industry, it is worth noting that according to an old tradition incorporated in the chronicle of Geoffrey of Monmouth (c. A.D. 1136) the bluestones were derived from Ireland. It is also a fact that under the right conditions it is possible to descry Wicklow from the crest of the Prescelly mountains.

Recession in the east Mediterranean

Enough has been said to make it evident that the Mycenaeans or their agents played a decisive part, both in fostering the development of native bronze industries in central and north-western Europe and in creating conditions that favoured the enrichment of chieftains whose wealth was conspicuously displayed by individual tumulus burial. It is possible also, though in the existing state of knowledge this is only a hypothesis, that Mycenaean skill and technical knowledge and the pull of the Mycenaean market were between them responsible for intensifying the winning of copper in central Europe, which made possible the far-reaching industrial changes of the Late Bronze Age in temperate Europe. It has been suggested that it was expansion from central Europe that precipitated the fall of Mycenaean civilization and helped to set in motion movements of peoples which troubled the whole of the east Mediterranean world during the first half of the twelfth century B.C. Of the existence of disturbances at this time there can be no doubt. We know from the records of Ramses III (1198–1166 B.C.) that the Hittite confederacy, previously threatened during the closing decades of the thirteenth, was broken up by an eastward thrust of population during the first part of the twelfth century, at a time when Philistines were settling on the coast of Palestine and Egypt herself was threatened by islanders from the north. Again, according to later sources, Troy VII A was destroyed some time around the end of the thirteenth or the beginning of the twelfth centry (between 1209 and 1183 B.C.); and Thucydides tells us that the Dorians entered the Peloponnese some eighty years later. Archaeology confirms that many of the leading Mycenaean cities were destroyed by people whose immediate source was Mount Pindus, but who probably originated in Macedonia. Yet many of the detailed analogies between central European, Greek and Anatolian material used to support the idea of movements from the Middle Danube area might equally suggest movement in an opposite or even from a third direction and no definite answer can be expected until the chronology has been more exactly worked out.

Urnfield cultures in central Europe

A notable feature of this time in central Europe was the adoption by the descendants of the Aunjetitz people of the practice of burying their dead in urnfields, a practice that presumable spread from Hungary and which, significantly, occurred at Troy VI as early as the fourteenth century B.C. Likewise the warts and fluting on the cinerary urns themselves have Hungarian affinities and fluted pottery had a very long history in Anatolia, as well as being used by the destroyers of Troy VIII A and of Late Mycenaean villages on the Vardar. The Urnfield cultures of central Europe are symbols of the independent potentialities of European peasants at a time when civilization in the east Mediterranean was undergoing a temporary eclipse. They are immensely significant as laying the basis on which, under Greek, Etruscan and Scythic influence, the prehistoric Iron Age civilization of Europe depended. The earliest Urnfield group was that established in Hungary and exemplified by the C-level of the mound at Tószeg. Another grew up in the old Aunjetitz territory of the Lausitz between the Elbe and the Oder and north of the Sudeten mountains and later spread east to the Vistula and south to Lower Austria. A third, of special importance to the genesis of the Hallstatt Iron Age civilization of temperate Europe, was located in the north Alpine area, where two distinct cultures flourished, namely the Knoviz of Bavaria and south-west Bohemia and the Hötting of Austria.

Copper-mining in the Tyrol

It was the Hötting people who were mainly responsible, under the initial stimulus of the Mycenaean market, for opening up the copper-mines of the Tyrol. The best explored mines are those of the Mühlbach–Bischofshofen area near Salzburg, which tapped deep veins of copper pyrites. The miners had bronze-headed picks, but their main weapons were fire and water. Veins would first be attacked where they outcropped, but as soon as the miners had worked themselves into the hillside they were able to bring the fire to bear on the ceiling as well as on the rock immediately ahead. Very soon it would be necessary to build a wooden staging to carry the rock-waste and support the fires, and under this a passage would be left for the air currents needed to keep the fires burning and the atmosphere clear. By the time the workings had reached a practicable limit they might be as much as 160 metres in length and 30 metres in height at the entrance. Such a mine at the peak would probably have called for a labour force of some 180 men, a third of whom would have been employed on felling the wood needed for fuel and staging purposes. The total quantity of crude copper produced by the Mühlbach–Bischofshofen mines during the Late Bronze Age has been estimated at around 20,000 metric tons.

Mining operations on such a scale greatly increased the supply of copper and it must be remembered that the collapse of the Mycenaean market soon left the whole of this to the peasant societies of prehistoric Europe. Some of the metal was undoubtedly exported, to be incorporated for example in the products of the Nordic bronze-smiths in their splendid heyday; but the bulk was used by the Urnfield people themselves, either directly or for fabricating wares for export. Among the techniques first practised by Urnfield people in temperate Europe was the art of hammering vessels, an art long previously practised in the east Mediterranean world. Socketed axes, the idea of which may have originated in central Eurasia, were among the numerous forms that required core-casting. The cheapness of metal made it practicable to turn out an increased range of tools, and these included such things as chisels, gouges and saws, which in turn made possible notable advances in wood-working. The scale and number of the urnfields, the highly organized character of the extractive industries and the advanced standards of bronze-smithing suggest a denser population and a more productive basis of subsistence than that which sufficed for the earlier peasant communities of much of Europe. Although there is evidence that the ox-drawn ard or light scratch-plough may have started to be taken into use during an earlier stage of the Bronze Age, it would seem that the Urnfield people consolidated a system of settled mixed farming that was to prevail over extensive parts of Europe down to the Roman period.

Expansion of the Urnfield cultures

It is hardly surprising therefore that after a period of consolidation in the north Alpine area, during which they elaborated their way of life and accumulated wealth from copper- and salt-mines, the Urnfield people should have entered on a phase of further expansion which took the form of a series of thrusts over a period of centuries and continued into the time during which iron had come into use for tools and weapons. The expansive power of the Urnfielders, based in the first instance on an enlarging population, was enhanced by the mobility made possible by a fuller use of horse-drawn vehicles and given a sharp cutting edge by the slashing swords first introduced to central Europe from Asia Minor during the disturbed period that ushered in the break-up of the Hittite empire and the decline of Mycenaean power. The expansion of the Urnfield people, by displacing the populations that existed in the territories into which they first penetrated, brought about movements of population far more widespread than those involved directly in their own migrations. Moreover, through their control of vital commodities like copper and salt and as a result of their pre-eminence as metal-smiths, they exercised an important influence through the medium of trade, and it is often difficult from the imperfect evidence of archaeology to determine the precise historical significance of particular Urnfield influences.

The Urnfield expansion is significant both on account of the movements of population and of trade that it set in motion and because it laid the economic foundations of the last major phase in European prehistory, a phase in which iron tools were destined to play a role of increasing importance. South of the Alps Urnfield influence penetrated to the Po Valley and Latium, and round about 1000 B.C. a distinctive culture marked by cremation cemeteries and known as Villanovan began to develop between the Po and the Tiber on the basis of the old Appennine civilization. The Villanovans placed the ashes of their dead either in biconical urns, decorated in the Apennine style and covered either by a small cup or by a crested bronze helmet, or in urns shaped like storehouses with entrances high up in the walls and of a type probably derived from the Middle Elbe. They grew prosperous by intensifying the exploitation of Tuscan metal resources initiated long previously, probably under Minoan influence; developed a rich bronze industry, of which many of the leading forms, including swords with antennae-like projections at the base of the hilt, razors, helmets, girdles, safety-pins or fibulae and cult objects, were of Danubian derivation; and in due course adopted iron-working. North of the Alps on the other hand Celtic-speaking people seem actually to have penetrated as ethnic groups as far west as Catalonia and ultimately as far north as southern Britain, incidentally setting in motion a number of groups with traditions formed in the Middle Bronze Age. The earliest incursion seems to have passed through the Belfort gap into south Alsace and north Franche-Comté. Late movements during the first quarter of the first millennium B.C. reached as far south as the Saône, pressed forward in a westerly direction towards the Atlantic coast, and during the latter half of the eighth century B.C. crossed the south of France to complete the movement into Catalonia. Meanwhile a distinctive bronze industry grew up in the Atlantic zone of Iberia, based on Cantabrian copper and Galician tin, the original stimulus for which was probably given by refugees from the Loire region displaced by the westward thrust of Urnfielders. By the seventh century B.C. the region had apparently entered into active trade relations with Brittany and the British Isles, a commerce that greatly enriched the later bronze industries of the islanders.

Southern England was strongly influenced from across the Channel by the economic growth and ethnic expansion of the Urnfield people. Doubtless it was through trade that such continental types as socketed axes and slashing swords first came into the country, and it must be significant that it was during the opening centuries of the first millennium that the distribution of the products of metallurgical industry was reorganized on Continental lines and the travelling tinker replaced by the more elaborate organization implied by large hoards of finished wares or of scrap. How far the introduction of iron-working was accompanied by the intrusion of new people is another matter. The so-called 'Celtic' system of agriculture based on the cultivation of short, broad fields by means of ards or light scratch-ploughs, had almost certainly existed in southern Britain since the beginning of the second millennium; and the round houses, antler combs and many pot forms of the Iron Age peasants had certainly been present since the Bronze Age.

Protogeometric Greece

As we have seen, the catastrophes which temporarily eclipsed Aegean leadership redounded to the economic advantage of central Europe, and set in motion changes which transformed the way of life prevailing over extensive tracts of the then barbarian world. Even in Greece itself the disaster failed to impair the basis on which civilized life was re-created during later centuries. The destruction of Mycenae and of other urban centres is a fact attested by archaeology, whoever the attackers, traditionally referred to as Dorians, may have been in particular cases. Urban sophistication gave place to rustic simplicity; economic life reverted very largely to the activities immediately concerned with subsistence; trade languished; and crafts like masonry-building, gem-cutting and writing fell into desuetude. Yet even at a material level the decline was not unrelieved; Protogeometric pottery may have been ruder in some respects than Mycenaean, but it was by no means without merit; and the importation of iron ornaments and weapons marked the onset of a new era in European technology. Moreover, the break was by no means equally marked in all the Greek lands. If Mycenaean civilization was destroyed in the Peloponnese, substantial continuity was maintained in Attica,

Boeotia and Ionia, and it can hardly be a coincidence that it was in these latter regions that, to quote Miss Lorimer, 'all Greek poetry, both archaic and classical, all the great forms which the literature of Europe was destined to imitate and elaborate through the centuries, have their ultimate origin'. No doubt it was this continuity also that helps to explain why it is that Greek mythology, with the gods dwelling on Olympus in subjection to Zeus, is Mycenaean in conception and the Greek temple a descendant of the Middle Helladic megaron. Again, it is a striking fact that the oriental influences that brought Classical civilization to birth were transmitted through territories like Rhodes and Cyprus, where Mycenaean civilization had been subject to the least disturbance.

Genesis and diffusion of iron-working

As so frequently happens, the decline of one phase of culture marked the genesis of its successor. Thus the fall of the Hittite Empire at the beginning of the twelfth century B.C. was the immediate cause for the spread of iron technology. Although much more widely spread in nature than copper and still more than tin, telluric iron did not come into general use until much later than bronze, even though insignificant quantities were occasionally produced accidentally in early times in the course of such activities as firing pottery in closed kilns. Traditionally the earliest skilled iron-workers practised their craft in the lands bordering the southern shore of the Black Sea, and it is significant that the first historical references occur in the archives of the Hittite kings at Boghazköy. There are grounds for thinking that the Hittites, conscious of the advantages conferred by iron weapons in war, guarded the secret of their production and restricted exports to daggers, personal ornaments and the like, designed as presents for rulers of foreign states. What is certain is that it was not until the downfall of the Hittites that iron-working spread for example to Palestine, where it soon came to be applied to general economic activities such as farming in the shape of hoe-blades, ploughshares and sickles. It must have been from Anatolia or Syria, probably by way of Cyprus, that the Greeks of the Protogeometric period obtained their sword- and dagger-blades and in due course the knowledge needed for establishing their own iron-working industry.

The alphabet

It was in the same historical context and from the same quarter that the Greeks derived the alphabet. The fall of the Hittites, the decline of Egypt, following the death of Ramses III (1166 B.C.), and the collapse of Mycenaean power combined to play into the hands of the Phoenicians, a Semitic trading people of the coasts of Lebanon and Syria, who even managed to enjoy political independence from the twelfth to the ninth centuries. During an early phase of this period and most probably by c. 1100 B.C. the Phoenicians had evolved, probably to assist them in the conduct of their commerce, the first alphabetic script, the actual symbols of which were adapted from Egyptian hieroglyphs. Considering that the alphabet had to be adapted to the needs of a non-Semitic language, the agreement between the symbols on the earliest Greek inscriptions and those of the Phoenician alphabet is so close as to leave no doubt of their source, in addition to which the names and order of letters and the direction of writing from right to left in many inscriptions are all features of early Greek practice and only readily explained on the hypothesis that the alphabet was originally devised for inscribing a Semitic tongue. The probability is that the Phoenician script was first adopted around the mid-ninth century B.C. by Greek traders based on the Asiatic coast of the Aegean and operating through the Phoenician trading station on Cyprus. Although devised and spread in the cause of commerce, the alphabet was doubtless a main factor in reducing the Homeric poems, hitherto passed on by word of mouth, to their final form, probably towards the end of the eighth century, just as it was destined in its variously modified versions to transmit down to our own day the literature of Western man.

Greek colonies

Ever since Neolithic times the coasts and islands of the Aegean had been the subject of exploration by mariners eager for trade or new areas for colonization; at the height of their power the Mycenaeans had posts as far west as south Italy, Sicily and the Lipari islands and trade connections over broad tracts of Europe from Iberia and southern Britain in the west to the Ukraine and even Transcaucasia in the east. It is a sign of their renascent energy that the Greeks of the Geometric period not merely caught up with, but in due course eclipsed their predecessors. This is particularly true of the Euxine, into which Mycenaean trade had penetrated only feebly and settlement not at all. Already during the eighth century B.C. Ionian Greeks had begun to explore the northern shore of Asia Minor and in due course trading stations were established at Trebizond and Sinope, the first for loading iron, copper and gold from Transcaucasia and the latter perhaps for transhipment into larger craft. Doubtless it was the adventures of these pioneers which nourished the myth of the Argonauts in search of the Golden Fleece that we find incorporated in the *Odyssey*. During the following century exploration was extended to the western and northern shores and here no doubt the leading attractions were the fish that abounded in the rivers of south Russia, the Cimmerian Bosporus and the Sea of Azov, and which were traded dried or preserved in jars; the salt that could so conveniently be prepared in the great estuaries; and the honey and wax, known to have abounded in medieval Russia and of which the importance was already implied by Herodotus. In addition to its importance as a source of food and metals, the Euxine also offered scope for settlement, and numerous colonies sprang up at favourable points on the coasts. Among the most prosperous were those which paid tribute to and lived in profitable harmony with the Scyths, such as Olbia at the mouth of the Bug and close to that of the Dnieper, Pantikapaion on the west shore of the Bosporus and Tanais at the head of the Sea of Azov.

In the Mediterranean the Greeks met formidable rivals in the Phoenicians and Etruscans. To begin with they had to content themselves with establishing colonies in south Italy, from Calabria to as far north as Naples on the west coast, and in Sicily. They were effectually prevented from venturing further over the open sea by the Phoenicians, who had founded Carthage and other colonies on the Tunisian coast and established depots on the coasts of Sicily and Sardinia as early as the eighth century B.C. Assyrian pressure on the trading cities of the Lebanese and Syrian coasts first made it possible for the Greeks to spread to Egypt and Cyrene and ultimately to the western Mediterranean, where they founded Massilia (Marseilles) around 600 B.C. and Emporion (Ampurias) on the modern Catalan coast, approximately 550 B.C. From Massilia Greek traders reached out to remoter parts of Europe for tin and other materials. By the middle of the sixth century they had ventured through the Straits of Gibraltar to Tartessos, the modern Cadiz, probably to collect Asturian tin. But once again Greek enterprise was affected by events far away at the east end of the Mediterranean. The destruction of the Ionian cities by the Persians weakened the Greeks and made the Carthaginians powerful enough to close the Straits of Gibraltar. One effect of this was to deflect the Greek quest for tin to the deposits of Morbihan and Cornwall. These were reached by way of the Carcassonne gap, the Garonne river and the Biscayan sea-route with a port of call at Corbillo by the mouth of the Loire.

Athenian repulse of Persia

The overwhelming of the Ionian cities also constituted a mortal threat to the Helladic homeland where the arts of Classical civilization were already beginning to develop. Before long Athenian support for Ionian rebels incurred the active enmity of Darius, who set his armies in motion to stamp out the distant source of disaffection. Conversely, it was the defeat of the Persian army at Marathon in 490 B.C. and the destruction of the fleet ten years later at Salamis that, in dispelling the Persian menace, ushered in the greatest age of Classical Greece. That this proved to be brief was due to a fatal flaw in political life: the existence of so many sovereign city states in a land as small as Greece was bound to lead to destructive rivalry and conflict. In the event the state which emerged as victor from the Peloponnesian war (431–404 B.C.) was the most disciplined, but also the most philistine. With the predominance of Sparta the most creative, though not necessarily the most influential, phase of Classical art and thought was over. Before long the emergence of a strong Macedonian kingdom under Philip II (359–336 B.C.) put an end to the Greek city state as a political entity of importance. Yet in other respects Philip's achievements were immensely significant, since they made possible the conquests of Alexander the Great and so ultimately brought within the sphere of Hellenic influence the ancient civilizations of western Asia and Egypt and prepared the way for the expansion of the Roman Empire in the east.

The Etruscans

Both on the Italian mainland and in the North Tyrrhenian sea the Greek colonists encountered the Etruscans: a people of non-Indo-European tongue, whose literature has yet to be deciphered and whose origins have long excited interest. The idea that the Etruscans arrived in Italy with a ready-made culture from the Lydian homeland in western Asia Minor attributed to them by Herodotus has few supporters today. The culture which appeared in full view around 700 B.C. between the Arno and the Tiber was in essence no more than an enrichment of that of the Villanovans, explicable in terms of economic growth and the impact of exotic influences; Phoenician, Cypriot and Greek. The Etruscans drew their wealth from the deposits of copper, iron and tin in the mountains and from their own skill as metal-workers. From their early homeland they gained control over most of western Italy north of the Greek zone though, except in the north, they nowhere crossed the Apennines or disturbed the Italic bearers of the old Apennine culture: Elba was seized early on account of its iron deposits and Corsica fell into their possession as a result of a sea-victory in league with the Carthaginians over the Greeks around 540 B.C. In the course of the sixth century Etruscan civilization spread widely over the old Villanovan territories in the Po Valley and southward as far as the Campanian plain, where the northern Greek colonies on the Gulf of Naples were enveloped.

Whereas the Villanovans were essentially villagers, the Etruscans preferred, like the Greeks, to live in stone-built towns with public buildings: it was after all Etruscans who first enclosed the Seven Hills of Rome with a wall and converted a cluster of Villanovan villages into a city with forum and temple. The most impressive signs of their wealth are furnished by their tombs, great stone chambers domed or vaulted and heaped over with earthen mounds: the scenes painted on the inner walls, no less than the sculptured urns, the bronze figures, mirrors and vessels, the ivories, the imported Greek vases and the exquisite gold-smithery testify to a society that was not only affluent, but sophisticated and highly stratified. Politically the Etruscans were organized in self-governing cities, each with its dependent terri-tory, a system which, as with the Greeks, was favourable to a high level of culture, but which was unable long to survive the pressure of larger and more coherent units. The overrunning of their terri-tories in the Po basin by Celtic-speaking warriors between 450 and 350 B.C. began the process of disintegration which the Romans did so much to accelerate. By the middle of the third century B.C., indeed, Etruria had submitted to Rome, even if culturally the absorption was not complete until just before the beginning of the Christian era. Although the Roman republic ostensibly owed its birth to the expulsion of the Tarquinian dynasty and its growth was largely at the expense of the Etruscan state, Roman civilization was deeply indebted to the Etruscans: apart from their capital city and its forum, the Romans owed them many of their leading characteristics, such as their prowess with drains, their system of land survey by centuriation, their preoccupation with divination by the *haruspices* and, in the fasces, their very emblem of authority.

The Scyths

By the middle of the sixth century B.C. the Phoenicians, Carthagians, Greeks and Etruscans had thus between them settled the coasts, islands and peninsulas of the Mediterranean Sea and had already begun to penetrate by means of trade and exploration the extensive territories to the north that still remained prehistoric. Before tracing the impact of these influences on the heirs of the Urnfield and earlier prehistoric inhabitants of western and middle Europe, it will be convenient to consider the nomad peoples of the Eurasian steppes, who contributed important influences of their own to the cultural life of the Celtic and Teutonic peoples. Everywhere the natural grasslands of the steppe were defined on the north by the forest zone. At their western extremity the steppes came down to the shores of the Euxine, and east of the Volga they graded on the south into deserts. In this way the steppes formed a natural corridor linking the northern margins of China with the Altai, the southern Urals, Caucasia and the southern Ukraine, along which nomad horse-riders could move rapidly. Moreover, the fact that the nomads depended for their bare existence on the natural pastures of the steppe meant that pressure at any one point was liable to involve progressive displacements of population over vast territories.

To gain a living from the steppe called for a highly specialized knowledge of animal husbandry and a notable degree of cultural adaptation, notably in riding, clothing and habitations, so it is hardly surprising that well-defined nomad groups did not make their appearance until well into the first millennium B.C. One of the first indications dates from the end of the ninth century, when forerunners of the Huns began to harass peasant cultivators in the frontier lands of North China, and it may well have been the driving of these raiders to the west by the Chou emperor Suan that set in motion the widespread displacement of nomad groups which brought the Scyths to south Russia, probably around 700 B.C. Although mainly concentrated in the south Ukraine and the Kuban, the Scyths penetrated in some numbers into Hungary, where they formed immediate neighbours of the central European Celts, with whom they appear to have intermixed in Hungary and Transylvania. The Scyths were pre-eminently nomads: by the fifth century B.C., it is true, some groups in contact with settled peoples had adopted agriculture and even occupied townships on the Dnieper and in the Crimea; but the overwhelming proportion were at home on the open steppe. There they subsisted to a large extent on mare's milk and cheese, helped out by game and fish. Ever on the move from one pasture to another, the men rode on ponies, on whose harness they lavished the best materials and the most skilled craftsmanship, and the women and children reclined in waggons under the shelter of felt roofs. It is likely that when stationary they lived in felt tents which, to judge from the frozen tombs of the Altai, where such things survived in a wonderful state of preservation, had wool-pile rugs and brightly worked wall-hangings. Leather, wool, felt and fur provided materials for clothing, which in the case of men included soft boots, trousers for riding, jackets pulled in tight round the waist to allow maximum freedom in the use of the bow while in the saddle, and conical hats. They wore plenty of jewellery, and bronze mirrors of Greek manufacture or copied from Greek models were common possessions.

A notable feature of Scythic culture was the decorative art manifested in metal belt-plaques, harness-fittings, scabbards, dagger-hilts, drinking-vessels and jewellery and also in wood-carving, leather- and felt-work and even tattoo marks. Although much of the metal-work was executed by alien craftsmen and though the art derived elements from south-west Asia and Ionia, Scythic art was essentially barbaric in style and feeling. It was animated above all by a lively feeling for animals—stags, goats, lions and birds of prey prominent among them—such as one might expect to animate men who spent much of their life in the open and for whom hunting was a main interest. Yet there is a strong tendency towards stylization: the artist sometimes combined several aspects of a single animal into one representation, or he might use parts of one creature, such as the head and beak of a bird of prey, to enrich a representation of another quite different one; nor did he hesitate on occasion to contort and manipulate the beasts to conform to some decorative pattern. Among the tricks which the Scyths could have derived either from China or from south-west Asia, and which they probably transmitted in turn to Celtic art, was the rendering of projecting muscles on shoulders, haunches and other joints by means of curls.

As might be expected of a people to whom war, the chase and the management of animals were all-important, Scythic society was strongly masculine and authoritarian. This is strongly brought out in the burials, which seem to have provided a main focus of religious sentiment and which incidentally have yielded by far the greater part of our information about the Scyths. The dead were buried under barrows in chambers roofed over with timber and provided with grave-goods. In the case of the leaders the tombs were sometimes of vast size and the grave-goods of outstanding wealth. The barrows of the royal Scyths in the Alexandropol region of South Russia, for example, might range up to from 9 to 21 metres in height and from 122 to 375 metres in circumference and the chamber might exceed 12 metres in depth below the old ground surface. The archaeological evidence strongly bears out the account left by Herodotus, who records that the body of the dead leader, having been embalmed, was laid on a waggon and for a period of forty days was drawn in procession round his territory. The great man would be accompanied to the grave, not merely by material possessions, such as clothing, jewellery, weapons, food, drink, drinking-vessels and containers, but also by his favourite horses, his wife and his chief servants, recalling the practices of the Han emperors of China or from much earlier times those of the Sumerian rulers, witnessed by the contents of the royal graves at Ur.

Hallstatt Iron Age

The spread of iron-working north of the Alps gave rise to a new group of cultures which takes its name from the cemetery of Hallstatt near Salzburg. Although most of the bearers of Hallstatt culture must have been direct descendants of the Urnfield people, the ruling class probably stemmed in part from the old Tumulus culture, and in part from immigrants from the east. The most notable find relating to the earlier phase of the Iron Age Hallstatt culture, defined by the characteristic long swords of bronze or iron with scabbards having metal terminals, or chapes, of winged type, are the burials of the chieftains. Instead of being cremated and deposited in flat urnfields, they were now inhumed under timber chambers covered by substantial burial mounds. Some of the richest burials in the cortical area of Austria, Bavaria and Bohemia have yielded remains of four-wheeled waggons that remind one vividly of the funeral carts described by Herodotus in connection with the burial of Scythic leaders. Although they had adopted iron-working for some purposes, the Hallstatt peoples made great use of bronze: for instance, they used a variety of vessels, helmets, shields and greaves of sheet bronze in the north Italian style, as well as a variety of smaller objects and ornaments; and on occasion they even made their characteristic swords in this metal. Whether these were really designed for fighting from horseback, as many have held, is far from certain. There is no doubt that the Hallstatt warriors rode horses, but there is no proof that they used them for true cavalry fighting; it could well be that they treated them, as the La Tène and other early charioteers did their vehicles, as means of transporting warriors to the most advantageous point for ground combat. In any case their ability to ride, which they doubtless owed to impulses from the east, enabled them to spread fairly rapidly over the old Urnfield territories in the west, down the Rhine to the Low Countries, into the Alpine area and across France to northern and central Iberia. In an opposite direction elements of Hallstatt culture appeared in several distinct Urnfield groups, among them the Lausitz culture, regarded by Polish prehistorians as the basis of the Slav people; the East Alpine, occupying much of the Middle Danube basin; and the Bosnian, extending over much of Yugoslavia south of the Sava and the Danube. The wealth of personal armament and above all the widespread prevalence of military defences in the form both of hill-forts and marsh-fortresses like Biskupin in Poland leave one in no doubt that the period was one of warlike activity, but how far the diffusion of Hallstatt types was due to mere fashion, how far to raids by warriors and how far to anything like folk-movements are problems which need to be considered on their merits in particular cases.

During the final phase of Hallstatt culture, defined by short swords and beginning around 500 B.C., the centre of gravity seems to have moved west, and it was then that Greek influence, stemming from the colony at Massilia and passing up the Rhône and across to the Upper Rhine and Danube, began to play directly, at least on the upper classes of Celtic society. The most numerous imports from the Greek world were concerned with wine-drinking, which seems to have been taken up by Celtic chieftains almost as a symbol of status: amphorae, still retaining traces of the pitch commonly added to wine in the Mediterranean down to the present day, pottery wine-cups, bronze mixing-bowls and flagons of Rhodian type combine to give a convincing picture of a trade symbolizing an influence that was to do far more than transform the drinking habits of the Celtic aristocracy. Another striking instance of Greek influence at this time is given by the brick bastions of the Heuneburg hill-fort near the headwaters of the Danube.

La Tène

During the last quarter of the fifth century a new art style, taking its name from the famous votive find of La Tène at the eastern end of Lake Neuchâtel in western Switzerland, came into being in the territory between the Upper Danube and the Marne. Many elements of La Tène art are most easily explained by the break-down of Classical Greek motifs like the tendril and the palmette (an ornament with narrow divisions somewhat resembling a palm-leaf), in the hands of craftsmen schooled in the geometric Hallstatt style. Some of the earliest vehicles of Greek art to reach the area in question were bronze wine-flagons with beaked spouts, manufactured in the Etruscan workshops of the Po Valley, but carrying Greek patterns on the handle-attachments, which crossed the Alpine passes in the course of trade; it was not until the conquest of the Po Valley by Celtic-speaking people and the inauguration of Cisalpine Gaul around the middle of the fourth century that contacts with Italo-Greek art proceeded on a broader front. The fantastic treatment of animals or parts of them was on the other hand almost certainly derived from the Scyths, who as we have seen were immediate neighbours of the Hallstatt peoples in east central Europe. Celtic society was organized on an aristo-cratic basis and the finest products of La Tène art flashed in bronze or gold on the helmets, shields, spears, scabbards, harness-mounts, lynch-pins and terret-rings (driving rein rings) of warriors, their horses and their chariots as well as on the head, limbs and clothing of their women; but some of the basic motifs were reflected in the work of humble potters and wood-carvers. From its original focal area La Tène art spread east into the

Danube Valley, where was probably made the silver vessel found in the bog of Gundestrup in Denmark, south into Cisalpine Gaul and west and north over France, the Low Countries and the British Isles. Over the whole of this territory it continued to flourish until replaced by Roman provincial culture within the advancing frontiers of the Empire; and on the far north-west perimeter of Europe, in Ireland and the highland zone of Britain, it continued to survive until much later historical times.

During the prehistoric La Tène period the Celtic peoples of Gaul and Britain borrowed much from their more civilized contemporaries in the south. Thus, the revival of chariots was almost certainly due to contacts with the Etruscans. Again, during middle La Tène times the rotary lathe, used mainly for working wood and shale, reached south-west Germany from north Italy, where it had been introduced by the Etruscans, and from there spread widely over temperate Europe. The rotary quern, invented in the Graeco-Roman world for large-scale milling by means of donkeys and slaves, was introduced to barbarian Europe in the portable form used by legionary troops. The native coinage developed in Gaul stemmed from two main sources: the gold coinage was modelled on Macedonian staters; and the silver one on coins of Massilia and the western Greek colonies. The appearance of native coinage in Gaul, and in due course in southern Britain, marked an important advance in political consciousness and organization and it is significant that the late La Tène period also witnessed the development in Gaul and South Germany of the considerable fortified townships or *oppida* described and in some cases stormed by Caesar.

Expansion of the Roman Empire

Meanwhile the tiny and rather rustic Roman republic, born in 509 B.C. of the eviction of the Tarquins, was making ready to extend the boundaries of the civilized world. By the time the Gauls irrupted into Italy around 400 B.C. the Romans had begun to dominate their Latin neighbours, but it was not until the victory of Sentinum in 295 B.C. that they finally emerged as the dominant power in middle Italy. In the second stage of their expansion they consolidated their hold on Italy as a whole: they began by bringing under control the Greek colonies of Magna Graecia, went on to evict the Carthaginians from Sicily in the course of the First Punic War (264–241 B.C.) and within the next twenty years had subdued the Po Valley. The third stage, during which they gained control of the Mediterranean, was initiated by the Second Punic War (218–201 B.C.), which not only brought them Spain, but also, as a result of the battle of Zama, Carthage itself and with it full control of the straits of Sicily; further than that, through the Carthaginian alliance with Macedon, Rome became involved in campaigns in the east Mediterranean which led indirectly to the conquest of Pergamum and so to Roman intervention in the affairs of Asia. The annexation of Syria and Crete in 62 B.C., and of Egypt in 30 B.C., virtually completed the encirclement of the Mediterranean, which became in effect a Roman lake. Meanwhile the fourth and final phase of expansion, during which the Romans incorporated within the empire most of the remaining territories of the Celtic La Tène peoples, had already been initiated with the conquest of the rest of Gaul by Caesar between 59 and 51 B.C. The subjugation of Britain, much of the southern part of which had since Caesar's incursion been subject to strong influences from Roman Gaul, was begun by Claudius between A.D. 43 and 47 and completed even beyond the Firth of Forth by Agricola (A.D. 78–84), appointed for the task by Vespasian. By the death of Trajan in A.D. 117 the Empire had reached the Rhine–Danube line, which it was destined to hold until the collapse of imperial authority in the west; and beyond this it had extended to the Low Countries, the enclave between the Middle Rhine and the Upper Danube, and the province of Dacia.

The Germanic Iron Age and the Migration Period

Meanwhile, beyond the most extended limits of the Empire the forces that were ultimately to disrupt it were gathering strength. The heirs of the Nordic Bronze Age had acquired a knowledge of iron-working from the south by around 400 B.C.: during the ensuing four centuries they drew their main inspiration from the Celtic La Tène peoples with whom they came into contact on their southern borders; but during the opening centuries of the Christian era they came predominantly under Roman influence. By means of trade, to quote just one instance, bronze accessories of wine-drinking, manufactured in Italy, Gaul or the Rhineland, were taken into use by prosperous farmers as far north as the Trondelag; but even more important than trade in many respects was the return of individuals from service in the Empire. Thus the free Germans were growing in wealth and knowledge at a time when the inhabitants of the Roman provinces were being thwarted by bureaucratic interference and fiscal exactions; moreover the provincials' power of war-like resistance was progressively lowered by the very peace secured within the frontiers by an army in which the barbarian element was ever on the increase. Beyond the frontiers the small possibility of internal growth allowed by subsistence farming and the barrier to northward colonization set by the adverse climate of Sub-atlantic times led inevitably to southern thrusts of population. The first of these identified in history was the drive of the Teutones and Cimbri from northern Jutland, that began in 120 B.C. and was only checked by the destruction of the Teutones on the field of battle near Aix-en-Provence in 102 B.C. More widespread movements occurred during the second century A.D., when for example the Goths crossed the Baltic from their homeland in south Sweden and drove north of the Carpathians down to the region of Olbia on the north-east shore of the Black Sea. Such movements as these increased the flow of new ideas back to the old homelands.

It was from the Goths in their new territories that many exports from the Roman world, and art conventions from the steppes, reached the north. Another feature to spread north was the runic script, first adapted from the Latin in all probability by the Marcomanni of Bohemia, a script that was to reach Britain with the Anglo-Saxon invaders and to survive in Scandinavia in full flower down to the Christian Middle Ages.

Although it has been argued that westward thrusts of Huns from the steppes, by engaging the eastern Germans delayed their assault on Italy, in the long run it was the complex system of folk-movements which they set in motion that brought down the Empire in the west. The death of Theodosius I in A.D. 395 and the division of the Empire, the Latin west falling to Honorius and the Greek east to Arcadius, was the signal for wholesale invasions. The full brunt of these was borne by the western half of the empire. Although the formal end, symbolized by the deposition of Romulus Augustulus, was delayed until 476, the invasion of Italy and the sack of Rome by Alaric and his Visigoths in 410 was really decisive in that, bereft of an effective head, the provincial limbs proved unable to withstand the multiple and often lightning thrusts of the barbarians (Pl. VIII). No account of these can be offered here, but it is important to recognize a primary distinction between those of the eastern and western Germans. Whereas relatively small bands of the former, Visigoths, Ostrogoths, Burgundians, Lombards and Vandals, penetrated great distances and left little ethnic trace behind—the last-mentioned for example passed through Gaul and Spain and across North Africa to fall upon Rome from the Carthaginian shore—the latter, spreading only over neighbouring territories, laid the foundations of Anglo-Saxon Britain and Frankish Gaul.

The spread of Christianity

The prehistoric peoples beyond the old imperial frontiers were first brought within the sphere of civilization by Christian missionaries. Although subject at times to severe persecution, Christianity spread widely throughout the Empire during the Antonine period (138–92) and between 313 and 325 it achieved a settled status through its recognition by Constantine and the clarification of its doctrines at the council of Nicaea. When the western Empire collapsed, much of its ecclesiastical organization survived even though in the areas most overrun by barbarians there was some relapse into paganism. Thus the continuity of civilized life in south-east Britain was so disrupted by the Anglo-Saxon invaders that Christianity had to be reintroduced from Rome when more settled conditions set in by the end of the sixth century. In the long run the Anglo-Saxons brought about an enlargement of the Christian world by displacing Christians from the most populous parts of the Roman province and driving them to the remoter parts of Britain and even across the sea to Ireland. As a result thriving centres of Celtic Christiantiy grew up in northern Britain and in the far west, separated from the remainder of Christendom by a welter of Germanic barbarians, and it was only during a lengthy period after St Augustine's mission (597), in the aftermath of which the Synod of Whitby (663–4) was an outstanding episode, that the two were reunited. Even so the Celtic church continued as in a sense a separate force, making for example a distinctive contribution to the conversion of Bavaria and West Germany.

The bringing in of northern and eastern Germany had to wait on political progress. The defeat of the Huns at Troyes (451) and the conversion of the Frankish ruler Clovis to Christianity encouraged the emergence of a well-founded state under the Merovingian dynasty (486–751). Great advances were made under Charlemagne, who extended the Frankish frontiers to the Elbe and the Pyrenees and was crowned in the year 800 as emperor of the Romans at the hands of Pope Leo III. Yet the ninth century was to witness the temporary return of conditions reminiscent of those prevailing some four hundred years earlier, with Vikings taking the place of Germans and Magyars that of Huns: the former issued from Scandinavia to ravage the coasts of the Baltic, the North Sea, the Western Isles, the Irish Sea, the English Channel, the Bay of Biscay and even the west Mediterranean; and the latter, of remotely east Ural origin, were pushed by the advancing Petcheneg hordes from their immediate homeland in the Ukraine across the Carpathians into the Middle Danube basin, where their forays terrorized more settled peoples.

It was not until the middle of the tenth century, after half a millennium of unrest, that the German kings Henry the Fowler and Otto were able to establish more or less settled conditions in central Europe, the latter beating the Hungarians decisively at Lech and reviving the Holy Roman Empire at his crowning in 962. The extension of Christianity and indeed of literate civilization itself to the remaining parts of Europe was the work of missionary endeavour from Rome and Byzantium, the twin capitals of the Roman Empire. Henry and Otto had carried the frontier up to the Oder and the closing years of the first millennium were marked by a series of dramatic advances, among them St Adalbert's mission to Prussia (997), the adhesion of Hungary (1000), the conversion of Olaf Tryggvason, king of Norway (995–1000) and a former Viking, and the establishment of Christianity in Sweden, whence in the twelfth century missionaries crossed to Finland. Meanwhile Byzantine missions had already before the end of the ninth century gone among the Bulgars, Croats and Serbs. In 988 Vladimir the prince of Kiev introduced Christianity to his dominions, which extended north to Novgorod over territory crossed by the old trade routes linking the Swedish Vikings with Byzantium. Pressure of nomads from the eastern steppes led to Novgorod taking the lead from Kiev during the later twelfth century, but during the fourteenth and fifteenth centuries Moscow rose to prominence, and when at length the ancient capital of the East Roman Empire fell to the Turks it was to the metropolitan of Moscow that the headship of Orthodox

Christianity passed and it was the principality of Moscow that formed the core of the future Russian Empire. It was the expansion of Muscovite power and Orthodox Christianity that brought the remaining areas of prehistoric Europe within range of literate tradition. By the death of Ivan III in 1505 the frontiers had reached the Arctic territories and the Urals and the prehistory of Europe was to all intents and purposes concluded.

A counterpart to the northward expansion of Christianity, which followed the achievement of more stable conditions towards the end of the first millennium, is to be seen in the staying and reversal of Islamic expansion in the south. Within twelve years of Mohammed's death in 632 his followers had overrun much of the Byzantine Empire, including Cyrenaica, Palestine, Syria and Iraq, and in addition Persia and Armenia; and by 700 they had added to their conquests the rest of North Africa, Afghanistan, West Turkestan and north-west India. At the peak of their power in the mid-tenth century the Moslems had come near to engulfing the entire Mediterranean, having occupied most of Spain, as well as Provence, Sicily and south Italy, and threatened Asia Minor and Byzantium itself. From this point of view the stability that made possible the Crusades came to Christian Europe only just in time: in the event not only was all Spain regained by the middle of the thirteenth century, but the fall of Byzantium was delayed sufficiently long for it to be in some respects an advantage to western Christendom.

The age of exploration

By the middle of the thirteenth century Christendom was no longer on the defensive in the west and was indeed ready to reach out into other continents. Already by 1260 Venetian and soon after Genoese merchants had begun to establish trade relations with China from bases in the Crimea using the same route as that followed a thousand years previously for conveying silk to the Roman world; and during the earlier half of the fourteenth century envoys were reaching China by sea from the Persian Gulf. The conditions on which this eastern trade was based ceased to exist when the Mongol was replaced by the Chinese Ming dynasty (1368/70) and xenophobic influences regained the upper hand. The Europeans had to turn elsewhere for the spices and other eastern produce to which they had become accustomed. A new age of geographical discovery and as it turned out a new era in the history of mankind was inaugurated, in which the lead passed from the Mediterranean to the nations of the Atlantic sea-board. The Portuguese began by edging round the west coast of Africa and by 1498 had succeeded in reaching India by way of the Cape of Good Hope. Meanwhile, six years before Vasco da Gama's culminating exploit, Christopher Columbus, a Genoese holding the commission of Ferdinand and Isabella of Spain, made landfall on one of the Bahama islands and before returning planted a small colony of Spaniards on Haiti. Christendom had thus in the course of two or three centuries initiated a process that within the ensuing three or four was destined to bring the whole world within the purview of literate civilization.

CHAPTER 8

AFRICA

By comparison with the role it played during the earlier stages of prehistory Africa, as we have already seen, had, except for part of its Mediterranean coastal zone, already relapsed into provincialism during the Late Pleistocene. From this time much of the continent remained a kind of cultural museum in which archaic cultural traditions of modes 2 and 3 continued to adapt to ecological change and even on occasion to display idiosyncratic variations without contributing to the main course of human progress. For this reason, quite apart from the more fortunate biological endowment of parts of south-west Asia, it is hardly surprising that Africa should have failed to share in the original break-through to modes of subsistence based on farming. It is highly significant that just as traces of Advanced Palaeolithic culture were restricted to the parts of Africa closest to south-west Asia, so also the earliest traces of agriculture and stock-raising on African soil are concentrated in the corner nearest the Levant. Radiocarbon dating shows that even in this zone farming was not established much before the middle of the fifth millennium B.C., that is over a thousand years after it had begun in south-eastern Europe.

Yet there is much to be said on the other side. Africa may have been restricted in the adoption of settled life based on farming in relation to south-west Asia and even to parts of Europe, but it remains to emphasize its positive achievements. For one thing the Nile Valley, profiting from its proximity to Asia but also from its huge potentialities for growing food, gave birth to one of the great urban and literate civilizations of the ancient world, one that owed its continuity to the manner in which it was insulated by geography and by the low standard of technology of most of its neighbours. But the Dynastic civilization of Egypt was not the only contribution made to the human story by the peoples of Africa during the last ten thousand years. The mere fact that the arts of farming spread slowly and belatedly meant that the Africans were able to adapt a knowledge of cultivation and stock-raising to suit their own particular circumstances, including the nature of the varying types of environment found in the continent. When they first began to make serious inroads on the equatorial forests in the interest of horticulture they did so as pioneers; and the culture they created in West Africa is one which through the slave trade and its aftermath has coloured the whole image of Negro achievement as this has impressed itself on the imagination of the outside world. Quite a different adjustment was made in the Sahara or on the grass tablelands of East Africa by such peoples as the Tuareg and the Masai with their strongly pastoral economies. Nor, again, should we forget the contribution made by those groups that survived by hunting in the remoter forests of the Congo or in the Kalahari desert. The later prehistory of Africa reminds us that there are indeed more ways of contributing to the heritage of mankind than by guiding the main lines of technological advance.

Mesolithic hunters

During the period of transition from the Late Pleistocene to Neothermal times, say between 12,000 and 7500 B.C., the flint industries of North Africa, the Oranian or Ibéro-maurusian of Morocco and the Eastern Oranian of Cyrenaica, shared the same leading features: they were marked by a predominance of backed blades of medium size and by smaller proportions of flake scrapers and burins. In this they agreed with the Kebaran and Nebekian cultures of the Levant and the Zarzian of the Zagros which were broadly contemporary with their initial phase.

It was not until Neothermal conditions were well established that we find indications around the middle of the seventh millennium of a marked change in flint technology which by then conformed to mode 5. The Upper Capsian industries of the Maghreb, centred on Tunisia and Constantine, and the allied Libyco-Capsian that immediately overlies the Eastern Oranian in the Haua succession, though still showing substantial proportions of backed blades, were marked above all by a truly microlithic element. The microliths, which were fabricated in some cases by the notch technique, comprised crescents, triangles and elongated trapezes. At this time also there is evidence for the use of ostrich eggshells, complete ones as containers and fragments as beads. Another significant innovation was that geometric patterns were sometimes engraved on the shell in the form of dotted or continuous lines.

Lithic industries in mode 5 also occurred during Neothermal times over extensive tracts of East and South Africa, as well as appearing in parts of West Africa. The earliest, that named after Magosi in northern Tanzania, occurred with a high degree of uniformity as far south as the Cape. Over this region we find industries with diminutive points of Still Bay type, associated with small blades removed from prepared cores by punches, and backed blades and lunates shaped rather like a thin section of a tangerine with the straight edge sharp and the curved one blunted by steep flaking. There seems little doubt that the Magosian, along with more or less parallel cultures like the Hargesian of Somaliland, was in its turn a source of the even more widespread microlithic industry, characterized by small double-ended scrapers and lunate insets for arrows and known after the South African locality of Wilton. This first appeared during the succeeding Makalian wet phase and at the extremities of its distribution lasted down to modern times. Other industries included in what South African prehistorians term their Late Stone Age are the variant of the Wilton named after the Nachikufu caves in north-east Zambia, found in the savannah woodland country north of the Zambezi and marked in its earliest stage by narrow pointed microliths; and the Smithfield of the Vaal and Upper

Orange rivers, an industry with special forms of scraper, but lacking microliths, the general aspect of which is doubtless related to the nature of the raw material, a variety of indurated shale. In the course of their long history the microlithic industries underwent many changes and were enriched by contact with more advanced cultures. In East Africa the art of potting was early acquired from neighbouring groups, but in South Africa this was a more recent trait. Among other features that appeared only in the younger stages in South Africa may be mentioned stones bored from faces to give an hour-glass perforation and polished stone axes and beads made from ostrich and mollusc shell. Both in the Horn of Africa and in South Africa itself lithic industries corresponding to mode 5 lasted down to the spread of iron-working, which first reached Rhodesia on its way south during the first millennium B.C., indeed, microlithic industries in the Wilton tradition were still being made when European influence began to penetrate South Africa. It seems probable, though it is by no means proved, that the makers of the later Wilton industries were Bushmen. Although at present confined to the Kalahari desert, where certain groups have recently been the subject of intensive ethnographical research, these hunters formerly ranged over the whole of the eastern part of South Africa into which they came at an unknown period from the north. The Bushman's way of life is basically the same as that which archaeology leads one to infer for the Wilton people and, moreover, they made beads of eggshell, weighted their digging-sticks with bored stones and used the bow and arrow for hunting; a main difference is that they now tip their arrows with bone or iron, but in times gone by arrows were armed with lunates set in resin with the sharp edges exposed.

The presence of more or less naturalistic rock-paintings over broad tracts from Tanzania and Malawi, south through Rhodesia and Zambia to the eastern zones of the Transvaal and Orange Free State and on to the Cape and South-West Africa, has attracted widespread interest because of their supposed affinities to ones of Advanced Palaeolithic age in eastern Spain. A more sober view of the African paintings is now taken, for many of them were almost certainly executed during the last two or three hundred years by Bushmen; moreover, the east Spanish are now generally considered to be of Neothermal age. Yet there is little doubt that some of the African paintings are of prehistoric age and that they were executed by makers of Wilton industries. Again, it is generally accepted that the rock-engravings found in the interior of South Africa were made by the Smithfield people within whose territory they are confined. The practice of this rock-art, like the wearing of personal ornaments, are features common to parts of North Africa and the Sahara.

Early farming in Lower Egypt

One of the main difficulties in tracing the earliest farmers of Lower Egypt is that the Nile must have eroded or buried under silt the great majority of early sites. One of those to survive is Merimde on the west side of the head of the delta, a huddle of flimsy huts of oval or horseshoe plan. The villagers made monochrome pottery by hand; shaped axeheads and maceheads from polished stone; flaked hollow-based arrowheads and knives or daggers from flint; and carved a variety of things from bone, including barbless fish-hooks of the same general class as those of the Natufian culture. They caught hippopotami and fish, but also planted cereals which they stored in large jars as well as in basket bins or silos. One way in which they differed from the early farmers of the Fayum is that they buried their dead among their dwellings. According to radiocarbon analysis the culture already flourished in Lower Egypt during the first quarter of the fifth millennium; and if the pottery from the upper part of level VIII in the Haua Fteah in Cyrenaica belongs to the same tradition this date can be put back to the middle of the millennium. On the other hand the date from El Omari suggests that villagers may have preserved the same pattern of culture down to the Middle Predynastic period.

If the evidence for Neolithic settlement in the Fayum depression is fuller, this is due partly to the better conditions of preservation and partly to the care with which the environmental setting has been studied. Around the middle of the fifth millennium to which the Neolithic occupation can be assigned on the basis of radiocarbon analysis, that is at the peak of the Altithermal phase of climate, conditions were much more favourable than they are today. The level of the lake stood *c.* 55 metres higher and forest trees and swamps existed in what is now an arid environment. At this time the Fayum was no isolated oasis. It formed part of a territory linked to the Nile Valley as far south as the Sudan and extending thence in a westerly direction along the southern margin of the Sahara, a territory in which fish, crocodiles and hippopotami were then able to flourish. That the Fayumis took advantage of this is shown by their equipment for hunting, including barbed bone harpoon-heads and flint arrowheads of winged form; but the important thing is that they were farmers.

The Fayumi people kept sheep or goats, cattle and swine, and cultivated emmer and flax. The equipment used in harvesting, storing and grinding the grain, like the cereals themselves, were those developed long previously in western Asia. The silos lined with coiled basketry, in addition to carbonized cereals, yielded fine baskets, used in all probability for sowing, and wooden reaping-knives with flint blades set in slots, like the much older bone ones of the Natufians. Although fire-holes were noted in the mounds of midden material, no definite traces of dwellings were observed, from which it has been inferred that tents or similar structures were used. Numerous axe- and adze-blades made from polished flint or stone suggest that timber was nevertheless utilized on a considerable scale and it may prove that more substantial dwellings were in fact made. Traces of linen show that weaving was practised. Pots were made by hand in simple shapes, mainly undecorated flat-based bowls without handles, spouts or other features. Apart from shells, some of which were brought from the Red Sea and the Mediterranean, and beads of amazonite or microcline felspar of uncertain, but certainly exotic origin, the Fayumis made do with local materials and their economy was of simple subsistence type.

Badarian of Upper Egypt

Other communities of relatively simple farmers, depending on flint and stone for their basic technology, established themselves in Upper Egypt, notably in the region near Badari, where they seem to have laid the basis of the Early Predynastic culture. Traces of the temporary settlement of such early farmers were found at Hammāmīya stratified below Early and Late Predynastic levels, but the bulk of our information comes from burials. The Badarian peasants cultivated emmer and barley which they harvested with reaping-knives set with bifacially flaked sickle-teeth and stored in clay silos; and they kept cattle and sheep or goats, though not apparently swine. In addition they hunted, using arrows tipped with heads of leaf- or hollow-based and winged form. As craftsmen they also wove, made baskets and turned out pottery by hand. This latter comprised bowls and open dishes, commonly black inside and near the rim, the lower part of the body being red or brown through oxidization; the finer ware was finished with a burnished rippled surface and patterns were sometimes made on the inner face of open vessels by means of burnished lines. Flint, stone and bone were freely used, but copper appeared only in the form of beads that had been hammered into shape, presumably from native metal. The dead were interred in a contracted attitude in oval trench graves clothed in linen with skin outer garments, as a rule with the head at the west end, facing south and so lying on their right side. The men were clean-shaven, but wore their hair long; and the women plaited theirs and wore ivory combs carved with animal heads. Finds of stone palettes, occasionally with red pigment or with malachite, suggest the use of cosmetics. Perforated shells were used for head-dresses, girdles and necklaces; and anklets, bracelets, rings and ear- or nose-plugs were also worn. A feature of Badarian practice of special significance for the future was their careful burial of domestic animals wrapped in textiles.

Among the graves with Badarian grave-goods were others with distinctive, though evidently closely related, furniture, which is commonly attributed to a separate culture named after the site of Der Tasa. Although no radiocarbon or absolute dates are available for the Tasian it is generally held on not very impressive evidence to have preceded the Badarian. The absence of copper beads, on which some stress had been laid, could well be due to chance; and in any case the presence or absence of small trinkets of native copper has no real economic or technological significance. The distinctive beaker pots, slender, with round base and flaring rim, are decorated by incised patterns that suggest basketry prototypes.

Early Predynastic Egypt

The Early Predynastic or Amratian culture has been found at Nakada sandwiched between the Badarian, from which it apparently developed, and the overlying Late Predynastic. Radiocarbon dates suggest that it existed during the second quarter of the fourth millennium. Some marked changes are apparent. Whereas the villagers of Merimde and Badari camped on spurs overlooking the Nile and the Fayumis settled the margins of the Fayum lake, the Predynastic peoples seem to have been the first to exploit the possibilities of the naturally irrigated valley. The size of the Naqada settlement, an aggregation of mud and reed huts at least 92 metres across in either direction, and the number of the graves in the cemetery both suggest enlarged social units. Schematic representations of a variety of animals painted or scratched on pottery may have been intended as symbols of totems and it is significant that similar ones recur as emblems of nomes or territorial divisions during the historic period. It may well be therefore that the Amratian villages were occupied by totemic clans. Their technology was still basically lithic, copper continuing to be used only in its native form and for such small objects as pins with rolled heads. On the other hand, flint was no longer obtained merely in the form of surface nodules; it was now mined and the roughing out and manufacture of tools was carried out on the site of the quarries. Bifacially flaked arrowheads continued to be made in numbers, including leaf and triangular as well as hollow-based forms. The finest pieces were fish-tail lanceheads and long dagger-blades, which had been ground into shape before being subjected to a final process of superbly controlled pressure flaking. This process, the object of which was no doubt to impart a surface finish, was also applied to polished flint axes and adzes. In general Amratian pottery was coarser than Badarian, probably because the Predynastic people were beginning to develop elegant stone vessels, cylindrical ones from alabaster and footed ones from basalt. Black-topped ware continued to be made, but a new departure was White Cross-lined ware in which patterns recalling basketry, together with others depicting animals, men and boats, were applied in dull white paint to a polished red surface. To judge from the clay figurines found in the graves, men appear to have gone unclothed apart from penis sheaths and sandals, though they wore plumes in their hair, and both sexes went in for a variety of ornaments, most of them elaborations of ones used by the Badarians, such as ivory combs carved with animal figures, glazed beads and a variety of bracelets. Stone palettes show that making up was still popular and indeed their more elaborate character—they might be shaped to animal profiles—suggests an even greater accent on cosmetics. In addition to personal ornaments the dead were accompanied by food and figurines, which might be carved from ivory, as well as being modelled more roughly in clay, in graves that were still simple holes in the ground.

Late Predynastic Egypt

The Late Predynastic culture, represented by Nakada II, extended further north into the northern part of Middle or the southern part of Lower Egypt and indeed takes its name from Gerza near the entrance to the Fayum depression. In the extreme south, however, it never displaced the Amratian in Nubia, nor at the opposite extreme did it penetrate northern Lower Egypt with the Delta, which was occupied by a quite different culture, represented by the settlement of Maadi near Cairo and by the cemetery of Heliopolis on the margin of the Delta. The Gerzean culture probably arose in Middle Egypt on an Amratian basis enriched by the permeation of cultural elements of Asiatic origin. Thus, whereas Black-topped pottery continued to be made for a while, White Cross-lined ware gave place to Decorated ware, painted in Asiatic fashion with dark red paint on a pale buff ground, to represent the natural markings of the stone vessels on which the forms were based. Stone vessels themselves continued to be made and the use of hard porphyry marks a further advance in an exacting craft.

A highly significant innovation was the introduction of metallurgy, which had appeared in western Asia a thousand years or so previously: in addition to the small objects which the Badarians and their immediate successors had made from native copper, the Gerzeans were now able to cast flat axes, ribbed daggers and flat knives. Swallow-tailed blades and curved knives continued to be thinned by polishing and finished off by controlled pressure-flaking, which on the latter might take the form of oblique, parallel fluting of extreme regularity. On the other hand new features to appear at this time, almost certainly from Asia, included the widespread use of blades struck from carefully prepared prismatic cores, and the introduction of chisel-ended or transverse arrowheads and pear-shaped stone maceheads. In place of glazed stone, faience began to be manufactured, a complex substance consisting of an artificial core of finely powdered quartz grains cemented by fusion and coated with a glass glaze. Important raw materials were obtained from a distance: copper came from the eastern desert or from Sinai, but lead and silver were imported from Asia, and lapis lazuli from an ultimate source in northern Afghanistan, presumably by way of Mesopotamia. In this latter connection it is significant that a local copy of a Meso-potamian cylinder seal of Protoliterate type was found in one of the Gerzean graves at Naqada. Boats made of bundles of reeds, but of substantial size and provided with cabins, served for the transport of materials like mined flint or stone vessels on the Nile. These native boats were propelled by oars, but foreign-looking ones with upturned prow and stern painted on Gerzean pots were fitted with a sail. For overland portages asses were used, and it should be noted that wheeled vehicles, though long known in Mesopotamia, were not introduced in Egypt until the New Kingdom, which began *c.* 1570 B.C.

Gerzean society was firmly based on farming, and hunting had markedly declined as an economic activity. The villagers lived in more substantial houses, rectangular in plan and fitted with a wood-framed doorway in the side. Graves were no longer orientated regularly and it is noteworthy that they began to show a greater range of wealth in terms of burial offerings, some being provided with ledges, others with compartments separated off by wattle partitions, to contain extra offerings; the most one can say is that during Gerzean times there were signs of a growth in wealth accompanied by a more integrated social structure.

Unification of Upper and Lower Egypt

The ancient Egyptians attributed the unification of their country to a single individual, Menes, whom they supposed to have welded the twenty-two nomes of Upper and the twenty nomes of Lower Egypt into a single realm and to have initiated in his own person the First Dynasty of pharaohs. In reality the process must almost certainly have been a gradual one, lasting for at least two or three generations. The unification is unlikely, for one thing, to have been accomplished without a good deal of fighting, and we have evidence for this on a number of well-known archaeological objects. For instance scenes of royal conquest are carved in low relief on either face of a great stone palette some 2 feet in length from the old royal capital of Hierakonpolis in Upper Egypt: one (Pl. IX) depicts King Nar-mer, the crown of Upper Egypt on his head, despatching an enemy with a stone-headed mace and surrounded with captives and enemy dead; and the other shows the same ruler, this time with the crown of Lower Egypt, confronting four chiefs of nomes and surmounting a heap of decapitated enemies. It is interesting to note that two animals are depicted on this latter face with their necks intertwined, a convention also found on a dagger handle from Gebel el-Tarif, but only at home in Mesopotamia. Another knife-handle, this time of ivory from Gebel el-Arak, has been carved to show on one face combats between men and boats with standards and upturned ends and on the other a man dompting two lions. This last is especially interesting because the man is wearing a hat and skirt of Sumerian type and because the whole scene recalls the Sumerian epic of Gilgamesh.

The occurrence of elements of Mesopotamian origin among the representations on these key objects raises the question how far the unification of Egypt was brought about by foreign influence or even by alien intruders. There can be no doubt of the existence precisely at the period of transition from the Predynastic to the Protodynastic or Archaic period of Egyptian history of innovations that stemmed from Mesopotamian sources of Protoliterate (Jamdat Nasr) age. In addition to the cylinder seals and the art motifs already mentioned, one could cite brick architecture, which after a long history in Mesopotamia appeared suddenly in Egypt during the First Dynasty in the construction of tombs and which exhibited a series of detailed agreements, such as the size of bricks, the use of three rows of stretchers alternating with one of headers and the decorative use of buttresses and recesses. Another innovation to appear about the same time was writing, with ideograms, phonetic signs and determinatives, even though at first mainly as an element in monumental art rather than for the practical purposes for which it had been devised in Mesopotamia.

Dynastic Egypt

Yet it has to be emphasized that, important though Asiatic impulses undoubtedly were at this decisive juncture, the civilization that emerged in the Dynastic period was essentially Egyptian, the culmination of a thousand years or so of prehistory in the Nile Valley, distinct from and in some respects in marked contrast to that of Mesopotamia. The continuity of Egyptian civilization from its prehistoric beginnings down to the Hellenistic Age and even to the spread of Islam owes much to geography. Whereas the inhabitants of Sumer had to contend with rich and warlike mountain dwellers both in the east and north, as well as with occasional incursions from the western desert, the ancient Egyptians were comparatively insulated in the Nile Valley. They were not so remote as to be cut off from the stimulus of Asiatic civilization, deriving from that quarter first the arts of agriculture and then metallurgy and the techniques of incipient civilization, but they were far enough off to escape invasion, save at periods of exceptional weakness; and even when this did occur their civilization was too deeply rooted to be much affected by temporary political domination. Meanwhile the economic wealth conferred by the Nile floods and the cultural advantages derived from proximity to Asia ensured that the Egyptians were at all times so superior that they had nothing to fear from their neighbours in the deserts on either side or in tropical Nubia.

The main political danger was rivalry between Upper and Lower Egypt arising from the narrowness and great length of the alluvial zone of the Nile. It was because of this that the conquerors from the south found it worth while to set up an important centre at Memphis to match their old capital at Hierakonpolis and that down to the end of the New Kingdom the pharaohs wore the two crowns. The River Nile provided a physical means for uniting the country, but it was the supremacy of the pharaoh that guaranteed that unity. As a divine ruler he symbolized the whole community and it was his unchallenged sovereignty that engendered confidence and stability. The whole administration was carried on by authority delegated from the pharaoh, whether through governors of nomes or through officials of the central government, one of whose main concerns was to channel a sizeable proportion of the social surplus into the hands of the ruler. The importance of leading officials even during the Archaic phase of the Dynastic period is witnessed by the scale and richness of their tombs recently explored at Sakkara. On the other hand the supremacy of the pharaoh is well displayed on one of the great ceremonial stone maces from Hierakonpolis, showing Nar-mer raised up nine steps on his throne, confronted by captives and attended by a priest, a sandal-bearer and fan-bearers. Another shows the 'Scorpion' ruler presiding at the opening of a canal, a symbolic act emphasizing how the people of Egypt depended for their very sustenance on the mediation of the pharaoh. From the beginning crops must have benefited from the natural irrigation brought about by the Nile flood, but for any great extension of the fertile zone it was necessary to cut channels and lift the Nile water into them by some such device as the *schaduf*. The increase in population that seems from all appearances to have marked the Predynastic period suggests that some such works must have been initiated before the end of the prehistoric period. On the other hand the institution of a highly centralized government, while in itself expensive to maintain, made it possible to undertake public works on a scale not hitherto possible.

In addition to centralizing sovereignty and administration, the pharaohs were careful to promote an official religion. This was centred on the solar cult whose priests evolved a cosmogony, accounting for the genesis of nine main deities, at their headquarters in Heliopolis (the ancient Egyptian On), a little north of Memphis. Of the progeny of Ra-Atum, the sun-god, the most influential was Osiris, lord of the regions of the dead, whose cult was a direct counterpart. Preoccupation with death, or rather with the continuance of life after physical death, played an immensely important part in the life of ancient Egypt. The basic belief was that the spirit could survive only if the body was adequately preserved and provided with what was needed for its well-being in the after life. As the Egyptians grew richer and their social structure became more elaborate the tombs of the more important members of the community took on a monumental form and were furnished richly to accord with the position in life of the dead. By the First Dynasty substantial structures of sun-baked bricks, known as Mastabas, began to be erected over the graves of prominent people, and by the Third Dynasty stone was employed for royal tombs. The first or Stepped Pyramid, erected by Zoser at this time, was built over a Mastaba, already twice enlarged, the burial being made amid a maze of passages and rooms at the foot of a deep shaft beneath. The Old Kingdom was symbolized above all by the regular pyramids which began to be made in the Fourth Dynasty and reached an early climax in the Great Pyramid built for Cheops and his queen. The dimensions of this structure— approximately 231 metres square at the base, which covered over 5·3 hectares (13 acres), and rising, when complete, to a height of 147 metres—are impressive in themselves, but the great cause for wonder is the sheer labour involved in the preparation and transport of the stone. Approximately 2,300,000 blocks, weighing on the average some $2\frac{1}{2}$ metric tons, were used and the mere transport of these by manpower would have involved the labour of perhaps 100,000 levies for a three months' spell in each of twenty years, the time it took to complete the work, according to the story recorded by Herodotus; and in addition to this a permanent force of masons and labourers would have been needed on the site, perhaps as many as 4000 in all. When it is recalled that upwards of twenty pyramids, none so large, but all substantial, were erected during the Old Kingdom alone, the overwhelming force of the idea behind them, the conservation of the bodies of the pharaoh and his consort and their provision for life after physical death, and the almost incredible concentration of the forces of an essentially poor society on the needs of one man will be even more apparent.

By contrast, no trace of the houses or even of the palaces of these divine rulers survives. For the purposes of transient life even the greatest were content to live in flimsy structures, while lavishing their power and substance on the construction and provisioning of their own tombs. In this respect the difference between Egypt and Sumer is marked, even when we remember the riches of the Royal Tombs of Ur. Although in abstract terms civilization had progressed by way of the same broad stages of development, the actual expression or form of the two civilizations was markedly distinct. Nourished by the Nile and sheltered by protective deserts and their own superior technology, the ancient Egyptians were able to maintain their way of life with remarkably little change over something like three thousand years of recorded history. The breakdown of central authority that marked the end of the Old Kingdom would in an Asiatic state almost certainly have led to alien domination, but in Egypt it was the local nomarchs who profited and when the royal power was re-established with the Middle Kingdom (c. 2132–1777 B.C.) the construction of pyramids was begun again as though no interruption had been. During the second intermediate period, it is true, Egypt fell under the yoke of foreign rulers, the Hyksos or Shepherd kings, but it is significant that their eviction (1573/70 B.C.) inaugurated, in the New Kingdom, the greatest phase in the history of the land, during which Egyptian armies warred against the leading powers of western Asia and campaigned as far east as the Euphrates. Even during the period of decline that followed the close of the Twentieth Dynasty (*c.* 1090 B.C.) and witnessed conquests by Assyrians, Persians and Greeks the fundamentals of Egyptian civilization survived: indeed, under the earlier Ptolemies, whose rule began with the death of Alexander in 323 B.C., the Egyptian state experienced something of an imperial revival; and independence was only ended with its conversion into a province of the Roman Empire on the death of Cleopatra in 30 B.C.

The early spread of food-production in Africa

Ancient Egypt owed its history to the twin facts of being near enough to share in the basic advances made in the creative zone of south-west Asia, while at the same time being remote and self-sufficient enough to mature and conserve its own distinctive civilization over what in terms of other and later traditions must be accounted an immensely long period. For the rest of Africa the consequences were less happy. The ancient Egyptians, secure in their homeland, made no conscious effort to extend their civilization or even their sphere of influence over other peoples: they defended their frontiers and during the New Kingdom extended these far into south-west Asia; but in their African homeland they contented themselves with holding their neighbours at arms' length. This is not to say that the ancient Egyptians refrained from all contact with other African peoples: apart from anything else they were compelled from time to time to campaign in Nubia, they employed Libyan mercenaries and they even sent trading expeditions to the land of Punt, activities which between them must have resulted in some limited amount of cultural interchange. The fact remains that pharaonic Egypt, in itself technologically sheltered and conservative, served even more as a buffer than as a mediator of higher culture. The greater part of Africa outside

Egypt, except for Mauretania in the far west where the copper deposits of Akjoujit were apparently exploited, most probably under the influence of Beaker prospectors from Spain, passed directly from the Stone to the Iron Age.

The concept of stock-raising and the cultivation of crops, like the manufacture of pottery or polished stone tools, spread to North Africa from two directions. They came to Cyrenaica from the Levant, the source from which Egypt itself received its basic Neolithic economy. The animal bones from the Haua cave indicate that sheep or goat were introduced abruptly at the same time as pottery-making. That the people who adopted Neolithic traits were nevertheless the indigenous population is shown by the flint-work which remained basically in a mode 5 tradition: the only new feature was the use of pressure flaking for finishing arrowheads, a technique that it is worth remarking could have come as well from Africa south of the Sahara as from the Lower Nile. Further west the Maghreb, comprising Tunisia, Algeria and Morocco, offered a much more substantial terrain for food-producing societies. Once again the body of the population was indigenous and continued to make most of their flint implements after the Capsian pattern, but here there are indications that 'Neolithic' innovations came directly by way of the Mediterranean. One is that some of the pottery was decorated by the impression of a deckle-edged shell like a cardium; and another is the presence of domestic cattle—conspicuously absent from the Haua—both among food-refuse and in the repertoire of the rock-engravers of the Fezzan.

So far as East and South Africa are concerned—and this applies in large measure to the Sahara—the source of 'Neolithic' innovations was the Nile Valley. In discussing the Neolithic occupation of the Fayum the point was made that during the Altithermal phase of climate the Sahara was far more favourable to settlement than it has since become. This finds ample reflection in the rock-engravings of such territories as the southern Atlas,

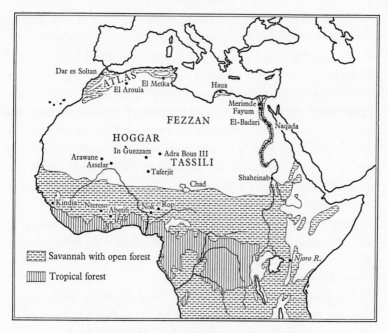

6. The expansion of food-production in Africa

the Fezzan, the Hoggar and the Tibesti massif. These depict in what are now arid regions big game like elephant, buffalo, rhinoceros, giraffe, hippopotamus and crocodile, the last two of which require a really damp environment. Another indication of this is the occurrence of skulls of markedly Negro type both at Asselar and at Shaheinab, well to the north of the area in the central African forest. Evidence of this kind implies that the Sahara was then relatively easy to cross, and not merely from the Nile to the Atlantic but north and south from the Maghreb to the Niger and *vice versa*. Again, the southern part of this territory between *c.* 12° and 20° of latitude North was at this time suited to sedentary life on the banks of rivers and lakes rather than requiring, as it has done in modern times, a more nomadic mode of life. The widespread occurrence of pottery in the South Saharan sites suggests a settled mode of life, but this does not necessarily imply, any more than it did in the Russian taiga during the third millennium, the practice of either stock-raising or agri-culture: where hunting and fishing were combined in the imme-diate neighbourhood of lakes and rivers, catching activities would have been sufficient to account for what we see. On the other hand the pottery-making people of Shaheinab certainly combined goat-herding with hunting and fishing as early as the last third of the fourth millennium. Again, it is significant that barbed bone harpoon-heads, adapted to fishing and closely re-sembling those from the Fayum and Khartoum, have been found at many sites in the South Sahara from Tchad (Artiena) to the Hoggar (Meniet) in the north and as far west as Mali (Arawane) and Mauretania (Taokest); and further that the pottery of the Ténéré culture (e.g. Adrar Bous III), as well as its flint adzes, resembles that of Shaheinab.

The precise timing and course of the desiccation of the Sahara have yet to be worked out, but it is probable that by the opening of the second millennium B.C. people were being displaced to the Maghreb or southwards to the savannah with open forest. Until more information about the organic residues from settlements is available the beginnings of food-production in this territory must remain obscure. What can be said on the basis of the archaeologi-cal evidence is that polished stone axe-blades of a kind needed for clearing forest were a significant component of the material equip-ment of each of the early pottery-making groups identified in this zone. If crops were in fact grown it is likely that they would have included indigenous millets and, in the case of Guinea, rice (*Oryza glaberrima*). The most widespread cultural group equip-ped with polished axes and pottery in the savannah zone is that known from the rock-shelters and caves of Guinea (e.g. Kindia district), Ghana (Rop) and highland Nigeria (Nok): in each case the basic stone industry is microlithic (mode 5) and plainly in-digenous in origin, but the pottery, no less than the polished stone blades, is exotic and the tooth-stamp decoration on some of it recalls wares from the Maghreb. By contrast we have in Ntereso on the Volta River in Ghana a village which yielded a number of Saharan forms like winged arrowheads, bone fish-hooks and barbed harpoon-heads in addition to the familiar comb-decorated pottery and polished stone blades.

Pastoralism in East Africa

Meanwhile there is solid evidence that pastoral economy spread south from the Sudan into the Horn of Africa and down into Kenya. There it is linked in the archaeological record with cultures featuring stone bowls and pestles used presumably for crushing wild plant foods, by coil-built pottery decorated in a variety of styles including some suggesting basketry prototypes, and by lithic industries with lunate microliths like those widespread in the Late Stone Age of Africa. The precise age in terms of years of the sequence formed by the Hyrax Hill, Gumban A, Gumban B and Njoro River cultures cannot yet be told, but it is suggestive that a faience bead of a kind that spread most widely during the period 1500–1300 B.C. has been found with a burial at Nakuru assigned to Gumban B. There is no certain evidence that pastoral activities spread further south until much later, but isolated 'Neolithic' traits, like polished stone axes and pottery, were adopted by Nachikufu and Wilton groups in Zambia and Rhodesia and even as far south as South Africa.

The diffusion of iron-working

The first people in Africa to make general use of iron tools were presumably the inhabitants of Carthage, founded near the site of modern Tunis by Phoenicians from Tyre at a date set traditionally at 814/13 B.C. From Carthage the new technology spread east along the coastal tract of Libya, and the possibility has been mooted that it may have been carried south across the Sahara to West Africa. The more likely hypothesis is that it came to West, as to East and South Africa, from Meroe, some fifty miles above the confluence of the Nile and the Atbara, the capital of Nubia or Ethiopia between the fifth century B.C. and the third A.D.

It is possible that iron-working may have been practised by bearers of the Nok culture of the Nigerian highlands as early as the third century B.C. Yet a convincing pattern of radiocarbon dates has still to be established for this part of Africa and until it has been the status of the Nok culture and the context of iron-working in West African prehistory must remain uncertain. In the eastern half of Africa iron-working was associated with standard pottery wares: in Kenya, Ruanda, Uganda and Tanzania it appeared with dimple-based pottery by the first century A.D.; and in Zambia and Rhodesia around A.D. 300 with channelled ware.

Quite apart from its value in providing more effective tools and weapons the manufacture of iron increased men's ability to clear the ground for crops. In the savannah and open forest there is, it is true, no certain evidence that the Iron Age farmers were much more advanced than their Neolithic predecessors. At a site like Kalomo in Zambia they lived in round huts, kept dogs and cattle and a few sheep or goats and cultivated kaffir corn (*Sorghum caffrorum*). The creation of gardens in the forest for cultivating such food-plants as yams and bananas was a new and probably later development. It was also one of immense demographic importance. The discovery of stone axe-blades in forest zones must not be taken as proof of Neolithic clearance since these were used alongside iron ones down to modern times. To judge by recent practice, burning as well as felling was involved quite apart from the labour needed for planting tuber-cuttings in ridges, keeping them mulched and providing poles to support the vines. The result was to make possible densities of the order of 500 to 2·6 square kilometres. The species of yam cultivated in Africa today include some species of certainly south-east Asian origin (e.g. *Diosoresceae alata*, *esculenta* and *bulbifera*), but others (e.g. *D. cayenensis* and *rotunda*) were indigenous to Africa. When and

how the Asiatic species reached Africa and whether the indigenous species were domesticated before or after the introduction
of Asiatic ones are still open questions. Botanically the cultivars
introduced to East Africa compare more closely with those of
south-east Asia than of India and ethnology points in the same
direction: the outrigger boats of the east coast and the xylophones
of wide distribution can both be derived most plausibly from
south-east Asia; and the Malagache language of Madagascar has
Malayo-Polynesian affinities.

Prehistoric Africa and the literate world

The spread of farming over the Mediterranean zone of North
Africa laid the basis for successive civilizations. In a variety of
ways these influenced the parts of Africa that remained prehistoric. For instance it was by diffusion from these that iron-working spread over much of prehistoric Africa. Again, the zone of
literacy expanded in the course of time. By the beginning of the
Christian era a new state had arisen in the north of modern Ethiopia centred on Axum some 483 kilometres south-east of Meroe;
and during the fourth century A.D. its ruling class adopted
Christianity. Further west camel-riding Mohammedans moved into
the zone of savannah between the Sahara and the equatorial
forest and there set up emirates which still influence the course of
history in Nigeria. The further spread of civilization was limited
by two natural barriers, the mountain massif of Ethiopia and the
equatorial rain-forest extending from the Great Lakes to Liberia.
Sheltered by these, prehistoric societies continued to flourish
until they were temporarily incorporated into the overseas
possessions of European states.

Before this happened the ivory and gold of prehistoric Africa
had long attracted the interest of overseas traders. The coast of
East Africa was open to the maritime commerce of the Indian
Ocean and the Arabian Sea. When various cultivars and certain
elements of material culture were introduced from Indonesia is

still to be decided. In the case of the gold trade more is known because of successive excavations at a number of sites in the neighbourhood of the Mashonaland goldfields. At the best known of these, Zimbabwe, the first inhabitants lived simply, made channelled ware pots and managed on their own resources. Gold ornaments appeared in Period 11 (c. 600–eleventh century A.D.) and at the same time cylindrical glass beads of a kind known from Arabian, Persian and Indian sources. Period III, marked by houses with solid mud walls and compounds built of dry-stone walling, saw the introduction of opaque beads of oblate form that were undoubtedly of Arabic origin. Period IV, beginning with the appearance of the Portuguese late in the fifteenth century, saw the peak of material welfare: there was greater skill in the quarrying of stone and in its construction; superior black burnished pottery was made; and the Portuguese connection brought imports of Indian and Indonesian glass beads, as well as Chinese pottery, including Ming porcelain.

Meanwhile the Portuguese in finding their way to India had perforce explored the coast of West Africa. Between 1433, when Henry the Navigator began to open up the coast of West Africa and 1488, when Dias first rounded the Cape, successive expeditions had identified the main gold-bearing rivers. The castles they built on the Gold Coast were forerunners of the many defended posts established by the north European nations who followed them in the quest for gold and in due course for slaves. The slave trade brought untold misery to its immediate victims, but the long-term evils that flowed from it have mainly affected the host countries of the Western world. Our concern here is rather with the impact of European trade and exploration on the indigenous cultures of Africa. In the long run, and more particularly since the interior of the sub-Saharan regions has been opened up by modern transport and communications, the effect has been to draw the country within range of modern science and technology, to bring its economy within the world market and finally to

Some key radiocarbon dates for North Africa

			B.C.
First Dynasty	Sakkara, tomb of vizier Hemaka	C 267 av.	2933±200
Middle Dynastic	El Omari, Egypt	C 643	3306±230
Early Dynastic	Naqada, Egypt (SD 36–46)	C 811	3669±280
	(SD 34–8)	C 810	3794±300
Neolithic	Adrar Bous III, Niger	SA 100	3190±300
	Shaheinab, Sudan	C 753	3110±450
		C 754	3396±380
	Dar-es-Soltan, Morocco	GrN 2805	4250± 82
	Haua Fteah, Cyrenaica:		
	(level VI, upper)	NPL 41	2910± 97
	(level VI, lower)	NPL 40	3850±108
	(level VIII, upper)	NPL 42	4420±103
	Merimde, Egypt	U 6	4180±110
	Fayum, Egypt	C 457	4145±250
		C 550	4441±180
Capsian	El Mekta, Algeria	L 134	6450+400
	Haua Fteah, Cyrenaica:		
	(level X, surface)	GrN 3541	5050+110
	(level X, middle)	GrN 3167	6450+150
Oranian	Haua Fteah, Cyrenaica:		
	(level XIV–XV)	NPL 43	1,800+173
	Taforalit, Morocco	L 399E	10,120+400
			9950±240

stimulate the growth of modern political institutions. Fortunately for the integrity of African culture and society, European influence was for some centuries mainly confined to the coast. If the equatorial forests kept many Africans prehistoric down to recent times at least it kept them African. The peoples south of the Sahara were able to conserve their heritage of music, sculpture and socio-political styles to a substantial degree intact. The sculptures that nourished the modern school of Paris were specifically African. The bronze plaques of Benin depict in some instances Portuguese soldiers, but the art-form they embody was already ancient. Like the bronze and terracotta heads of Ife they continued a tradition already manifest in the terracottas of Nok (Pl. X).

CHAPTER 9

INDIA

The Indian sub-continent shared fully in the cultural pattern prevailing during Middle Pleistocene times. The Soan industries of the Punjab compare in their dependence on pebble tools and their associated flakes with those known from south-east Asia to North China; and the hand-axe and cleaver industries of the peninsula form so to speak an eastern outlier of a great province extending across south-west Asia, Africa and southern Europe. The situation during the Upper Pleistocene was very different. It is true that the Indian Middle Stone Age industries share in the trend towards a greater reliance on flakes, but from the point of view of technique they compare very unfavourably with those of the Levalloiso-Mousterian cycle found over much of the northern part of the Palaeolithic world. The comparison is even more unfavourable for the later stages of the Upper Pleistocene: nothing really comparable with the Advanced Palaeolithic cultures of the territory between the Atlantic and the Iranian plateau, cultures which formed the very seed-bed of Old World civilization, has yet been found in India.

Food-production must have spread to the sub-continent as it did to Europe, but the circumstances were very different. Whereas over much of Europe the new way of life was introduced by societies who made their pottery by hand and whose technology rested above all on the polished stone axe, societies which appeared as early as the beginning of the sixth millennium B.C. in the Aegean area, in the case of India it was first brought in some three thousand years later by people using the potter's wheel and well acquainted with copper metallurgy. In stadial terminology settled life began in India in a 'Chalcolithic' context and such 'Neolithic' societies as made their appearance were chronologically retarded and geographically marginal: like the 'Neolithic' societies of much of Iberia they were symbols of peripheral poverty rather than of an advancing vanguard.

Microlithic industries

Among the problems of Indian prehistory is the status of the microlithic industries found over so many parts of the subcontinent. Lithic assemblages comprising lunate microliths with a few triangular and trapezoid variants, scrapers and burins, together with an occasional stone macehead with hour-glass perforation, are known from east Rajputana to the Gujarat and Bombay; from the central plateau, including the Vindhya hills but extending east to west Bengal; from the Tinnevelly region close to the extreme tip of the peninsula; and in Ceylon. The notion that these developed directly and without external influence from indigenous flake industries remains a speculation. Equally hypothetical is the notion of an early and as yet quite undocumented spread from the Iranian plateau or its eastern flanks. There remains the possibility that they may have been developed from indigenous sources under the impact of the chalcolithic intruders. Although we have no evidence that they made microliths, the painted pottery communities of the Quetta region certainly struck the kind of small blade from which such could easily have been made: and it is no less certain that microliths of lunate and trapezoid form were a product of the highly stylized blade industry developed by the Harappans and inherited by the chalcolithic villagers of the Malwa and the Deccan. It will be easier to reach some conclusion when we know more of the chronology of microlithic industries found in isolation from pottery or other signs of settled life. The discovery of a microlithic industry in the deposit immediately underlying the Harappan settlement of Rangpūr near the head of the Gulf of Cambay is suggestive so far as it goes, but is quite insufficient to tell us whether the Gujarat was occupied by microlith makers before the first arrival of chalcolithic farmers. As to the other end of the scale, nothing is more likely than that isolated pockets of hunter-fishers continued to fabricate microliths down to a comparatively late period. Reports of microliths made of recent bottle-glass on the other hand, when checked, have been found to refer to irregular lumps or flakes of no great relevance.

Chalcolithic farmers in Baluchistan and Sind

It is beyond debate that a way of life based on stock-raising and cereal-growing reached India from the north-west. The most important source was undoubtedly Iran. Turkmenia cannot be entirely excluded, especially in the light of the high radiocarbon date (c. 5000 B.C.) for the hand-made pottery, charred cereals and sickle-blades from the upper level of the Ghar-i-Mar Cave near Aq Kupruk on the northern margin of the Hindu Kush. On the other hand there is no evidence for really early farming communities in North-west Pakistan, even if the name site of the Harappan civilization is situated suggestively far north. The concentration of early sites is found in the region of Quetta on the natural route from the Balan Pass. To judge from the radiocarbon date for the original settlement at Kile Ghul Mahammad impulses were reaching northern Baluchistan from Iran by way of Seistan and the valley of the Helmand River as early as the middle of the fourth millennium B.C. Excavation of the covering mound has shown that the first permanent settlers were already making copper tools and turning their pots on the wheel before applying painted decoration. By the middle of the third millennium this type of culture was being practised over an extensive area of western Pakistan. The designs used by potters of communities sharing the same general level of culture displayed regional and temporal variation just as woven rugs have done in the same area down to the present day. Thus, the Zhob potters of northern Baluchistan and the makers of Togau ware that extended down into the southern part of the country applied friezes of humped oxen with stylized elongated legs in a manner that compares tellingly with that seen on painted vessels from the mounds of Hissar and Sialk a thousand miles or so to the west on the inner flanks of the Elburz and Zagros Mountains of Iran. Oxen were conspicuously absent from the repertoire of the Nal and Amri potters, who shared a common culture but occupied differing habitats, the former keeping to the higher ground, the latter to the foothills and the lower Indus plain, and whose wares can be distinguished through the use of polychrome paints by the Nal potters, as well as by elements of design. Although animal forms occur on Nal pottery, the designs on both wares are predominantly geometric, reminding one of those employed in basketry, textiles and rugs. On the other hand, the makers of black-painted Kulli pottery, direct successors of the Nal potters, were fond of depicting bulls, though in this case tethered to trees in precisely the same style as those found on painted vessels from Susa and Early Dynastic Sumer. This stylistic borrowing is matched by the westward extension of Kulli ware, both to the high ground forming the hinterland of the Makran coast and even more strikingly to the island of Abu Dhabi off the Trucial coast on the south shore of the Persian Gulf. This suggests that the people who made this pottery may have played a key role in linking the great riverine civilizations of Mesopotamia and the Indus Valley.

The Harappan civilization

Although what we know of the Harappan civilization rests entirely on the basis of archaeology, it is already recognized as one of the great historic achievements of the human race. It has been so on account both of its scale and of its distinctive style and character. Even the great metropolitan centres of Mohenjo Daro on the west bank of the lower Indus and Harappā itself on the east bank of the Ravi, are nearly 644 kilometres apart; and modern research has greatly enlarged the extent of the civilization beyond Sind and the Punjab. Traces have been found as far west

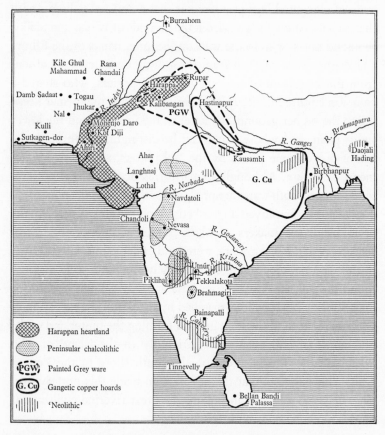

Harappan heartland

Peninsular chalcolithic

Painted Grey ware

Gangetic copper hoards

'Neolithic'

7. India in the second and third millennia B.C.

as Sutkagen-dor on the Makran coast and in the north-east nearly 1,609 kilometres away at Rupar close to the foot of the Simla hills. To the south, many sites have been traced in the states of Western India and in the Gujarat at the head of the Gulf of Cambay, 1,126 kilometres or so from Sutkagen-dor and Rupar.

The civilization extending over this vast territory possessed an unmistakable identity. There seems no reason to suppose that the urban, literate civilization of the Indus was derived from that which had earlier grown up in the Tigris–Euphrates basin. Al-

though it started later everything about it emphasizes its independent character. Considering that both had roots in the Iranian
plateau, the surprising thing is not so much the general similarity
as the differences which appear in every particular feature, whether
in the styles and forms of pottery, metal-work and seals, or in the
scripts or even in political style. When the civilizations of Sumer
and Harappā came into contact it was as independent entities
making easily recognizable products. It needed no particular
acumen to detect Harappan seals when these turned up on
Sumerian sites or conversely what are probably Harappan copies
of Sumerian cylinder seals at Mohenjo Daro. The implied contacts
gave the first clue as to dating, since the context of Harappan seals
in Sumer was Akkadian (c. 2300–2000 B.C.). Radiocarbon analysis
confirms 2300 B.C. for the opening of the Harappan civilization
and suggests that it lasted down to the seventeenth century B.C.
The evidence for contact opens up the question of how trade
relations were established and carried on. Present evidence
suggests that the initial probes came from each direction. We
have already seen that the makers of Kulli ware spread from south
Baluchistan into southern Iran and that their pottery turns up
in the south-east corner of the Persian Gulf. On the other hand,
inscribed tablets from the time of Sargon to that of the dynasty
of Larsa point to active maritime trade from Sumer to Dilmun
or Telmun, tentatively identified with Bahrain where suggestive
evidence has since been brought to light by Danish excavators.
Perhaps Bahrain—and other islands may also have been involved
—served as an entrepôt between the Tigris and Euphrates and the
Harappan ports of the Makran, or even of the Bay of Cambay.

The use of stamp seals and red-on-black painted pottery and
the fact that so many of the materials worked by the urban
craftsmen, such as gold, silver, tin, alabaster, turquoise and lapis
lazuli, came from Baluchistan, Afghanistan or Iran itself, are all
pointers to the ultimate source of the Harappan civilization.
Excavations at Amri have shown, it is true, that Harappan modes

intruded on a culture, which as we have seen had a wide distribution in south Baluchistan, and can hardly therefore have developed directly from it. On the other hand, the pre-Harappan levels at Kot Diji, dating back to the first half of the third millennium B.C., have yielded pottery and fortifications which seem to anticipate those of the more mature civilization. No doubt excavation will in the future throw an even sharper light on the transition from village to urban life in the Indus basin, but no analysis of forms or types can dim the courage and enterprise of those who took the decisive steps of embarking on city life in a territory much of which was menaced by floods. Even more surprising in some respects is the way in which a homogeneous civilization was kept running so smoothly for a period of centuries over a territory greater in extent than that presided over by the pharaohs of Egypt or the kings of Ur.

The salient points of the Harappan civilization have often been described, especially as these relate to the main centres. Although an overall homogeneity prevailed it must be understood that there were marked variations in wealth as between the great metropolitan centres, and the much more numerous ones of more modest size which bulk so much less in most of the accounts. The major centres were dominated by substantial citadels, the one at Harappā being about 273 × 546 metres across. These were enclosed by walls with breast-high parapets, fortified at intervals by brick towers. For cities to be dominated by centres of power was common form, whether in the ancient world or for that matter in medieval Europe, but instead of enclosing palaces or temples, the Harappan citadels contained what appear to be collegiate buildings associated with bathing tanks. Whether the governing authority was in fact monastic, it was certainly effective. The very streets of Mohenjo Daro, about a mile square, were laid out on a grid-system, though one that was slightly irregular. Although the streets were unpaved an effective system of drains and brick-lined wells was provided. The city seems to have been divided into quarters. The better-off citizens lived in courtyard houses built of fired bricks and fitted with bathrooms. The artisans on the other hand occupied rows of mud-brick cottages clustered round metal-workers' furnaces and flour-grinding floors, reflecting the subdivision of labour prevailing in a society already far removed from subsistence agriculture. Huge granaries built of timber frames on massive brick podiums to withstand flood-waters testify alike to central planning and a subservient countryside. Little is known of religious practices or beliefs, but at an intellectual level the civilization was held together by a pictographic script, unhappily not yet deciphered and occurring only in the briefest of inscriptions, and by a common system of weights and measures that assisted the spread of homogeneous planning and encouraged exchange and trade. Precious raw materials were obtained from every quarter: as already noted many came from the Iranian plateau and its eastern bastions; rich supplies of copper were available east of the Indus in Rajputna; sought-after timber was probably floated down from Kashmir and the Himalaya; and amethysts were probably obtained from the Deccan. How these goods were paid for is uncertain, but fragments of a cotton textile adhering to a silver vase from Mohenjo Daro suggest that cloth may have been an important source of income and the Harappans were also skilful carvers in elephant ivory, a raw material greatly sought after in antiquity.

The question arises how so extensive and apparently well-ordered a civilization came to an end. The suggestion that the Harappans were toppled by Aryan-speaking invaders no longer seems so attractive as when it was first advanced. If radiocarbon dates are as correct for the end as they seem to be for the beginning of the civilization, then this must have come some centuries before most scholars would be inclined to place the Aryan intrusion; and in this context it is worth remarking that evidence for the famous massacre came from the deep south at Mohenjo Daro rather than from the northern metropolis. Was there not rather some ecological explanation? The suggestion of a marked worsening of climate seems not to be borne out by the evidence, but the possibility has recently been pressed that flooding may have been responsible for tilting the balance between the city-dwellers and their environment at least in the lower Indus basin. This is in many ways an attractive hypothesis. It would explain why a progressive decline was noted at Mohenjo Daro some time before its abandonment, whereas no signs of this were observed at Harappā far beyond the direct effect of flooding. It is undeniable that the earliest occupation at Mohenjo Daro is buried some 12 metres below the existing flood-plain and that the massive platforms of the granaries as well as other architectural features point to the ever-present menace of flooding. Perhaps further boring and geological study will one day provide a convincing mechanism for flooding sufficient to overwhelm the heart of the culture. Meanwhile it is worth recalling that the effects of deforestation resulting from the firing of so many bricks have been considered a contributory factor in upsetting the always delicate balance between man and nature in the Indus Valley.

Post-Harappan chalcolithic cultures in the Indus and Ganges basins

Precisely when Aryan-speakers first entered the sub-continent is still open to discussion, though it may be relevant that documentary sources, notably the archives of clay tablets at the Hittite capital of Boghazköy, point to the arrival of Aryan-speakers in Asia Minor during the fifteenth and fourteenth centuries B.C. In so far as we can picture them from the epic-chants, hymns, prayers and spells that make up the Rigveda, the Aryans were copper or bronze-using barbarians, who gained their living from stock-raising and cereal farming, occupied timber and thatch houses and used horse-drawn chariots for sport and war. Although providing useful clues this generalized tradition hardly allows us to identify Aryan-speakers with any particular assemblage of archaeological material. Even so it is suggestive that archaeological finds dating from post-Harappan times in north-west India display intrusive features that point to Iranian sources.

One may first mention Jhukar ware whose users camped among the ruins of Chanhu Daro rather as the Anglo-Saxons did in the deserted cities of Roman Britain. The painted designs on the pottery incorporated traditions derived ultimately from Kulli, Amri and Harappan sources, but the associated metal-work, notably pins with rolled-over heads and the shafthole axe, showed exotic traits and pointed much further west, as did certain of their beads and seals.

Next one may point to the earliest trace of settled life yet recognized from the Ganges basin namely the culture of the earliest inhabitants of Hastinapur, a mound some 93 kilometres north-east of Delhi. Although sherds of their ochre-coloured pottery have been noted at other sites in the region, the vessels are still too fragmentary for valid comparisons further afield. What is quite certain is that the first inhabitants and their immediate successors used copper tools but were ignorant of iron. Indeed, it may well prove that they founded the school of metallurgy whose products in the form of hoards of copper tools and weapons are well known from Bihar and Bengal as well as from the Upper Ganges basin. Most of the objects were cast in primitive flat moulds and in this respect compare with Harappan metal-work. On the other hand many of the forms, including types of barbed harpoon-head, were local in character.

With a third group of material we are on firmer ground, namely that from the second occupation of Hastinapur. Here the pottery, Grey ware of high technical quality and sparingly decorated in black paint with parallel stripes and circles, betrays undoubted Iranian inspiration. The fact that Painted Grey is found distributed widely between the basins of the Sutlej and the Upper Ganges and Jumna at the very heart of early historic India is only one more and by no means the last confirmation of the vital part played by Iran in the development of Indian culture.

Chalcolithic communities in Malwa and the Deccan

The demise of the Harappan civilization was followed in the northern parts of peninsular India, as well as in the Indus and Ganges basins, by the appearance of copper-using societies based on agriculture and stock-raising, societies that may or may not have been Aryan-speaking. In many respects the communities established in Malwa between the mid-sixteenth and the mid-fourteenth centuries B.C., notably at Navda Toli and Maheshwa, and in the northern Deccan at Chandoli and Nevasa in the fourteenth and thirteenth centuries B.C., were economically poorer than the Harappans. Yet though they occupied villages rather than cities and no longer wrote inscriptions or even made seals, they still used copper artifacts in some abundance as far south as Chandoli at the head of the Krishna basin and continued to make their pots on the wheel and decorate many of them in black paint on a red ground. They also carried on the highly stylized production of stone blades from long cores prepared by lateral flaking, blades in many cases used as knives, saws or reaping-knife blades, but occasionally also for conversion into lunate or trapeze-shaped microliths for setting in composite tools or weapons. Certain traits like the steatite and faience beads found at Navdatoli no longer occur south of the Narmada basin. Conversely, at Nevasa and other sites in or south of the Godavari basin we encounter for the first time polished stone axes.

Polished stone axe cultures

Three main groups of peasant communities marked by polished stone axes and hand-made pottery have so far been recognized in India. One, comparatively little known, is that in Kashmir, the most notable site of which so far investigated is Burzahom near Srinagar. The lowermost level at this site, dated by radiocarbon to early in the second millennium B.C., has yielded polished stone axes, bone harpoon-heads and other forms and hand-shaped steel-grey ware, including flasks with flaring neck, the affinities of which have still to be defined.

A second group, centred on Assam, Bengal, Bihar and Orissa, but extending down the east coast of India, is mainly represented by stray finds of polished stone axes and adzes. The latter include shouldered four-sided forms of a kind well-known in south-east Asia and South China. Adzes of this kind have recently been excavated at Daojali Hading in Assam in company with grey pottery marked on the outside by impressions of paddles wrapped in cord or textiles, another cultural trait common to south-east Asia and China. Although the culture was apparently established in Thailand during the first half of the second millennium B.C., it seems likely that its influence did not penetrate north-east India until several centuries later.

The third centre of polished stone axe industries occupies the basins of the Krishna and Cauvery Rivers in south India. The people who made the axes depended to an important extent on herds of cattle and the ash-mounds which are their most prominent memorial apparently arose directly from this. As careful investigations at Utnūr have shown, they cover the post-holes of timber enclosures that were evidently intended to protect the cattle at night from wild predators, and analysis of the ash itself shows that it represents burnt cattle-dung. The most likely explanation is that from time to time dung accumulated in the enclosures got ignited by the fires maintained to give added protection against wild animals. Radiocarbon analysis suggests that the ash-mounds began to form at the beginning of the second millennium B.C., that is some five hundred years before the establishment of chalcolithic societies in Malwa and the northern Deccan. On the other hand the presence of a few objects made of copper at key sites like Bramagiri and Piklihal reminds us that there must have been a substantial degree of contemporaneity between the two groups. Even more to the point is the fact that the 'Neolithic' communities of southern India practised the sophisticated technique of striking blades from long cores prepared by lateral flaking apparently first developed in India by the urban-dwelling Indus valley people and, as we have seen, also carried on by the chalcolithic peoples of peninsular India.

Spread of iron-working

It is common ground that the working of iron must have been introduced to northern India from the west before spreading south into the peninsula. The latest date for the introduction of iron-technology into India must surely be 516 B.C., when Darius conquered the northern part of the province and converted it into the twentieth satrapy of his Persian Empire. Some prehistorians have interpreted certain passages in the Rigvedic literature as if these referred to iron-working and go on to argue on the basis of a few iron artifacts from deposits containing the distinctive Painted Grey ware of northern India that the new technology had been introduced as early as c. 800 B.C. All this is open to doubt. The Painted Grey ware culture was, as we have seen, basically chalcolithic. At Hastinapur and other sites it consistently gave way to northern Black Polished ware, the pottery which occurs as far south as Godavari with the first appearance of iron-working. Beyond the Godavari iron-working spread into a zone where polished stone axes continued in use down to the third century B.C. The introduction of iron-working was accompanied by the adoption of Black-topped ware and the practice of burying the skeletons of the dead after removal of the flesh either in urns, clay sarcophagi or megalithic cists built of large stone slabs and sometimes provided with a hole for inserting more bones.

The Mauryan Empire

The creation of a satrapy by Darius had much less effect on India as a whole than the overthrow of the Achaemenid Empire by Alexander the Great and his triumphal entry into India by the Kabul River and the Khyber Pass. The first effect was political.

Some key radiocarbon dates for India

			B.C.
Pre-Harappan			
Damb Sadaat I, Baluchistan	Amri ware	L 180B	2400±350
Kot Diji, Sind	Layer 14	P 196	2471±141
Kile Ghul Mahammad, Baluchistan	Preceramic	L 180A	3500±500
Harappan			
Mohenjo Daro, Sind	Final Harappan	TF 75	1650±110
Lothal, Gujarat	Layer 10	TF 136	1965±130
Ahar, Rajasthan	Range at 11·3 m.	(V 56)	1765± 95
		(V 57)	2025± 95
Kalibangan, Rajasthan	Range	TF 150	1790±100
		TF 139, 145, 147, 151, 163	
		TF 160	2110±100
Kot Diji, Sind	Layer 4*a*	P 195	1975±134
	Layer 5	P 179	2211±151
Peninsular chalcolithic			
Nevasa, Bombay	Topmost chalcolithic	P 181	1250±122
Navdatoli, Madhya Pradesh	Trench 1,		
	Layer 2	P 205	1344±125
	Layer 3	P 204	1499±127
	Layer 6	P 202	1553±128
'Neolithic'			
Bainapalli, Madras	At 1·8 m.	TF 349	1390±100
Tekkalakota, Mysore	Range	{ TF 239	1445±105
		{ TF 266	1675±100
Burzahom, Kashmir	At 2·9 m.	{ TF 129	1720± 90
		{ TF 128	2255±115
Utnūr, Andhra Pradesh	Phase IIA	TF 167	1940±110
	Phase IB	BM 54	2170±150

Alexander encountered a multiplicity of warring kingdoms and he was able to prevail by playing off one petty ruler against another. Yet, if he succeeded in his aim of conquering the Indus basin, it was his intervention that stimulated centralizing forces in north India. His death at Babylon in 323 B.C. gave the signal for something like a national rising and led to the establishment by Chandragupta Maurya of a dynasty that marks the effective beginning of Indian history. The fall of the Persian Empire also made its effect felt in the cultural field. When Chandragupta set about building and embellishing his capital city at Pātalipura he was able to attract refugee craftsmen and so obtain a valuable accession of technical ability and artistic skill.

As we know from the report of a resident Greek, Megasthenes, the Mauryan king created an elaborate bureaucracy to administer his realm. His other main achievement was to link together the Gangetic and Indus plains whose cultural and political history had hitherto run on separate lines. This in turn provided the solid base needed by his grandson Asoka for extending the Mauryan Empire as far south as Mysore. One of the main forces impelling Asoka was his missionary zeal for the teachings of Buddha (c. 560–480 B.C.), to which he was himself a convert. Indeed, it was his habit of inscribing propaganda for his new-found faith on rock-surfaces, a habit in itself deriving from Persian example, that more clearly than anything else defines the extent of his Empire. Yet in the event Buddhism as we know failed to endure in the land of its birth, only to survive in Ceylon and the wider world to which it spread. It needed fresh invasions and conquests in the north by Arabs, Afghans, Pathans and others of Moslem faith to detach any substantial part of the Indian population from Hinduism, a religion stemming in large measure from the Aryan-speaking conquerors, but which apparently had its roots as far back as the Harappan civilization of the Indus basin.

CHAPTER 10

CHINA AND THE FAR EAST

CHINA

Chinese civilization originated and took the form destined to endure in essentials down to modern times in the basin of the Hwang-ho or Yellow River. There are two main reasons for this. First and foremost the basin lies athwart what has always been, until the rise of modern sea-power, the main entrance into one of the largest fertile land-masses of the world, the great roundel of territory between the mountain zone of Inner Asia and the Pacific Ocean. Although the mountains and the ocean provided barriers behind which cultural traditions were able to establish a continuity of development analogous in duration to that of ancient Egypt, Chinese civilization first developed and has ever since been quickened by impulses from outside.

The Chinese people themselves were of course firmly rooted in their homeland long before external impulses began to transform their way of life. Preliminary examination of skulls from the Upper Cave at Choukoutien and from Tzŭ-yang in Szechwan shows that the Chinese physical type had already emerged at least as far back as the Late Pleistocene. Again, there can hardly be any doubt that as Neothermal conditions became established the river valleys and coastal regions of China in particular were inhabited, even if sparsely, by peoples of Chinese stock who supported themselves by varying combinations of hunting, fishing and gathering. If comparatively little is yet known about these people, this is partly due to their reliance on flaked pebble tools too crude to attract casual attention, but which have now in fact been identified as far apart as North China, Szechwan and Kwangsi (the modern North Vietnam). In the latter region excavations in the limestone caves of Kweilin and Wu-ming have disclosed such pebble tools alongside ones of antler and bone and stone mace-heads having hour-glass perforations.

There can be no question therefore of the Chinese people invading China and bringing with them cultivated plants and the Neolithic arts. It was much more a case of new concepts and techniques being absorbed by an indigenous population, which rapidly expanded to the limits of the new technology. This brings us to the second reason why the Hwang-ho played such a vital role, namely the fertility and ease of working of the loess soil brought down in the form of alluvium and spread over much of the North China Plain from its source on the high ground of Shansi, Shensi and Kansu.

The new ideas by means of which this territory was enabled to support a growing and relatively settled population presumably reached it from central and ultimately from south-west Asia by the route skirting south of the Gobi and traversing Sinkiang by way of the Tarim basin and Kashgar, a route followed early in the Christian era by the silk trade between the Han and the Roman empires. By far the most important of these were ideas relating to the domestication of animals and plants, their maintenance and cultivation. No doubt other elements of the Yang-shao culture, the first to be based on farming in this region and one that takes its name from a prehistoric settlement at Yang-shao-ts'un in Honan, derive from the same source, including for instance the idea of painting pottery. Yet it is important to make it clear that many elements in the material culture of the earliest peasant cultures of North China stem from hunter-fisher sources indigenous to a large tract of east Asia. As we know from the Jomon culture of Japan (p. 241) cord-marked pottery was in use in that country for thousands of years before the introduction of agriculture; and in Manchuria and the Baikal region of Siberia it was made by hunter-fishers whose equipment included other elements common to the early peasant cultures of China, notably polished stone rings, knives and projectile-points.

Yang-shao peasants

The earliest peasant societies to emerge in China cultivated the loess soils of low-lying areas either side of the middle course of the Hwang-ho in the province of Honan and Shansi. Next to be taken into cultivation were the lands extending south to the upper reaches of the River Huai and north to the frontier between Shansi and Hopei. Expansion to the higher ground of Honan and Kansu to the west came later and may even have been due to pressures exerted by the appearance of a new culture in the northeast, known from its name site in Shantung as Lung-shan. What is abundantly clear is that in some regions the Yang-shao culture persisted during the life of the Lung-shan and even ran parallel to the Shang Bronze Age in outlying regions.

Since they occupied loess soils it can be taken for granted that the Yang-shao peasants must have had to cope with deciduous forest and this is substantiated by the fact that swine formed the backbone of their livestock and that their houses were built round substantial timber uprights. Their leading crop was millet, though rice was introduced from the south before the end of the period. To begin with cultivation was probably carried on in temporary clearings by the slash and burn method, but since the loess was capable of retaining its fertility under prolonged cultivation permanent settlement is likely to have begun early. The lack of oxen argues against the use of the plough and it may be assumed that hoes were the main implement of tillage. Fairly heavy polished stone axe-blades were probably used for felling trees and lighter adze-blades served for dressing the timbers needed for building. In addition to and in connection with mixed farming wild animals were hunted by bow and spear and fish were caught by means of barbed bone hooks.

Like the Danubians who cultivated the loess of central Europe between one and two thousand years earlier, the Yang-shao peasants had a sufficiently certain food supply to make it possible

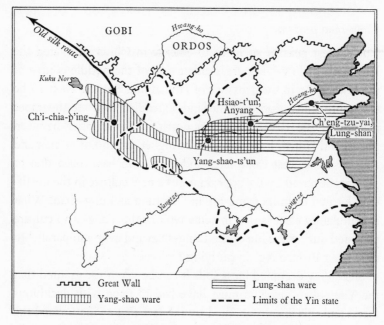

8. China: the prehistoric core of the earliest state

to live together in quite large village communities, like those explored at Pan P'o Ts'un in Shensi and Miao-ti-Kou in west Honan. Their houses, which might be rectangular or, less commonly, round in plan, had floors sunk into the subsoil, no doubt to keep out the cold; high-pitched roofs were supported on stout timbers; and walls were of wood and mud. Numerous storage pits bear witness to the key role of an assured food supply. Settlements were defined by curvilinear ditches and it is of interest that cemeteries were situated outside these. Again, potting, whether or not it was already a specialized craft, was apparently carried on outside the settlements. Pots were made by hand, often by the coil process finished off by beating the surface, but the rims were sometimes trued by using a turning board or basket. The commonest forms were open bowls or dishes, jars, including some of globular profile, and vases with sharply pointed base.

Most pots were of a coarse, mostly reddish ware with roughened surface. On the other hand a certain number of pots, whether for use or for burying with the dead, were painted with geometric designs, including spirals, and symbolic animal or anthropomorphic figures, before being burnished. Impressions on some of the coarser pots point to the plaiting of mats and to weaving and for the latter there is the added testimony of spindle-whorls.

Lung-shan and the southward spread of farming

A second and in some respects more advanced peasant culture developed in the eastern zone of the Hwang-ho basin. There are two main reasons for thinking that the culture termed Lung-shan after the name site in Shantung stemmed from the same tradition as that of Yang-shao. For one thing, despite the fact that the later culture was centred on Shantung and Hopei, a clear continuity can be observed at sites like Miao-ti-kou situated within the area of overlap. Again, there is a substantial degree of homogeneity between the two cultures: both depended on the cultivation of loess soils, though in the case of the Yang-shao these were primary and in that of the Lung-shan redeposited; both again employed polished stone arrowheads, knives and rings; and the coarse ware with paddle-impressed cord markings that predominates in each, although differing in form, shows a basic similarity of treatment. It is above all the finer pottery that makes it possible to distinguish the two groups. Lung-shan ware is notable in having a black fabric and being wheel-turned, thin-walled and burnished to a lustrous surface. Again, the Lung-shan potters devised a number of novel forms including three main kinds of cooking vessel—the *li* tripod with hollow feet for maximum exposure to the fire, the solid-footed *ting* and the composite *hsien* comprising a steamer resting on a *li* tripod—and various forms of cup or tumbler. In the final phase of the culture, sometimes accorded separate status as the Hsiao-t'un culture, the Lung-shan potters ceased to make Black ware and concentrated on Grey Paddle-beaten ware, a ware which it is interesting to recall was assigned to the earliest phase of Chinese peasant culture when it first came to light at such a site as Ch'i-chia-p'ing in Kansu.

This second stage of peasant settlement in China witnessed in the first place a more intensive utilization of the deciduous zone in the Hwang-ho basin, marked by increased clearance and reflected in the addition of cattle, sheep and even occasionally horses to the domestic livestock. The increasing wealth of settled communities based on this more intensive utilization of land was reflected in the need for improved defences, now met by earth-stamped walls and by the increased tension revealed by the practice of scapulomancy or divination from animal bones: both developments that were to be further developed during the ensuing Shang period. No less important for the future of Chinese civilization was the expansion which took place during this stage from the deciduous into the evergreen zone. Most of the peasants involved in this expansion subscribed to the Lung-shan culture and particularly to its final Hsiao-t'un manifestation. Farming was introduced first into the lower and middle Yangtze basin, whence it spread into Szechwan and south into the coastal provinces from Chekiang to Kuangsi and beyond into south-east Asia. In the coastal zone settlement was concentrated on the lower courses of rivers and on adjacent islands.

The importance of wood-working for house- and doubtless for boat-building is testified by the abundance and technical development of polished stone adze-blades, which were now frequently rectangular in section. Two methods were devised for facilitating hafting. In the Lower Yangtze and Huai basins and on the middle coastal zone the butts were reduced in thickness to produce stepped adzes, but on the South China coast the butt was reduced in width, leading to the shouldered form that was to attain so wide a distribution in south-east Asia. Crescentic stone reaping-knives and large polished stone hoe-blades confirm the continuing importance of agriculture, but huge shell-mounds like that excavated near T'an Shih Shan, some 500 metres long, 10 metres wide and 10 metres thick, show that sea-food contributed in a powerful way to diet. The commonest pottery was grey in colour and shaped and decorated by the use of paddles or beaters wrapped in cord or matting. Some of the finer wares of the maritime provinces had a distinct character, having been turned on the wheel and fired at temperatures of up to 1000°C., after being decorated by stamped designs that might include angular spiral forms.

The expansion of farming technology into South China and beyond into Vietnam, Malaya and Thailand was of vital importance in that it brought rice into the sphere of food-production, a food plant that in its wild form was at home in south-east Asia. The precise circumstances under which it was first domesticated remain to be worked out. For present purposes the significant fact is that its cultivation was already established during this phase in the Yangtze basin, as we know from impressions on the clay floors of houses of the Ch'u-chia-ling group in Hupei, a local offshoot of the Yang-shao tradition.

Decisive though the southward expansion of farming and the northward movement of rice-cultivation was to prove for the future, the creative centre of China remained on the Huangho for more than another thousand years. 'Neolithic' peasants continued their placid lives over much of western and southern China, as over Manchuria and Korea, and 'Mesolithic' hunters pursued their quarry over the sandy wastes of Mongolia, while the ancient heartland of China quickened to the glories of Shang achievement.

The Shang (Yin) Dynasts

When the city of Hsiao-t'un near the modern Anyang was first revealed by excavation the contrast it seemed to point with the peasant communities previously known was so great as to throw into some doubt the continuity of culture on the Hwang-ho. Here, after all, was a veritable city laid out in zones, with palace and artisan quarters and rectangular wooden houses set on terraces of beaten earth and with gabled roofs supported on rows of pillars resting on stone or even bronze bases. From this city the kings of the Yin or later Shang Dynasty ruled a stable and to some degree literate state, in which the art of the bronze worker had reached a high pitch of perfection and in which leaders rode to war and chase in chariots mounted on spoked wheels and drawn by pairs of yoked horses, vehicles recalling and surely in some distant way linked with those of Mitannian and Mycenaean princes far away to the west.

Clearly the citizens of the Shang state were living in a different world from that of the village communities that marked the apex of social life in past ages. The discrepancy has been mitigated to some degree by the excavations at Cheng Chou and Lo Ta Miao which show that in reality the city of Hsiao-t'un belongs, as the following table shows, to the latter part of the Shang Bronze Age.

Approximate dates B.C.	*Phases*	*Sites*
1150–1027	Shang V	Hsiao t'un (late)
1300–1150	Shang IV	Hsiao t'un (early)
1500–1300	Shang III / Shang II	Cheng Chou
	Shang I	Lo Ta Miao

There is wide agreement that the Shang culture developed from Hsiao-t'un or final Lung-Shan antecedents: not merely do Shang settlements frequently overlie directly layers with Hsiao-t'un Grey wares, but they share with them many significant elements of culture, notably in relation to pottery, defence and divination. On the other hand it is equally sure that certain aspects of Shang culture reflect the impact of ideas from the west coming in part by the same route as those that underlay the genesis of the Yang-shao culture. The sophistication of the Shang bronzes, no less than the absence of 'primitive' metal forms, point to the arrival of ideas from territories where bronze metallurgy had a long previous history. Again, despite the specifically Chinese character of much of the ornament and some of the forms of Shang bronzes, certain leading types, including knives with in-curving edge and certain forms of dagger, socketed axe and spear-head, are widely distributed over the steppe and forest zones from Baikal to the heart of European Russia. Detailed analogies be-tween Chinese pieces and finds from places as far apart as Seima on the Upper Oka, Turbino and Gorbunovo on either side of the mid-Urals and Minusinsk and Karasuk on the Upper Yenisei argue for lively contacts during the period between the fifteenth and the eleventh centuries B.C. over a zone covering some 100° of latitude. Indeed, remote links can be detected as far afield as the Black Sea coast of Bessarabia and far to the north with the hunter-fishers of Finland and middle Sweden. Having said so much it remains to emphasize on the one hand that the direction of influences is seldom known for certain and on the other that in any case most of the finest Shang productions are so emphatically Chinese in style as to be instantly recognizable as such. Thus, the stylized tigers and other beasts common to wide territories in Eurasia turned in the hands of the Shang into the conventional dragons that were to populate Chinese art for another three thousand years.

The increased wealth and individuality of the Shang culture should be viewed in the final analysis as products of a more intensive exploitation of the loesslands of the Hwang-ho. It was above all the growth of population, outcome of a thousand years of settled life based on mixed farming, that made possible the growth of cities, the subdivision of labour and the emergence of the new more highly integrated social structures needed to ensure the workings of a more complex economy and the safety of rich and concentrated communities.

Consumption of the fine things made in these workshops, such as bronzes, objects carved from jades and jars made of white kaolin or of earthenware with a thin greenish-yellow felspathic glaze, was concentrated in a small sector of society, the ruler, his retainers and warriors. The most conspicuous display of riches is that found in royal tombs that have escaped robbers. Such a one has been explored at Hsi Pei Keng a little north-west of the Shang city of Hsiao-t'un. Conspicuous in such burials are the bronze armament, notably halberds and spears, the bows and the chariots by which the lower orders were kept in their place; amulets and the ornaments carved from jade, products which in themselves display the investment of prolonged and skilled labour in a precious and notoriously hard material; and the splendidly ornamented bronze ritual vessels dedicated to ancestral rites. Even more striking in what they have to tell of the status of departed rulers is the evidence for the sacrifice of retainers on a scale reminiscent of the royal tombs of Ur. For instance the main chamber of the tomb at Wu Kuan Ts'un yielded remains of 24 human victims and 11 dogs; additional men, horses and dogs were slaughtered and buried in the ramps, the men in the attitude of guards; yet more crammed into the stamped earthen fill, including 34 human skulls arranged in rows; and for full measure headless bodies were dumped in groups of 10 in pits south of the main tomb.

Literacy, for which there is evidence from inscriptions on ritual vessels and much more abundantly on the bones and tortoise-shells used in divination, was also confined to quite a narrow section of society. The language used in the inscriptions was unquestionably Chinese, though due to reforms in the intervening period it is now only possible to read some 1500 out of 5000 ideographs. The inscriptions on bronze vessels were mainly concerned with the sacrifices to ancestors offered by the upper classes of Shang society as well as by the royal house. The questions scratched on animal bones and increasingly on tortoise-shells were likewise occupied to an important degree with sacrifice, but the health and movements of the king were also matters for concern, as were the times and seasons of hunting or warlike expeditions, questions as to crops and rains and, not least, the warding-off of untoward events. Answers were sought by applying heat and seeking to interpret the cracks so formed, a task of divination that might be carried out by the king himself or alternatively by appointed augurs.

The Shang or Yin state was still small in relation to modern China, being centred on the primary territory of the Lung-shan culture; yet it now included the Yangtze basin and extended as far west as the eastern part of Kansu and the province of Hupei.

Chou dynasty (1027–222 B.C.)

The Chous who issued from the borderlands of Shensi to sack the capital city near An-yang in c. 1030 B.C. were relatively barbarous, but like so many of their successors they soon absorbed the civilization of their subjects. To such effect did they achieve this that it was under their rule that the Chinese acquired the basic pattern of manners, customs and even philosophy that they were to retain down to modern times. To mention only one example, it was as a subject of the feudal state of Lu in the province of Shantung that Confucius (551–479 B.C.) propounded the philosophy that was to determine for so many centuries the outlook of such large numbers of his compatriots.

The age was also one of technical progress. During the opening centuries of Chou rule bronze remained the only metal for tools as well as for weapons. The introduction of iron round about the middle of the first millennium as a material for implements affected profoundly the productivity of farming and therefore of the economy as a whole. A point to emphasize is that this was apparently a Chinese innovation. Whereas in the west iron-working was first carried on by forging, and casting was delayed until the fourteenth century A.D., in China iron-working was initiated with casting, and forging only began in the third century A.D. Another invention that may be especially mentioned because of its role in protecting Chinese civilization is that of the cross-bow operated by a trigger mechanism made of bronze that first appeared late in the fourth century B.C.

Ch'in (222–207 B.C.)

Politically the Chou conquerors had found it expedient to divide up the Shang dominions into a number of fiefs and in this way they initiated something very like a feudal system. The re-emergence of a unified state was brought about under the influence of outside pressures. During the seventh century many of the western provinces of the Chou realm had already been overrun; and in the fourth and third centuries B.C. stretches of what was later to become the Great Wall of China were built against the inroads of nomads from Inner Mongolia. Ironically the wall was completed, basically in the form in which it has come down to us, though modified and refaced early in the Ming period, during the shortlived dynasty established by the Ch'ins who themselves had emerged as comparative barbarians from Kansu and Shensi.

Han (207 B.C.– A.D. 220)

The completion of the Great Wall in effect symbolized the end of the feudal period in China. It was left to the Han emperors to comprehend within one polity the whole territory from Manchuria to Vietnam and inland as far as the Pamirs and in so doing to shift the centre of gravity from the Hwang-ho to the Yangtze basin, a task only made possible by the degree of cultural homogeneity prevailing since the expansion. Having exerted their authority over the natural confines of China the Han established relations with the Roman Empire and entered on the stage of world history. Chinese silks and lacquers, both long-established manufactures of the country, were exported as finished products to markets in the Near East and further west. Almost certainly maritime trade flowed through the Malacca Straits to the east coast of India, over the Coimbatore gap and across the Indian Ocean. Overland it followed the route by which between two and three thousand years previously the ideas basic to settled life had reached the Hwang-ho and initiated the process that led in due time to the appearance of the fully independent civilization of China.

SOUTH-EAST ASIA, INDONESIA AND THE PHILIPPINES

One of south-east Asia's greatest claims to interest is that, together with Formosa and the maritime provinces of South China and the Philippines, it formed the main reservoir from which cultural traditions spread not merely to Indonesia but over great tracts of the Pacific Ocean. Another is that it was the probable home of rice-cultivation, the food crop which today supports a sizeable proportion of the human race. Yet there is no sign that the people of this part of the world in fact domesticated rice on their own initiative. As we have seen, it looks much more as if this step was taken under the impact of influences flowing down from the maritime provinces of China, but stemming ultimately from the Lung-shan culture of the north-west.

Hoabinhian culture

The culture borne by the aboriginal population of south-east Asia and South China is known as Bacsonian or Hoabinhian after localities in Tonkin, North Vietnam. In the archaeological record its most important fossil is a chopper-like tool made by detaching flakes from a stone pebble, either from one or both faces. Stone industries featuring these, together with flakes, have been found in a zone extending from Szechwan and Kwangsi in the north (see p. 221) to Vietnam, Thailand, Malaya and Sumatra in the south; and similar forms are known from Borneo to Java. The general similarity which existed, despite local and temporal variations as regards form and technique, over south-east Asia and bordering zones can most easily be explained by supposing that all the industries in question stemmed from the chopper-tool tradition established in the area as long ago as the Middle Pleistocene, with the proviso that almost nothing is yet known of intermediate phases.

A good deal is known about the animals taken for food by the Hoabinhians because they frequently occupied caves, favourable for the survival of animal bones. At Gua Cha in Kelantan, for instance, extensive heaps of bones belonging to two varieties of wild pig were found in the Hoabinhian underlying Neolithic deposits. At other sites quantities of deer, oxen and water turtles were found. Substantial shell-mounds on the north-east coast of Sumatra and in inland rock-shelters on the mainland point to molluscs as having played a significant part, at least locally, in diet. Again, stone grinding slabs, no less than excessive wear on teeth, argue for the importance of plant foods. The Hoabinhian deposits at Gua Cha incorporated a number of contracted burials unaccompanied by grave-goods. The physical type to which the skeletons belong agrees with that of the Oceanic Negritos represented today by the Melanesians and Papuans.

It will hardly be possible to make more definite statements about the nature of the relationship between the Hoabinhian aborigines and intrusive Neolithic culture until more systematic excavations to the standard of Gua Cha have been carried out. Meanwhile the discovery in caves like Khé-Tong, Quang-Binh, Annam, and Pho-Binh-Gia, Tonkin, of edge-ground stone axes and hand-made pottery, apparently intermediate between Hoabinhian artifacts and quadrangular polished stone adzes, suggests that in former Indo-China there was a phase during which the aboriginal population was to some degree acculturated before a fully Neolithic peasant economy was established. Some degree of overlap and acculturation is in any case to be expected, though circumstances no doubt varied over an area as large as that of south-east Asia.

Microlithic industries

Contrasting with this heavy equipment are the mode 5 industries, based on the manufacture from small flakes and blades of microliths intended for barbing or tipping spears or arrows. Among these are obsidian industries from caves in the Djambi district of inner Sumatra, from sites bordering a former lake at Bandoeng in western Java and from the Manila district of Luzon in the Philippines, each of which features microliths with steep retouch. An industry of broadly similar character, but using triangular hollow-based arrowheads as well, has been recovered from caves in the south-west Celebes with remains of animals, which, apart from the dog, were exclusively of wild species. Nothing definite can yet be said about the origins of these industries. Excavation in the cave of Nia in Borneo and on the Philippine island of Palawan shows that both were occupied well back in the Late Pleistocene, during certain phases of which they formed part of south-east Asia, yet it is still not possible to say whether or not the later backed blade industries of these territories were of autochthonous origin. In the case of Luzon and the Philippines which were off-shore islands even at the height of glaciation they must certainly have been intrusive. If the microlithic tradition of Indonesia stemmed from south-east Asia or developed in Indonesia itself, the off-shore occurrences might plausibly be derived from that quarter, but the possibility cannot be entirely ruled out that they came from the north and that indeed the whole phenomenon was of northern origin.

Quadrangular stone-adze culture of Indo-China, Thailand and Malaya

It is certain that south-east Asia was strongly influenced from the coastal territories of South China and it is more likely than not that these influences came at least in large measure by sea. We know from the distribution of cultural traits like quadrangular polished stone adzes and pottery marked by cord-wrapped paddles that mariners of Lung-shan tradition were navigating the South China Seas at this time. There is no difficulty in visualizing contact if not settlement on the coasts of Tonkin and Annam and indeed this seems the most likely explanation for the Neolithic finds in the upper levels of the caves and shelters of the Bac-Son massif of former Indo-China.

Whether the further westward spread of traits—and these extended as far as Assam and Bengal—was entirely overland or whether it may have been reinforced by way of the Gulf of Siam is still for discussion. What seems reasonably clear is that, if we may rely on a single radiocarbon date, strong Lung-shan traditions had influenced cultural life in western Thailand already during the earlier part of the second millennium B.C. The settlements and burials of Ban-Kao have recently yielded an abundant material. Lungshanoid affinities are to be found in all main categories. Thus polished stone artifacts include numerous quadrangular adzes including shouldered forms and a variety of beads and bracelets. A rich industry in shell included semi-lunar and rectangular knives and many forms, including fish-hooks and barbed and lanceolate varieties of arrowhead and spearpoint, were made from antler and bone, as in China. The pottery points strongly in the same direction though showing a certain measure of individuality. It included coarse brown and grey wares, as well as finer red and black ones. Several vigorous forms were apparently turned on a slow-moving wheel, including shallow, sharply carinated dishes; stemmed and footed bowls and dishes; jars with rounded or slightly carinated shoulder and sharply everted rim; and, not least, sharply carinated bowls mounted on hollow tripods strongly reminiscent of the Chinese *Li*. Yet the hollow legs on the Ban-Kao vessels, as on all those recognized from sites in other parts of Thailand and in Malaya, differ from the Chinese prototypes in being sealed off from the body of the pot, a difference which also involved holes in the sides to allow the escape of hot air when the vessels were fired. Since the original point of the hollow feet was to increase the amount of liquid in close contact with the fire, it seems evident that the Malayan and Thai potters were reproducing the outward form without appreciating the function of these conical legs. Despite the many analogies there-fore—and one should add the remarkable similarity to Lung-shan ware of the thin black burnished vessels, as well as the general lack of ornament other than paddle-imprinted cord marks on the bodies and feet of pots—one must agree that the early Thai potters, though inspired from China, nevertheless developed to some degree on independent lines.

The same applies and even more so to Malaya, especially as time went on. Quite marked differences can be noted for instance between the forms of the pots from the upper Neolithic levels at Gua Cha and Ban-Kao, even if in respect of technique they stood very close. Again, although both used stone rings and quadrangu-lar sectioned adzes, they did not make the shouldered form that extended from China to Bengal; instead they went in for adzes, as did their colleagues at Buki Tengku Lembu, having the working-edge bevelled obliquely from two directions to form a beak. Other stone forms included beaters with heavily incised face used for making the bark cloth used for clothing and a sophisticated form of stone bracelet having a pronounced keel.

The sea-going peoples of the Lower Yangtze and the maritime provinces of South China also crossed the Formosa Strait to occupy Taiwan. Pushing still further south they introduced the quadrangular stone adze, including both the shouldered and stepped form, polished stone rings, arrowheads and pottery, in-cluding forms shaped by cord-wrapped paddles, to the Philip-pines and beyond to the Celebes. Over this vast tract there was naturally scope for variation and we find, for example, that in the Celebes coarse pottery was supplemented by vessels decorated by incision in the form of meanders and various arrangements of shaded triangle. It is sometimes claimed that the southward expansion from the Yangtze basin was due to pressure from the Shang and in due course the Chou empires. Another and perhaps more likely explanation is that what we see is merely one expression of the basic drive to explore the environment shared not only by men of all races but by the lowliest forms of animal life: once proficiency in using boats had been attained vast new territories lay open to exploration and settlement; and as we shall see these included the great ocean tracts of the Pacific.

Dongson bronzes

Neither south-east Asia, Indonesia nor the Philippines experienced a phase of technology fully comparable with the Bronze Age in certain parts of the Old World. Yet, while stone tools continued in general use into the Christian era, a certain number of bronze artifacts, named after the rich settlement and cemetery of Dong So'n in northern Annam, found their way over these territories during the latter half of the first millennium B.C. and in the richer graves of Annam these were sometimes accompanied by objects made of iron. The leading types of Dongson bronze, which was commonly a lead alloy like that of Shang China, included daggers, socketed axes, hoes and spearheads, and kettledrums of a kind used by the Karens of Burma and western Siam down to modern times for calling up spirits, rain-making, casting spells on enemies and similar purposes. Scenes of horsemen wearing costume of Late Chou character point to the north and it has been suggested that the Dongson style and industry was introduced by barbarians from the steppe, who formed part of the movement that overwhelmed the Western Chou dynasty. Bronze working, frequently employing a strong lead alloy as in North China, may have been established in Annam by the sixth century B.C. Within a couple of hundred years bronze artifacts began to make their appearance in Indonesia. The Dongson bronzes affected only a small segment of the population, which remained as a whole in a basically Neolithic stage until the general use of iron was spread by Hindu merchants trading as far afield as Sumatra, Java, Bali and parts of Borneo during the early part of the Christian era.

Melanesia

Beyond the range both of the Dongson bronzes and of the Hindu traders who introduced iron tools to Indonesia the Melanesian islanders remained in the Stone Age down to the European period, so that as recently as the Second World War communities could be found in the interior of New Guinea in a 'Neolithic' state of culture. Rice was not eaten in Melanesia until modern times, and the natives lived mainly by cultivating such things as bananas, breadfruit, coconuts, taro and yams by the slash and burn method, helped out by raising pigs, dogs and chickens and by sea-food. For felling and working timber for boats and houses the Melanesians used adzes and axes of polished stone; many of these were of lozenge section, but some were four-sided. The axeheads were roughed out at places where the best stone out-cropped and were distributed probably through some form of gift-exchange over extensive territories. They made all their pottery by hand, using coil-building and shaping by anvil and paddle, the immediate and remote sources of which were Indonesia and South China. Melanesian prehistory must remain obscure until sequences have been established in the various islands and the age of suitable samples correctly determined by radiocarbon dating, but already it seems to be established that a culture resembling the earlier Neolithic of the Philippines had reached New Caledonia at the latest by the middle of the first millennium B.C.

JAPAN

By comparison with that of China Japanese civilization was relatively a late development. Indeed, it was not until the third century B.C. that the basis even of peasant society was laid with the introduction of rice-cultivation and the beginnings of the Yayoi culture. Until this time the inhabitants of the Japanese islands had subsisted by hunting, plant-gathering and to an increasing degree by fishing and the collection of shell-fish.

Preceramic settlement

The findings of radiocarbon dating suggest that the islands were settled already during the Late Pleistocene period and this after all agrees very well with the fact that at the peak of glaciation the main islands were joined not merely to one another but to the mainland of east Asia by way both of Korea and of Sakhalin and the Amur basin. The earliest inhabitants occupied caves like that of Fukui on Kyushu, but also open sites, among them Iwajuku, now incorporated in the volcanic Kanto loam of the Tokyo plain and Shirataki on Hokkaido in deposits of similar age. Since the early inhabitants frequently had access to easily flaked materials, including obsidian, their lithic industries are easily recognizable. They were in many cases based on the production of blades, including some micro-blades of a kind known to have been used as insets for composite tools over a large area of northern Eurasia and North America. Many secondary features can be paralleled in the Advanced Palaeolithic tradition of extensive tracts of the Eurasiatic land-mass, including the steep vertical retouch seen to advantage on the Kiridashi knives with their blunted sides and oblique cutting edges, the burin, the blade scraper and the bifacially flaked projectile-point, including stemmed forms that closely match certain ones from the New World.

Jomon hunter-fishers

The settled life made possible by a plentiful supply of shell-fish was very early accompanied by the manufacture of pottery. Even if some of the earliest radiocarbon dates are discounted, the over-all pattern obtained for successive phases of the Jomon and Yayoi cultures is reasonably consistent and strongly suggests that potting was carried on long before, perhaps several thousand years before agriculture was introduced. Although some of the earliest pottery, like that from level III in the Fukui cave, was decorated by linear strips in very low relief, the commonest mode of decoration was to imprint cord-markings on the surface, a method which lends its name to the Jomon culture. Japanese pre-historians have distinguished a number of chronological phases of development as well as regional variations in the Jomon culture. Here it will be sufficient to indicate in very broad outline some of the leading characteristics of the mode of life of the Jomon people. For the greater part of their history their only domestic animal was the dog, and it was only latterly that they began to cultivate millet, buckwheat and beans. As a rule Jomon man pre-ferred to live within reach of the sea to take advantage of a wide range of sea-foods: clusters of middens around Tokyo Bay and many other localities have yielded vast quantities of discarded shells of mussels, oysters and other shellfish and in addition plenty of fish-bones. Most of the fish taken for food were of kinds like mullet and perch that could be taken from inlets at high tide, but remains of shark, sting-ray and tunny show that boats, dug-out varieties of which have survived, must also have been used for angling. Jomon fishing-gear includes fishhooks with plain or externally barbed tip and harpoons or detachable spearheads, perforated for attachment to a line. In addition inland game, in-cluding deer and wild pig, was hunted by arrows tipped with hollow-based triangular flint heads flaked on either face, and wild plants were prepared for food by grinding stones and mortars. The Jomon people lived in settlements of trapeziform or circular houses, having floors lowered below ground-level and central fireplaces, around which were set timber uprights for carrying the thatched roof. Like other Sub-Neolithic peoples the Jomon hunter-fishers made pottery by hand, and this they decorated with simple geometric patterns imprinted with cords or shells or executed with grooves: in form the earliest pots were conoid, but flat bases soon appeared and as time went on handles and spouts were successively added; and from the first human figurines were made from fired clay (Pl. XII). Their flint-work, as seen in the arrowheads and numerous scrapers, was of a relatively high standard, but the stone axes were generally crude—to begin with, hardly more than natural pebbles lightly ground at one end.

Yayoi farmers

An altogether more advanced economy, one that laid an adequate foundation for the relatively wealthy society of the Protohistoric period, was introduced to northern Kyushu from Korea along with other elements of the Yayoi culture some time during the third century B.C., probably as an indirect result of the expansion of the power of the Han Dynasty of China. Although initially the Yayoi culture spread rapidly into western Honshu, reaching the Yamato Plain by around 200 B.C., its momentum slowed down, and it was not until A.D. 100 that it penetrated Tohoku. The interrelations between the Yayoi and older Jomon cultures were quite complex and it would seem that in some parts of the country there was some real continuity between them. The most important single innovation was probably the introduction of rice-cultivation, which by middle Yayoi times had created in the western part of the country a predominantly agrarian society. Tangible evidence of the new economy includes traces of paddy fields and irrigation channels; carbonized grains and also impressions of rice; and granaries raised on timber piles and approached by ladders. Stone continued to be used for axes, adzes and arrow-heads, but bronze weapons and mirrors were first imported from the mainland and then in due course cast in Japan itself, or alternatively copied in stone; and many tools began to be made of iron. As a further symbol of the sub-division of labour, it may be added that at this time the potter's wheel came into use.

Protohistoric Japan

Around A.D. 400 Japan entered on the Protohistoric phase that
only ended with the introduction of Buddhism towards the end of
the sixth century A.D. and the committal to writing between
A.D. 712 and 720 of traditional claims surrounding the imperial
dynasty. The main information about this intermediate period is
derived from very numerous tombs, often of monumental construction and occasionally occupying areas, including surrounding moats, of as many as 32·4 hectares (eighty acres). These testify
to increasing wealth and technical skill, a growing density of
population and a feudal organization of society with numerous
clans owing allegiance to the imperial clan. Clay models buried
with the dead indicate not merely the differentiation of town and
country houses, but the emergence of palaces and shrines. Already
during this period, coinciding more or less with that of the
barbarian migrations into the European territories of the Roman
Empire, the main social institutions of recent Japanese history
were in being. As if to emphasize the continuity, wooden Shinto
shrines have continued to be rebuilt on the same site and after the
same pattern as examples first erected during the Protohistoric
period. Again, though it seems likely that Shintoism itself was
first institutionalized in competition with Buddhism, its basic
belief in the need to offer thank-offerings and sacrifices to a multi-
tude of natural spirits, inhabiting such places as groves, mountain tops, sources of water or stones of unusual size, must surely
stretch far back into the prehistoric past.

NORTH-EAST ASIA

Hunter-fishers

The vast funnel-shaped territory of Siberia east of the Yenisei
and north of the Amur owes its interest largely to its position in
relation to the New World. Doubtless it was through this region
that the first immigrants must have passed on their way to America,

presumably at a time when the land-connection was still intact, and doubtless, also, when means of communication had been developed during Neothermal times, it provided a main avenue for cultural movements, not necessarily always in one direction, between the Old World and the New. On the other hand the climate of Siberia must throughout prehistoric times have imposed narrow limits on the possibility of local cultural development: even in modern times agriculture has been confined to the uppermost Yenisei and to the Angara Valley, and hunting, gathering and fishing have provided the main and for most of the region the sole source of food-supply. Yet, if the possibility of sharing fully in the kind of life permitted to peasant farmers, still less of progressing towards urban civilization, was denied to the prehistoric inhabitants of Siberia, this did not prevent them developing effective cultures based on various forms of catching activity or of acquiring elements of technique, such as potting, originally developed among communities based to a greater or less degree on food-production.

The best sequence of Sub-Neolithic cultures in Siberia is that established in the Angara Valley and Lake Baikal regions. Pottery first appeared in the Isakovo stage and comprised conoid jars with straight sides ornamented by net-impressions. Among the hunting-gear were bone spearheads armed by flint micro-blades inset in slots, a type found with a number of burials in the region lacking pottery and assigned on not very conclusive evidence to a distinct Khini phase of settlement. The device is also interesting because of its occurrence over northern Eurasia as far west as the Atlantic coast of Norway and as far south as Mongolia and Kansu; and because it turns up in North America in the context of the Denbigh culture of Alaska and the younger Dorset culture of the Hudson's Bay area. Other and more specifically Sub-Neolithic elements to appear in the Isakovo culture include partially polished adzes, polished stone knives and bifacially flaked arrowheads. In the later Serovo and Kitoi stages a greater emphasis seems to have

Radiocarbon dates for south-east Asia and Japan

SOUTH-EAST ASIA		B.C.
Malaya		
Gua Harimau, Perak	BM 43	1500±150
Gua Kechil, Pahang (level III)	GX 0418	2850±800
Thailand		
Ban-Kao	K 838	1770±140
JAPAN		
Preceramic		
Shirataki (loc. 31), Hokkaido	Gak 160, 210, 212	{12,850±350 {13,850±400
Yasimba, Honshu: hearth, micro-blades	Gak 604	12,350±700
Fukui cave, Kyushu (level VII)	I 946	8750±300
(level IX)	I 947	11,180±600
Initial Jomon		
Kojohama, Hokkaido: pit-house	I 550	5730±200
Omagari, Hokkaido: shell-mound	GX 281	4845±150
Natsushima, Honshu: shell-mound (shell)	M 769	7500±400
(charcoal)	M 770/1	7290±500
Kishima, Honshu	M 237	6450±350
Early Jomon		
Misato cave, Hokkaido	I 553	4850±225
Orinoto, Honshu: shell-mound 31 cm.	Gak 379a	2780± 90
60 cm.	Gak 379b	2810± 90
Middle Jomon		
Tokoro, Hokkaido: shell-mound	Gak 188	2200±400
Nakazawra, Hokkaido: house	I 552	1875±175
Kamo, Honshu	M 240	3150±400
Ubayama, Honshu: shell-mound	{C 548 {UCLA 279	2596±200 2620±150
Uenae, Hokkaido	W 322	1280±160
Hormouchi, Honshu: shell-mound	N 59	1830±110
Kusaka, Honshu: shell-mound	Gak 170	1110±110
Yoshigo, Honshu: shell-mound	N 94	920±250
Yayoi		
Kori, Honshu: shell-mound	M 239	400±200
Toro, Honshu	M 70	0±130

been placed on fishing, for which lures, barbed spears and fish-hooks were used. In the Glaskovo stage, contemporary with the Bronze Age in south-west Siberia and probably with the Shang dynasty, the pottery shows signs of contact with North China.

Abundant traces of Sub-Neolithic people at the level of those of the Baikal area are known from the Lena Valley and even from as far east as the Kolyma. Over all this territory the hunter-fishers continued to combine the use of burins and bone tools inset with micro-blades with coarse, hand-made pottery, a sherd of which from a late site in the Lena Valley was found, significantly, to have had fish-scales mixed with the clay as tempering. Further east there are indications of well-developed maritime cultures. The Old Bering Sea culture probably grew up during the centuries immediately B.C. on either side of the strait and it occupied the coast of the Chukchi peninsula as far west as the Bear Islands on the north. Middens at the mouth of the Amur River suggest that coastal settlement may have begun there as far back as the middle of the second millennium B.C., and in this context it is worth recalling that the Jomon people who occupied the main island of Japan possibly several thousands of years previously were primarily coastal midden-dwellers. Whether or not the modern Ainu are remnants of the Jomon people as was once thought, it is certain that they retreated before the Yayoi cultivators until by the end of the first millennium B.C. they were concentrated on Hokkaido; it was probably about this time and doubtless under the same pressure that they spread northward into Kamchatka and the Kurile Islands. The native peoples of north-east Siberia remained prehistoric down to the Russian colonization of the first half of the seventeenth century.

CHAPTER II

AUSTRALASIA AND THE PACIFIC

AUSTRALIA

Migration route to Australia

Modern research has shown that Australia, like the New World, was settled by man much earlier than had until recently been thought. The fact remains that the continent was not occupied until a comparatively advanced stage of the Late Pleistocene. When he first arrived man encountered an archaic flora, recalling that of the Secondary era of geological time, and a fauna of monotremes and marsupials, the most primitive and next most primitive of the three groups into which mammals are divided. The reason why these backward groups survived is that biologically more advanced ones were cut off from south-east Asia during the Pleistocene by passages of open sea. Even at the peaks of glaciations when ocean levels were much lower and most of Indonesia, including the great islands of Sumatra, Java and Borneo, was joined to the continent by the now submerged Sunda shelf, the Makassar channel between Borneo and Celebes, no less than that between Bali and Lombok, was an effective barrier for land-forms. Some Asiatic species it is true seem to have crossed the Wallace Line but none traversed that defined by Weber dividing the Moluccas from Celebes and passing east of Timor.

So long as the Sunda shelf was dry land there were periods during the Pleistocene when man could occupy most of Indonesia west of the Wallace line without having to traverse open water, and indeed Java has yielded some of the key human fossils dating to the Middle Pleistocene; nor should we forget that, to judge from radiocarbon dates, the great caves of Nia in Sarawak and of

Tabon on Palawan Island, an outlier of the Philippines that would nevertheless have formed part of Borneo at a time of low ocean levels, were already occupied well back in the Late Pleistocene. To cross the zoological divides noted by Wallace and Weber involved the use of boats or at least of some kind of float to traverse several successive passages of open sea. Having once got into Australia, which at the time of low sea-levels would have been joined to New Guinea on a broad front by the Sahul shelf, there was nothing to prevent movement overland across the continent to Tasmania which would likewise have formed at this period part of the mainland.

The mere fact that sea passages were so much narrower during the late-glacial period makes it more likely that man first got into Australia at this time rather than later when much wider stretches of open sea would have had to be crossed. The evidence of technological stagnation available from excavation indeed suggests that the first Australians were effectively marooned when sea-levels rose in Post-glacial times, cutting them off from New Guinea and Indonesia; and to the south the Tasmanians were effectively insulated by the Bass Strait.

Tasmanians

It is no surprise that the Tasmanians should have been the least advanced of the inhabitants of Australasia at the time of its penetration by Europeans, since they were the most remote and isolated. This makes it all the more unfortunate that they should have been exterminated before any complete record of their culture was made. From accounts written after their extinction it would seem that economically and technologically they were subject to much the same limitations as the earliest inhabitants of Australia. The Tasmanians had only a very limited range of equipment. They had no bows and depended for weapons on wooden clubs and spears having their tips hardened in the fire. They seem indeed to have lacked entirely the more sophisticated

248

hafted weapons for which we first have evidence in Australia some thousands of years after Tasmania had been cut off by rising ocean levels. For subsistence they depended on what they could gather or hunt by the simple weapons available to them. As might be expected they lived in small bands widely distributed over the country and rarely settled in any one place for more than a brief time. Although Tasmania was not lacking in resources and extended over some 67,340 square kilometres (26,000 square miles), the aboriginal population at the time of the white occupation is not thought to have amounted to more than from two to four thousand. Individual hunting bands rarely exceeded fifty people and much of the year was passed in smaller groups. Wind-breaks of tree branches and bark provided rudimentary shelter. There was little scope for the sub-division of labour beyond that between the sexes, and technology was correspondingly simple. The Tasmanians were ignorant of pottery and depended on chipped stones for their basic implements.

Prehistoric occupation seems to have been restricted in the main to the coastal zone, and the temperate rain forest in the interior was apparently ignored. Since much of the coastal zone of the mainland period must now be submerged, it is unlikely that even intensive excavation will reveal traces of the earliest settlement. So far the oldest evidence of human occupation comes from a midden at Carlton River and from a depth of 10 feet in the undisturbed filling of a cave at Rocky Point on the north coast. According to radiocarbon these both belong to the seventh millennium B.C. Caves and open middens alike have yielded plentiful evidence for diet. Shell-fish were commonly eaten. Apart from these seals provided most of the animal food, ranging from half to four-fifths of the meat consumed. Fishing also played its part and parrot-fish provided more than a third of animal food at Rocky Point South. Birds were taken, and marsupial bones, although not abundant, reflect hunting in the hinterland.

Physically the Tasmanians were basically Australoid but they displayed certain features, notably a tendency to round-headedness and woolly hair, that are displayed by the Negrito peoples of New Guinea, the Celebes, Philippines, Malaya and the Andaman Islands. This led many of the earlier anthropologists to interpret them as in fact Negritos. Some went so far as to claim that the Tasmanians preserve traces of an original Negrito immigration that was overlaid in all but a few localities like the Atherton Highlands and Melville Island by a later Australoid one; and others that they were the outcome of a more recent wave of immigrants coming directly by sea from the Negrito zone and by-passing the Australian continent. Contemporary opinion inclines to quite a different explanation and supposes that the Tasmanians owed their special features to genetic change in a small population isolated from the mainland by the formation of the Bass Strait during Neothermal times.

Australoid migrations

The Australoids, with wavy hair plentifully distributed on their brown bodies, long heads with low foreheads and prominent brow-ridges, noses with low and broad roots, prognathous jaws, large palates and teeth and small chins, preserve a stage in the evolution of *Homo sapiens* probably anterior to the emergence of Negroids, Mongoloids, Whites and American Indians. It seems likely that they came from South Asia and it is significant that pockets of Australoids are found, though mixed with other strains, in Ceylon and possibly in South India. The route followed by the migration from south-east Asia passed through Indonesia and is marked by the fossil skulls from Wadjak in Java and by people still living on some of the lesser Sunda islands. Further it would appear that some of the Australoids, instead of pushing south, continued north of New Guinea to Melanesia, where they are still to be recognized in the Bismarck Archipelago and in New Caledonia. Physically the recent aborigines appear substantially homogeneous even if regional varieties exist. The fossil material on the other hand, though still rare, already falls into two groups. Crania from Talgai and Cohuna, neither closely dated, agree broadly with the Wadjak fossil and the recent aborigines. Those from Mossgiel, Keilor, a few miles north-west of Melbourne, and from nearby Green Gulley, however, display loftier, well rounded brows.

Like the Tasmanians, the Australian aborigines still (Pl. XIII) were limited by the possibilities of food-gathering and hunting, though possessing highly complex social institutions. The population at the time of the discovery is estimated to have amounted to some 250,000 to 300,000, giving an average density about the same as that estimated for Tasmania. On the other hand people were very unevenly distributed over the 7,640,500 square kilometres (2,950,000 square miles) of continental territory; much of the western and central parts were either desert or too arid to support more than very sparse settlement. Recent aboriginal habitation has been concentrated in the far north, along the extensive coastal territories, in the forested area of the south-east and in the valley of the Darling and Murray Rivers, but it has to be remembered that this was due largely to the effect of British colonization in the temperate south-east. Again, one should remember that the main climatic and vegetational zones, and by consequence the distribution of population, must have shifted considerably within the probable span of human settlement: for instance at the height of the Pleistocene ice age the zone of equatorial rain forest would have contracted and the northern parts of Australia would have been noticeably easier to penetrate than they later became. Again, there is evidence that at the height of the Neothermal phase, when the equatorial rain forest had returned to northern Australia, the interior of the continent was subject to a desiccation sufficiently marked to affect profoundly the dispersion of human populations.

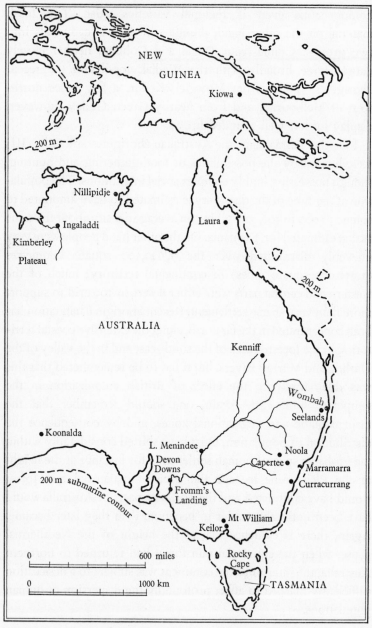

9. Some key sites of the Australian Stone Age

The earliest settlement of Australia

There is a growing body of evidence that man was already present in Australia well back in the Late-glacial period. Lack of precise observation at the time of its accidental discovery in 1940 of the well-known human cranium from Keilor, Victoria—a skeleton discovered in 1965 is still in course of study—leaves some uncertainty about its age. Nevertheless a sample from the presumed level of the cranium suggests that it dates from within fifteen hundred years of the end of the fourteenth millennium B.C., and possible traces of human activity at the same locality gave a radiocarbon age around three thousand years older. Radiocarbon dates centring on the seventeenth millennium B.C. have also been determined for a deposit with stone artifacts in Koonalda Cavern, some eighty feet below the level of the Nullarbor plain in South Australia, and a presumed hearth at Lake Menindee in New South Wales. Finally, it may be noted that determinations from the lower levels of rock-shelters at localities as widely separated as Kiowa on the New Guinea highlands, Kenniff Cave in southern Queensland and Noola in New South Wales show that stone industries of apparently unspecialized type were flourishing during the ninth and tenth millennia B.C., if not earlier.

The most important clues to the material culture of the earliest Australians are the stone industries found in the lower levels of rock-shelters. In addition to the sites already mentioned as dating from the Pleistocene a number of finds of comparable material date from early in the Neothermal, including stratified rock-shelters at Laura (Queensland), Ingaladdi (Northern Territories) and Seelands and Marramarra (New South Wales). Much remains to be learned about regional and temporal variations, but certain gross characteristics stand out already. One element in the early tool-kit was the uniface chopper-tool, usually a pebble with flakes removed from one or more edges. On the other hand tools of this kind were used throughout prehistoric times and into the nineteenth century A.D. The early stone-workers were mainly pre-occupied with producing flakes the main purpose of which seems to have been to shape wooden artifacts. It is a moot question how far the convex scrapers, notched and spurred tools and heavy plane-like implements were consciously shaped and how far they resulted from use. There is no sign that any of these tools, which compare in their broad characteristics with those known from Tasmania, were designed for hafting. All could have been and some could only have been manipulated directly in the hand. Yet the edge-ground stone axes that apparently came into use already during the Early Stone Age must have been mounted on handles.

There is still some uncertainty about whether and to what extent the makers of these Early Stone Age industries practised rock-art. At Kenniff Cave lumps of colouring matter, such as might have been used for painting the body, artifacts or the roof and walls of rock-shelters, were found throughout the deposit, even if no pieces showing signs of use in the form of striations were found in an early level. The occurrence of rock-engravings at several localities in Tasmania may be significant in view of the absence of stone tools of Middle Stone Age forms. Recent work at Koonalda increases the probability that rock art was practised during the Early Stone Age.

Middle Stone Age

A new era in Australian prehistory was ushered in by the intro-duction of fresh cultural elements which seem to have begun to filter into Australia early in the third millennium B.C. Although horticulture was apparently introduced early in the New Guinea Highlands, the inhabitants of the continental mainland on the other hand continued to subsist exclusively by hunting, catching and gathering indigenous species down to modern times and indeed steadfastly resisted the efforts of the earliest colonists from Britain to conscript them to agriculture. The only species to accompany man was the dingo, an animal between the wolf and the jackal in size and which compares with the pariah dog of southern Asia. The dingo, a true-breeding wild species, was present at Fromm's Landing (no. 6) on the Lower Murray River before the end of the second millennium B.C. When it first reached Australia is still unknown.

The innovations best represented in the archaeological record are those embodied in stone artifacts. In the sequence of Kenniff Cave, for example, a marked change can be seen in levels dating from the beginning of the third millennium B.C. in the forms of stone implement and in their technique of production: above all there is the appearance of smaller forms adapted to mounting on wooden shafts or handles. The most important of these are backed blades and microliths made by shaping narrow flakes or bladelets by means of steep secondary flaking in the manner of mode 5 and small 'pirri' points with flat surface flaking on the convex face and the base thinned to facilitate hafting. It must be significant that the earliest occupations of rock-shelters dating from this period on the Lower Murray river at Devon Downs and Fromm's Landing (no. 6) have yielded both these classes of implement, and that more or less close analogies can be found for each in the Celebes and Java. Yet it must be emphasized that within continental Australia microliths and pirri points are by no means always associated in the same assemblages. On the contrary their geographical distributions, though overlapping, differ widely. The pirri points, which occur extensively in northern latitudes of Australia, sometimes in association with bifacially flaked points, are restricted in the south to those parts of the eastern half of the continent north and west of the Murray River, apart from outliers in the Darling and Paroo valleys. Backed blade industries including microliths, scrapers, fabricators (lames écaillés) and a few burins, on the other hand, are concentrated in the south-east, though known from west Australia, and so far are absent from the far north.

Both pirri points and microliths were evidently designed to be mounted as the tips and in the latter case also as the barbs of weapons. The absence of the bow both from recent aboriginal equipment, except in certain coastal areas open to outside influence, and from representations in the prehistoric art, suggests that the weapons concerned were spears. Among elements carried forward from the Early Stone Age were stone axeheads roughly flaked into shape and having the working edge ground. In recent aboriginal culture similar axeheads were mounted in wrapround handles and held in position by resin of the kind obtainable from *Spinifex* grass. Other tools were crescentic (*elouera*) or scraper-like (*tula*) stone flakes which in recent aboriginal culture were mounted like adzes and used for finishing wooden artifacts.

Food refuse of the kind obtained in plenty from the Lower Murray rock-shelters shows that kangaroo and wallaby played an important role as suppliers of meat and it was no doubt in hunting these, as well as for taking certain of the larger birds and fish, that barbed spears were most needed. At the same time many small animals like lizards, small birds or fish could have been taken by hand or by means of snares. The Murray River people certainly also collected crayfish and molluscs as well as birds' eggs. Plants are seldom represented in the archaeological record, but there seems no doubt that they as well as insects and larvae would have played an important part in diet. Organic materials, more especially wood, bark and vegetable fibres, were also vitally important in technology. On the other hand animal bone, to judge from sites where this material was well preserved, contributed relatively little and this may help to explain why burins did not occur in larger numbers. One of the few bone artifacts represented in the archaeological record is the double-pointed *muduk* used as a gorge for killing birds and fish.

To judge from the frequent conjunctions of engravings and paintings with rock-shelters having Middle Stone Age deposits, it would seem that symbolic art, and the beliefs and ritual observances that went with this, was intensified at this time. Several categories can be distinguished. Rows of deeply incised vertical lines have frequently been observed on rock-shelters containing backed blades and microliths in New England. Particularly rich panels of paintings were found in Kenniff Cave and the neighbouring Toombs shelter in southern Queensland. These include large numbers of stencils of human hands, mostly negative, but some positive, of a kind widely distributed in Australia and significantly present in New Guinea and the Celebes as well as further afield; an extremely interesting series of representations of artifacts, including wooden shields, spear-throwers, boomerangs and hafted stone axes; and an exceptionally large-scale human figure. As a rule human representations are highly schematic and on a small scale. A particularly fine series from Moonbi in New England shows a scene with dancing figures and two circular and one vertical feature; perhaps this depicts an initiation dance of a kind known to have occurred in recent times on bora grounds, low embanked circles often connected by processional avenues, which, together with stone arrangements of uncertain age, provide the only monumental constructions from the aboriginal past of Australia.

Recent Stone Age

The Recent Stone Age, that which flourished when the first white settlers intruded and set up their colonies on the coast and which is only now coming to an end in remote areas, began with the disappearance of the backed blade industries characteristic of the previous age in the southern part of the continent. Precisely when this happened has yet to be closely defined. There is plenty of evidence that the inhabitants of rock-shelters in the Grafton area of New England and in the Sydney region were still fabricating microliths down to the middle or even the end of the first millennium A.D. Even more recent dates have been obtained for layers nearer the surface, but the intrusion of charcoal and other matter from more recent occupation is a strong possibility.

The most likely explanation for the disappearance, probably within the present millennium, of backed blade and microlithic industries is that the need which called them into existence came to be met in a different way: for example, if we are right to interpret the Australian microliths as the barbs or tips of spearheads, it is easy to see how the emergence of finely barbed wooden spears could have rendered them superfluous. The most striking feature of recent aboriginal technology is indeed the ingenuity and skill with which organic materials have been shaped to meet the needs of daily life. Thanks to the illustrations prepared by Angas for a work published in 1847 we happen to be well informed about the material equipment of the aborigines of the Lower Murray River at a time when the city of Adelaide was founded, men whose ash and refuse accumulated over the Middle Stone Age deposits of the Devon Downs and Fromm's Landing shelters and the smoke from whose camp-fires still blackens the overhanging rocks. Fishermen are shown precariously balanced in shallow canoes made from bark stripped from eucalyptus trees, examples of which with canoe-shaped scars can still be seen. The equipment they are using, and that of their fellows depicted on dry land, is made from a variety of wood, bark, fibre and bone. The only component of their equipment made of relatively permanent material was the edge-ground stone axehead shown mounted on its wooden handle. Yet no one who examines the wooden artifacts made by recent aborigines can fail to admire the skill with which they have been finished, often with a shallow parallel grooving, a finish imparted by the scraper-adzes whose blades show them to have come into use already during the Middle Stone Age.

Edge-ground stone axes, another inheritance from a previous age, were blocked out at quarry factories at the source of the raw material and only finished at the scene of use, often far away. The axe factories of Mount William above Melbourne, that remind one so vividly of Neolithic ones in Britain, were still active into the 1840s. In the northern parts of the continent stone spearheads continued to be made down to our own day. Leaf-shaped points flaked with great delicacy on either face, whose antecedents lie in the Middle Stone Age, have in recent times been identified with the Kimberley Plateau. So active was the tradition that when telegraph cables were first carried across the area it was found useful to place bottle-glass at the foot of the poles in hope of saving the insulators. In Arnhem Land on the other hand spears were normally tipped with tapered blades struck from cores so carefully prepared at the Nillipidje quarry that little or no secondary trimming was needed.

The widespread distribution of artifacts manufactured at outcrops of localized materials invites one to ask how this came about. Here we are helped by the observations made by anthropologists working in the field. It seems plain that the axes, spearheads and many other things no longer surviving in the archaeological record entered into a complex web of interchange the effect of which resembled that achieved by trade in our own society, namely the more or less even spread over extensive territories of materials or products found or made locally. Yet the driving force was not gain, still less the specialized function of a class of trader, so much as a means of recognizing the mutual obligations imposed by kinship. The widespread distribution of goods, of which the spearheads and axes were only examples, reflects in fact the strength and pervasiveness of the obligations that held together and to a large extent motivated aboriginal Australian society. In the same way the art, which though prehistoric in origin proliferated in modern times, whether in the form of rock-paintings, sand patterns, body painting or the ornamentation of artifacts, reminds us of the intricate web of totemic relationships established between the aborigines, the animals and other features of their environment and the ancestors from which their society and its setting alike were thought to have sprung.

When the handful of aborigines around Sydney Cove greeted Governor Phillip and his small armada in the year 1788 they are

Australian Stone Age

New Guinea	1	Kiowa: 0·91 m.	Y 1371	2890 B.C.± 140
		4 m.	Y 1366	8400 B.C.± 140
Northern Territory	2	Ingaladdi	GX 104	4305 B.C.± 135
Queensland	3	Kenniff: 0·61–0·62 m.	NPL 32	600 B.C.± 90
		0·76–0·84 m.	NPL 65	1880 B.C.± 90
		1·10–1·20 m.	NPL 66	3070 B.C.± 90
		1·70–1·72 m.	NPL 67	10,660 B.C.± 110
		1·77–2 m.	NPL 33	10,950 B.C.± 170
		2·23–2·30 m.	NPL 68	14,180 B.C.± 140
New England, NSW	4	Seelands	GaK 370	A.D. 420± 90
			V 24	2092 B.C.± 66
			V 27	4494 B.C.± 74
	5	Wombah	GaK 566	A.D. 420± 90
			GaK 568	1280 B.C.± 100
	6	Cambigne	V 39	A.D. 600± 75
	7	Jacky's Creek	V 41	A.D. 640± 70
NSW (remainder)	8	Lake Menindee	GaK 335	16,850 B.C.± 800
	9	Noola: 3 m.	GaK 334	9650 B.C.± 400
	10	Capertee: 1·72–1·92 m.	V 18	5410 B.C.± 125
	11	Lapstone Creek	ANU 10	1700 B.C.± 160
NSW (remainder)	12	Curracurrang: upper	GaK 689	A.D. 1110± 90
			GaK 688	410 B.C.± 90
		lower	GaK 482	5500 B.C.± 180
	13	Gymea Bay	NSW 6	A.D. 730± 55
South Australia	14	Koonalda	GaK 511	16,250 B.C.± 550
	15	Fromm's Landing:		
		level IV	R 456/2	1290 B.C.± 80
		level X	R 456/1	2900 B.C.± 90
Victoria	16	Keilor: cranium I	NZ 336	13,050 B.C.±1500
		hearth below	NZ 207	16,050 B.C.± 500
Tasmania	17	Carlton River	I 323	6750 B.C.± 200
	18	Rocky Point (S.)	GXO 266	6170 B.C.± 120

Note. There are growing indications that men first reached Australia substantially earlier than published dates suggest, possibly in the region of 30,000 years or so ago.

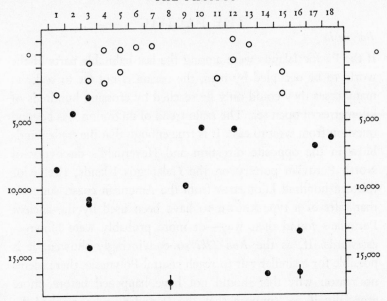

Chart illustrating the range of radiocarbon dates in the Australian Early and Middle Stone Ages. ● Early Stone Age; ♦ Hearths; ○ Middle Stone Age

recorded to have set up 'a horrid howl' and to have indicated 'by angry gestures with sticks and stones that the white man was not wanted'. To Phillips and his companions the aborigines must indeed have seemed ineffectual in the sense that their economy and weapons were such that they were unable to compete on anything approaching equal terms. Yet now that anthropologists have been able to learn more about them it is possible to appreciate more easily how effectively, despite the poverty of their material equipment, the native Australians had managed to come to terms with a wide range of environments, some of them, like the arid wastes of west central Australia, so severe that Europeans are only able to exist in them when supported by long lines of communication with their home bases. No less impressive since anthropologists have taught us to understand them have proved to be the complexity and ingenuity of their kinship system, their concepts and their art.

261

THE PACIFIC

Polynesia

If the Pacific Islands were among the last habitable parts of the world to be occupied by man, the reason is not far to seek: in many cases they could only be reached by crossing hundreds of kilometres of open sea. The main trend of migration was beyond question from west to east. It is true enough that the trade winds blow in the opposite direction and Heyerdahl's discovery of North Peruvian pottery on the Galapagos Islands, twelve or thirteen hundred kilometres from the American coast, suggests that rafts of a type known to have been used by the ancient Peruvians found their way—or more probably were blown—eastwards. If, as the *Kon-Tiki* so convincingly showed, it is possible for a similar raft to reach central Polynesia, there seems no reason why this should not have happened before, more especially if we suppose that the Peruvians who reached the Galapagos Islands did so involuntarily. It may even be that the megalithic masonry displayed on the façades of the mausoleums and temple platforms of Easter Island and the Marquesas owe something to Peruvian inspiration. Yet, even if this should prove to be the case, the fact remains that many lines of evidence point unambiguously to south-east Asia as the main source of the Polynesians and their culture.

Racially the Polynesians seem to have resulted from the intermingling of three main stocks, a predominant one, Caucasoid, the others, relatively weak, Mongolian and Negroid; and this ethnic mixture was apparently welded into a stable genetic unit on the Asian mainland. There is no suggestion that the Amerindians contributed in any way to the ethnic make-up of the Polynesians. The incidence of disease points in the same direction. Venereal disease, which originated in South America, was apparently unknown in Polynesia until introduced by Europeans. Conversely leprosy, encountered in Polynesia by the early European visitors, was absent from the New World until Europeans brought it there. Similarly with language: the relationships of the Polynesian languages, like those of Melanesia and Indonesia, rest unequivocally with Thai, Kadai and Li (Formosan). The same story is told by the plants and animals bred by the Polynesians for food. Except for the sweet potato, which possibly comes from Africa, all the plants cultivated by the Polynesians and nearly all the weeds of cultivation originated in Asia and must have been brought from there by man. Likewise the domesticated animals on which many Polynesian peoples depended for most of their protein, namely dog, pig and jungle cock, were all from southeast Asia and must have been carried, together with food plants and women, over great tracts of the Pacific Ocean in the canoes which made the whole colonization possible: and one has always to remember that it was possession of domestic animals and plants that alone enabled the Polynesians to expand apparently so rapidly over such an extensive kingdom of islands. This is not to say that Polynesian culture was a mere transplantation from the west. Its character can only be understood fully in relation to geographical circumstances. Here one must distinguish between west Polynesia, comprising Tonga, Samoa and the Ellice Islands, and the vast triangle of east Polynesia with its base between New Zealand and Easter Island and its apex in Hawaii. Although we still know very little in detail about the settlement of the west Polynesian islands, excavations at Vailele, on Samoa, have already revealed small clusters of simple pole-built thatched houses dating from the beginning of the Christian era, and it is likely that cultivators had spread there from Melanesia around 500 B.C. The early inhabitants of Samoa, like those of Tonga, made pottery, another trait that reached west Polynesia from Melanesia. Indeed pottery from Ha'atuatua on the island of Nuka Hiva shows that the craft had already spread across the Pacific to the Marquesas Islands apparently as early as the second century B.C., and it is of interest that the earliest Marquesans made polished adze blades of the same elliptical section as those of Melanesia.

Like the early Samoans, the Marquesans kept pigs, dogs and fowls, occupied small hamlets and built themselves simple thatched huts; but there is also evidence that they were building sacred sites and low stone burial enclosures. Evidently a simple form of village culture had already spread over Polynesia before the Christian era began.

A distinctively east Polynesian culture did not emerge until the latter part of the first millennium A.D. Its most important memorials, all the more remarkable when it is considered that they were built by peoples limited by a Stone Age technology, are massive stone structures, such as the Easter Island mausoleums (*ahu*), massive platforms encased by megalithic masonry and surmounted at their taller ends by free-standing stone figures, and the Marquesan terrace plazas (*tohua*) with their dance areas, images and temples. Structures on this scale bear witness to the size of the economic surplus won from tropical horticulture, but they also reflect the power of religion and the hierarchic structure of Polynesian society at this time. Again, the existence of a coherent culture, centred on the Society Islands and Tahiti, but extending over a huge area of the Pacific Ocean, testifies to outstanding ability in boat-building and navigation. This in turn explains the overriding importance of the adze in the Polynesian tool-kit, and the way in which a distinctive type like the tanged four-sided form was spread far and wide over so vast a territory. Along with navigation went fishing, and common forms of bone and shell fish-hook occur over vast areas. Their seamanship, no less than their megalithic structures, shows that the Polynesians were well able to operate in disciplined groups for specific ends.

To judge from oral tradition and the observations of early explorers, Polynesian society was structured to a high degree on hereditary leadership. For this reason alone great attention was paid to genealogies and the only way these could be perpetuated among non-literate peoples was through oral tradition. The question arises how much can safely be inferred from such traditions about the culture-history of Polynesia. Sir Peter Buck, in his *Vikings of the Sunrise* tells of navigators undertaking deliberate voyages, sailing by the stars, observing natural signs and seeking out island homes in the vast waste of the Pacific Ocean. Others, like Andrew Sharp, have minimized the purposefulness of Polynesian navigators and stressed the importance and frequency of accidental, involuntary travels. Of course we must be prepared to see in the surviving oral traditions an element of *post facto* rationalization and it would certainly be wrong to ignore accidental voyages. Yet the Polynesians when first encountered by Europeans were exceedingly proficient as navigators and commanded an extensive knowledge of distant places.

New Zealand

In considering the settlement of New Zealand, largest and most remote of Polynesian lands, surviving Maori legends have to be considered. According to these the country is supposed to have been discovered twice by accident, first by Kupe chasing a giant octopus, and next by Toi'ete'huatai pursuing two grandsons blown away from Tahiti in a canoe race. Tradition also insists on a massive immigration by the canoes of the Fleet setting out from the legendary Hawaiki in central Polynesia, supposedly around 1350 A.D. On genealogical grounds Kupe would have arrived some four hundred years earlier, about the same time as the date estimated from radiocarbon analysis for the first occupation of New Zealand.

When the east Polynesians reached New Zealand they not only arrived at the end of a lengthy voyage, but they must have found this temperate land very different from the tropics. Both these circumstances affected their economy. Of the familiar domestic animals of Polynesia only the dog had reached New Zealand at the time of European contact. As to cultivated food plants, a main source of food in tropical Polynesia, some, like the coconut, never reached New Zealand. Those that were introduced could only be cultivated with some difficulty and within limited regions: the yam was confined to the northern half of the North Island; taro and the common gourd could not flourish south of Cook Strait; and the all-important *kumara* or sweet potato could only be cultivated as far south as Banks Peninsula, about a third of the way down the South Island. The fact that New Zealand was situated on the climatic frontier of some of the basic food plants of Polynesia had two important implications: it meant that the original Maori, even if at first they did manage to introduce any cultivated plants, must have had to undergo a more or less lengthy period of adjustment during which they had to depend for their food largely on catching and gathering; and secondly that even when cultivation did get established—and it never did in the southern two-thirds of the South Island during the aboriginal period—it varied widely in intensity in different regions.

To begin with the immigrants, who brought with them Polynesian adze-blades and fish-hooks, apparently made do with hunting and gathering. Prominent among their victims were several species of moa, and it seems that these great flightless birds, in some cases larger than ostriches, were in fact exterminated by man. Smaller birds were also eaten, and the great encampment at Wairau Bar on the south side of Cook Strait reminds us of the importance of sea-food, as do the numerous fish-hooks found on Archaic sites. There is no certain evidence when the sweet potato was first introduced. The first clues that this vitally important tuber was being cultivated are the storage pits found on the more permanent settlements that began to appear on the North Island around the middle of the fourteenth century. It must have been hard to establish cultivation of the basic food plants even in favourable areas and it was not until around 1450 that we find in the North Island evidence of more systematic cultivation, more permanent settlements and the emergence of distinctively Maori culture. In the archaeological record specifically New Zealand

forms of adze began to replace ones common to the east Polynesian area, barbs began to appear on fish-hooks and pendants to
replace the moa-bone necklaces popular among the Archaic
people. During the Classic pre-European phase of Maori culture
(c. 1650–1800 A.D.) we find evidence for a growing economic
surplus. Instead of using this to build large-scale religious monuments the Maoris spent their increasing wealth on the great game
of war. Evidence of this can be found in the innumerable *pas* or
settlements defended by earthworks and timber palisades, as well
as by the proliferation of weapons. Conflict between rival tribes
headed by their warrior chiefs provided an outlet for aggression,
a means of buttressing self-esteem and a stimulus to production,
while adding glamour and excitement to social life. Only when
the balance was upset by firearms obtained through European
contact did fighting become a scourge leading to the decimation
of the Maori population. Even so, not all was lost. It was through
their prowess as warriors that the Maori were able to retain
sufficient lands to act as a base for the survival and ultimately
revival of the race, enabling it in due course to share in the modern
development of New Zealand.

The more favourable climate of the North Island meant that
Maori culture came to be mainly centred there. In the South
Island the new shapes of adze-blade, fish-hook and personal
ornament came into use, but outside the northern parts subsistence
continued to be won very largely by catching and gathering; and
after the final extinction of the moa this meant a marked concentration on coastal sources. One of the few sources of wealth on the
South Island were the greenstones, the nephrites of Westland and
to a lesser degree the serpentine of Milford Sound, stones which
were irresistibly attractive to the Maori on account of their hardness, their feel and their varying hues. Since the Maori population
was much denser in the north, most of the greenstone found its
way there to form prestige symbols for chiefs and leading figures,
personal ornaments including lobe-shaped ear-pendants and con-

Pacific Islands: early settlement

Marianas	Chalan Piao, Saipan I: midden	C 669	1529 B.C. ±200
New Hebrides	Tana	UCLA 734	420 B.C. ± 90
New Caledonia	Foue Peninsula: midden	M 341	850 B.C. ±350
Fiji	Viti Levu: midden	M 351	50 B.C. ±500
Samoa	Vailele: village	NZ 363	±120
Hawaii	Puu Alii: dune site	GrN 2225	A.D. 290± 60
Marquesas	Ha'atuatua Bay, Nuku Hiva: burial	1 AMNH 43	130 B.C. ±150
	fire lens, house	1 AMNH 48	A.D. 40±180
Easter	Ahu Tepeu: burial	M 732	A.D. 310±250
	Poike: oven	K 502	A.D. 380±100
New Zealand	Wairau, S.I.: oven	Y 204	A.D. 1010±110
	midden	NZ 50	A.D. 1100± 50
	Coramandel Peninsula, N.I.: midden	NZ 358	A.D. 1140± 50

ventionalized human figures (*hei tiki*) to hang round the neck, ceremonial adze-blades and *mere*, weapons used for striking and thrusting but above all for parade. Greenstone was of course only one item in a nexus of interchange by which cultivated plant foods found their way southwards. The fact remains that when Europeans began to colonize New Zealand they found the Maori people concentrated in the zone in which *kumara* was cultivated. This and the warlike character of the Maori explains why during the early stages of British settlement the South Island was the most prosperous part of the new Colony. Conversely, the end of the Maori wars in 1872 signalized a new phase in the history of New Zealand, a phase during which the natural advantages of the North Island began to reassert themselves.

THE NEW WORLD

EARLY PREHISTORY

The first immigrants

By comparison with most of the Old World the Americas were settled quite recently: no certain traces of human occupation have ever been found truly stratified in deposits of Early or Middle Pleistocene age, and it is significant that all hominid remains from the New World are of recent *Homo sapiens sapiens* type.

The earliest immigrants may be assumed to have followed the same route as a number of the larger mammals including reindeer or caribou and bison and mammoth, the two species most keenly sought by the prehistoric hunters. A drop in ocean level of around 40 metres would be sufficient to provide a land bridge across what is now the Bering Sea, and it is known that during certain phases of the Pleistocene, when large masses of water were locked up in extensive ice-sheets, we can think in terms of more than three times this amount. On the other hand, although Alaska was joined to Siberia for much of the Late Pleistocene, men could only have colonized the New World as a whole at times when ice-sheets were sufficiently contracted to leave a gap between the Laurentide ice-sheet centred on Hudson's Bay and that spreading from the Rocky Mountains. According to geologists the way south was blocked by a conjunction of the two ice-sheets during the final phase of the Pleistocene between *c.* 27,000 and 12 or 13,000 years ago.

Radiocarbon dating has made it sufficiently clear that both the Cordilleran region of the north-west and the High Plains to the east of the Rockies were occupied by advanced game hunters within a few centuries of the retreat from the Valders re-advance, the final stage of the Pleistocene Ice Age. Moreover, although, as we shall see, several elements of the Palaeoindian tradition were peculiar to the New World and must be accepted as indigenous developments, a number of generalized characteristics of their stone-working techniques can be matched in the Late-glacial cultures of Siberia and to a lesser degree of Japan, including the manufacture of bifacially flaked leaf-shaped points, punch-struck blades and bladelets and burins.

The immigration as early as the tenth millennium B.C. of bands of hunters equipped with a number of the basic industrial techniques of the Late-glacial Siberians can be accepted as a well-documented hypothesis. Whether the hunters whose projectile-points have so often been found with remains of bison or mammoth dating from the final Pleistocene were in fact the first immigrants is another question. The possibility remains that earlier people with a more primitive technology may have come through the gap during an interstadial phase of relatively genial climate before the formation of the Laurentide–Rocky Mountain ice-barrier. Some have indeed argued that the mere existence of stone industries of primitive appearance in the western states in itself points to this. Yet it is well known that people of relatively advanced technology are capable for certain purposes of producing artifacts of apparently crude appearance. The case needs to be established on the basis of positive evidence. It cannot be said that so far this has been impressive. In too many instances importance is attached to high radiocarbon dates obtained from burnt areas that are termed 'hearths' without convincing evidence that the fires had in fact been lit by men. At others—the famous Santa Rosa Island off the coast of California is a case in point—the artificial character of the artifacts associated with such 'hearths' is in itself suspect. At others, again, there have evidently been stratigraphic anomalies. For instance at Lewisville in Texas one of a number of 'hearths', two of which gave radiocarbon dates of more than 37,000 years, yielded a well-made projectile-point of the type first recognized at Clovis and dated on many occasions to the tenth millennium B.C., and 15·25 metres away, as if to emphasize the context, there occurred a well-made scraper of the same material. Again, when elaborate and extensive excavations were conducted at Tule Springs, Nevada, where 'hearths' dated to more than 23,800 and 28,000 years respectively were claimed to be associated with artifacts, they showed beyond reasonable doubt that the earliest trace of human occupation dated from *c.* 10,500 B.C.

The big-game hunters

The earliest occupants of the New World for which the evidence is abundant and incontrovertible were the Palaeoindian big-game hunters, whose projectiles, presumed to have been spears, were tipped with lanceolate stone heads having shallow flaking on either face. Logically, if these people came from Siberia, one might expect the earliest ones to have used projectiles with leaf-shaped heads pointed at either end like those used by Advanced Palaeolithic man in parts of the Old World. The fact that this form of spearhead is the one with the widest distribution in the New World, extending from the Yukon to the Argentine, certainly argues for a high antiquity.

The most northerly examples are the so-called Cascade points, a leading fossil of the Old Cordilleran culture found on the western slopes of the Rocky Mountains and extending from California to the Yukon, where it is represented by the so-called Kluane complex. Although so far no site of the Cordilleran group has been proved to be earlier than the eighth millennium B.C. the probability is that it represents a substantially earlier tradition. Further south the earliest spread of big-game hunters over much of middle and South America is defined by a similar form of projectile-point, named after the locality of Lerma and occurring over a wide territory from Mexico to the Argentine. In Mexico it has been found in cave deposits in the Sierra de Tamaulipas and among what were evidently butchered skeletons of *Mammuthus*

10. Early hunters in the New World

(*Archidiskodon*) *imperator* in an old lake bed at Santa Isabel Iztapan in the valley of Mexico. Similar points are known in some cases in certainly early contexts from many localities in South America from El Jobo in Venezuela, the Chillon Valley of coastal Peru and Lauricocha in the highlands, as well as from several places in the Argentine, including Ayampitin and the cave of Intihausi. At the same time it is to be noted that the projectile-points from the most southerly of the early sites, Fell's Cave on the Strait of Magellan, where extinct horses and ground sloths were being hunted early in the ninth millennium B.C., were of a distinctive form, lanceolate but having constricted tangs with fish-tail terminations. Points of similar form are known further north in South America from El Inga in highland Ecuador.

Although no find of Cascade or Lerma points has yet been proved to be as old as the earliest big-game hunting cultures on the High Plains east of the Rockies their geographical extent no less than their Old World affinities suggest that this may well be an accident of research. What is in any case worth remarking is that the big-game hunters seem to have occupied almost the whole of the New World as far south as the Magellan Strait within one or two millennia of their initial passage through the gap between the contracting ice-sheets. This in itself is a reminder that exploration of the environment is one of the basic drives of all animals. With his capacity for accumulating and sharing knowledge and the power conferred by his culture for adapting rapidly to new conditions it is hardly surprising that man should have excelled in this as in so many other fields of animal achievement.

The best known and most accurately dated groups of big-game hunters are those who pursued mammoth and bison on the High Plains east of the Rocky Mountains. What may relate to an early phase in this tradition are projectile-points whose basically leaf-shaped form is modified only by constricting one side of the lower end to form a weak shoulder. These were first recognized in the basal level of a cave in the Sandia Mountains of central New Mexico. The age of these points is still under discussion, but the fact that they are restricted to a single state suggests that they are unlikely to have been in use for any great length of time. Of far greater significance are the fluted points thinned along the middle by flakes struck from a concave base, a device apparently peculiar to the New World, though paralleled in polished slate in northeast Asia, and evidently intended to give a more secure attachment to the shaft. Two main finds are known, those named after the localities of Clovis and Folsom respectively, both in New Mexico. The earlier, the Clovis point, stratified at the name-site below Folsom points and several finds dated by radiocarbon to the tenth millennium B.C., was the larger and heavier, was more gently tapered and was fluted for only half the length. By contrast the Folsom point, which dated from the ninth millennium and almost certainly evolved from the Clovis form, was shorter, lighter, fluted almost to the tip and had its maximum width relatively near the obtuse tip. The reduction in size may well have come about through a change in the principal quarry. Clovis points were found with remains of mammoth at the name-site and at many others; eight specimens for instance were found with a single skeleton at Naco in Arizona and a single one with a still articulated skeleton at Dent in Colorado. On the other hand Folsom points have consistently been found with remains of bison. This was so at the name-site; at Blackwater Draw in New Mexico, where Clovis points were found in an underlying layer alongside remains of mammoth; at Brewster, Wyoming; at Lubbock, Texas; and at Lindenmeier in Colorado. The possibility suggests itself that the big-game hunters went first for mammoth, only transferring to bison when the former became scarce. Most of the sites first explored were kill-sites and it is hardly surprising that the artifacts should have comprised first and foremost projectile-points. Yet as we have already seen the Clovis site yielded a number of fine punch-struck blades and careful excavation of a site like Lindenmeier shows that the big-game hunters made a variety of scrapers for preparing skins, as well as knives and spokeshaves; it is further interesting in view of their ultimate origins in the Advanced Palaeolithic of Siberia that they made a variety of bone tools, including spokeshaves and eyed needles, as well as perforated stone beads and bone discs with incisions round the rim.

That the High Plains should have been an early focus of big-game-hunting culture is only what might have been expected in view of their position immediately south of the gap between the Rocky Mountains and Laurentide ice-sheets; moreover the pluvial conditions which must have existed at the end of the Pleistocene would have endowed the region with lakes and ponds and made it extremely attractive to herbivorous animals. On the other hand there is plenty of evidence that the big-game hunters rapidly spread far and wide. We have already seen how much of South America was occupied by hunters who tipped their spears with leaf-shaped blades. Similarly, the makers of fluted points spread northward as the ice-sheets contracted into Alberta and Saskatchewan and again and more importantly eastwards as far as North Carolina and Virginia in the south and Massachusetts, northern Vermont and even Nova Scotia in the north.

Over much of the territory first opened up at the close of the Pleistocene the big-game hunters had to adjust to the ecological changes that accompanied the onset and culmination of Neo-thermal climate. On the one hand in the Desert Basin, as it became, of Nevada and parts of California and other neighbouring states, they had to adjust to increasingly arid conditions; whereas in the east the spread of forest meant that specialized hunting had to give place to the more generalized food-quest that underlay the Archaic culture of the region. It was only on the High Plains themselves, the original focus of the big-game hunting economy in the New World south of the ice-sheet, that bison hunting continued to form the basis of existence for some thousands of years down to the end of the fifth millennium B.C. During this time experiments were made with many different kinds of spearhead to which modern collectors have given a bewildering variety of names. On the one hand there were forms (Midland, Plainview, Meserve, Milnesand) that retained the outline without the fluting of the Clovis and Folsom points; and on the other elongated forms, often with fine parallel flaking and commonly having tanged bases (Agate, Scotsbluff, Eden)—forms that in some cases spread and produced local varieties in more northerly territories like Alberta. Among the implements accompanying such tanged points were asymmetric tanged knives known after the locality of Cody in Wyoming, but more diagnostic in some respects were the grinding stones indicative of the growing importance of vegetable food that led ultimately to the incorporation of the High Plains themselves within the Archaic culture.

Desert culture of the Great Basin

In the Great Basin west of the Rockies the end of the Pleistocene was followed by conditions of increasing aridity. Here it was necessary to search for food, rather than pursue the specialized hunting of particular kinds of big game. Where opportunity offered, indeed, the Desert culture people killed their bison, antelope or mountain sheep, but often they had to be content with lesser game, carnivores like desert fox, bobcat, coyote or skunk or rodents such as desert wood-rat, bushy tail rat, gopher or kangaroo rat. In catching these and any other animals they could get, they used nets, snares and traps as well as darts tipped with chipped heads (lanceolate or stemmed and notched, sometimes with indented base) and propelled by wooden atlatls or throwers. Further, considerable reliance was placed on plant food, particularly seeds and rhizomes, the former of which seem to have been parched, abraded on grinding-stones and eaten as a kind of mush or gruel. The necessity to exploit every source of wild food in an inhospitable land meant that the Desert people must have lived in small groups and moved over considerable territories in the course of a year. Fortunately they were in the habit of sheltering at some periods in caves and under rock-shelters and the exploration of some of these—notably Danger Cave, Utah; Roaring Springs and Fort Rock Caves, Oregon; Leonard Shelter near Lovelock and Gypsum Cave, Nevada; and Ventana Cave, Arizona—has given us a remarkably complete picture of their equipment. The relatively small size of the shelters and the intermittent character of their occupation confirm the impression that they lived in small, nomadic groups. Their equipment was easily carried; they used baskets—at first twined, later supplemented by coiled—and a variety of nets, cordage and matting; their digging-sticks, fire-drills, darts and atlatls were easily carried; and even their milling-stones were portable. A depressing feature of their way of life is that the food-quest can have left them but little leisure and it is hardly surprising to find no evidence for decorative art—no sign of contrasting colours in their basket-work, no fringes to their leather garments and but few signs of personal ornaments. By the same token, though the Desert culture appeared with most of its basic traits already by around 7000 B.C., there were few signs of progress over much of the territory; the adjustment to an unfavourable environment once made, there was small inducement to change. Indeed, a similar way of life has lasted down to our own day in parts of California.

Archaic culture of eastern North America

By contrast with the Great Basin much of eastern North America witnessed a marked increase in forests and this helped to promote fishing, the gathering of shell-fish and the collecting of plants since it entailed the reduction of grazing for herbivorous animals. The Archaic culture began about the same time as the Neo-thermal climate and lasted down to the end of the second millennium B.C. The early stages, particularly well displayed in the sections at Modoc rock-shelter, southern Illinois, and at Graham Cave, central Missouri, showed a tendency for plant-gathering, represented by grinding-stones, to grow in time at the expense of hunting, marked by projectile-points. In many respects the Archaic resembles in the most general terms the Mesolithic of northern Europe. Specific features which support this European analogy include among others: the domestication of the dog, the absence of pottery, the utilization of antler and bone as materials for such things as harpoon-heads, the heads of fish-spears and fish-hooks, and in the later stages the polishing of stone for such purposes as axes, spear-thrower weights, bowls and plummets. A feature of the middle Archaic (5th–2nd millennium B.C.) which is surprising at first is the considerable use of copper for tools and weapons rather than ornaments; but the industry was of course based on the exploitation of outcrops of native metal in the southern region of Lake Superior and of detached fragments carried by glacial action over wide areas of Wisconsin, Minnesota and neighbouring states. It implied no knowledge of metallurgy, any more than did a similar utilization of native copper in more recent times by the Indians of the Copper River district of Alaska or by the Eskimo and Indians of the Coppermine River of northern Canada: as we are told by Samuel Hearne, who travelled in the latter area between 1769 and 1772, 'with the help of a fire and two stones, the Indians could beat a piece of copper into any shape they wished'. From such native copper the Indians of the Archaic period beat out awls, tanged knives, projectile heads with wrapped over sockets and broad spud blades similarly wrapped over at either side to grip the wooden handle. The products of this industry, though concentrated more densely in the area of production, were distributed by trade to the Laurentian area, New England and New York and as far south as the shell-heaps of the middle South. There is indeed plenty of other evidence for widespread trade in objects made of exotic materials among the Archaic people: for example, bowls of Appalachian steatite were traded as far as Florida and the lower Mississippi and objects made of shell were extensively traded from the south-east. The dead were cremated or buried flexed or seated and in either event might be scattered over with red ochre. Antler head-dresses of copper recall ones made from natural antler in the early Mesolithic of northern Europe.

HIGHER CIVILIZATION IN THE NEW WORLD

When the Spaniards first entered the New World they found two main zones of higher civilization, one in Mesoamerica, comprising the Aztecs and, in a state of some decline, the Maya, the other that of the Incas on the highlands of Peru. In between they encountered in Colombia and Ecuador a territory which had absorbed certain elements of civilization from either direction, but which did not itself attain either literacy or such a high degree of political organization. Many of the first scholars to interest themselves in the material traces of these civilizations were disposed, being European, to interpret them as the outcome of inspiration from the Old World. Leaving aside those who were mesmerized by the supposed journeys of the Egyptian Children of the Sun, sober scholars looked with more discrimination across the Pacific to south-east Asia and even to China for sources of these civilizations, for which they could see no convincing native origin. Against this, American scholars have by and large maintained that the higher cultures of the New World represented no more than intensifications of the indigenous American Indian cultures with which they shared a basically common style; that though more elaborate they were nevertheless subject to many of the same basic limitations *vis-à-vis* the Old World as were the lowlier ones—for example in the lack of the plough and wheel; and above all that they were grounded on the cultivation of distinctively New World crops. This does not exclude the possibility of early trans-Pacific contacts. For instance some authorities have remarked on close analogies between early pottery from Valdivia on the coast of Ecuador and Japanese Jomon wares; and others have doubted whether such a specialized process as tie-dying, by which patterns were produced on textiles by folding the material and tying it so as to prevent parts from coming into contact with the dye, can have been invented independently in pre-Incan Peru and Indonesia. On the other hand modern archaeology allows one to view such contacts, if indeed they existed, in perspective. By and large there can no longer be any doubt that the higher civilizations of the Americas were indigenous growths and that they were the outcome of progressive developments over many thousands of years.

The beginnings of food-production

The earliest civilizations of the New as of the Old World rested on the comparative security of domesticated sources of food-supply. In both, the process of domestication was the outcome of a lengthy and indeed hardly perceptible process and was far indeed from being a dramatic or sudden innovation. The cultivators of the New World suffered the disadvantage that they had no potentially domesticable animals comparable in utility as sources of food to sheep, goat, cattle or swine or as valuable as oxen and horses for traction; and the llama and alpaca when they were domesticated were important mainly for their hair. On the other hand, although they were compelled to cultivate them by hand even in the final stages of New World civilization, the Amerindians had an exceptionally large number of plants capable of domestication, several of which had great potential as sources of food.

The first point to emphasize about the food crops of America is that botanically they were distinct from those which supported the civilizations of the Old World. This, and the fact that both Mesoamerica and Peru were separated from the Asiatic centres by the Pacific Ocean or alternatively by vast tracts of north-west America and north-east Siberia ecologically beyond the possibility of farming under primitive conditions, makes it plain that farming, like the civilizations which it made possible, was the product of indigenous development. Another point, and one which finds some parallel in the Old World, is that domestication was a process that developed not at any one point or in relation to any one plant but over a wide territory and in relation to a variety of plants.

As to who was responsible for the development of farming in the New World, it must be evident that this can hardly have been the specialized big-game hunters whose projectile-points have left such widespread trails in prehistory. It must have occurred rather among people whose food-quest included the collection on an important scale of wild plants. As we have already seen in the case of the desert-dwellers of the Great Basin, it was possible for such a people to continue to crop wild plants for thousands of years without taking any perceptible step towards their domestication. On the other hand among other groups living initially at a comparable level a more dynamic relationship developed, one that led over some period of time to progressively more complete domestication and ultimately in some cases to the eliciting of new and much more productive varieties. This occurred in two main regions, certain parts of Mesoamerica, including the Tehuacàn valley, the Sierra Madre and the Sierra de Tamaulipas in northeast Mexico, and the valley of Mexico, and on the other hand the coast and highlands of Peru.

Important though it is to remember that many other plants were significant sources of food and raw materials there can be no doubt that maize was the most important single food-plant of the Amerindians. Its indigenous character has been shown by the fossil pollen recovered from deposits under Mexico City dating from long before the first men entered the New World. Study of the origins of its cultivation was hindered by the fact that no wild prototype continued to exist in the living state due to genetic drowning by cultivated forms. The great advances of recent years have been due to the convergence of a number of research interests: geneticists worked out on theoretical grounds the form of the hypothetical prototype; archaeologists digging in the Tehuacán valley in the central highlands of Mexico brought to light successive series of carbonized maize heads that became progressively smaller at the lower levels until they approximated to the predicted prototype; and physicists applying the technique of radiocarbon analysis have been able to date successive phases in the emergence of modern forms. The result is one of the most complete pictures we have of progressive advances in the domestication and intelligent breeding over thousands of years of a single food-plant. In the Tehuacán valley—and it may be emphasized again that there is no reason to think that this was the only or necessarily the first centre in Mesoamerica where maize was being gathered systematically at least as far back as 5200 B.C.—the first signs of domestication appeared already around 3400 B.C., yet it is significant that for more than another thousand years maize was only one of a number of plants under domestication—others including beans, gourds and squash—and that the inhabitants of the valley still continued to occupy caves and open camps and to depend substantially on the gathering of wild plants and on hunting. It was only gradually in the course of centuries that breeding elicited varieties sufficiently productive to yield a supply of food adequate for the formation of settled village communities, in which by the middle of the second millennium B.C. pottery began to be made. Finally, in the first millennium B.C. came the first appearance of irrigation by which the production of food was still further intensified, making possible the construction of the monumental ceremonial centres that appeared at this time.

As regards the Peruvian focus, it is fortunate that the arid climate of the northern coast has allowed exceptionally complete survival of organic materials, including invaluable evidence about the sources of food. One of the best-explored sites is a midden at Huaco Prieta in the Chicama Valley. Here traces have been found of subterranean one-roomed dwellings roofed by whalebones or timber beams. Between about 2500 and 1200 B.C. the inhabitants depended to an important degree on sea-food; they gathered molluscs, caught fish in seine nets weighted by stone sinkers and supported by gourd floats, and hunted porpoises. On the other hand they supplemented their diet to a significant extent by vegetable food. Investigation has shown that in addition to gathering wild roots, tubers and fruits they were already cultivating beans, gourds and squash, but it is interesting to note that maize was not included among their food plants. This is important because it brings out the point already made that the domestication of plants occurred gradually over a wide front and shows that maize was not everywhere among the first domesticates; indeed the indications are that maize when it did reach Peru came from Mesoamerica at the same time as Mexican and specifically

Olmec stylistic influences affected decorative art. In addition to domesticating food plants the people of the Chicama valley cultivated cotton, from the fibres of which they made a variety of bags, nets and fabrics. Like the desert people of the Great Basin they managed well enough without pottery and made great use of baskets and mats which they formed by the twining technique.

The rise of Mesoamerican civilization

The Classic civilizations which arose on the basis of food production both in Mesoamerica and on the highlands of Peru were preceded by Formative or Preclassic phases in the course of which their distinctive patterns progressively emerged. In the case of Mesoamerica the Early Formative stage can best be illustrated by the first substantial villages based on full-time maize cultivation to appear in the Tehuacán valley during the Ajalpán phase around the middle of the second millennium B.C. The earliest evidence for ceremonial sites did not appear until the Middle Formative. The most striking centre to be investigated is that which succeeded an Early Formative village at La Venta near the southern shore of the Gulf of Mexico. Here, dating from c. 800–400 B.C., we have a great rectangular plaza or court with a vast pyramidal earth mound at one end, long low mounds on either side and at the opposite end a complex of round and smaller rectangular structures, a very prototype of the ceremonial centres which served as symbols of the religious unity of communities over extensive territories. Especially worthy of note at La Venta were stone stelae up to 51 metric tons in weight carved in the so-called Olmec style which featured human beings combining a curiously infantile expression with a jaguar-like snarl of varying intensity. Another remarkable aspect of this site was the discovery in pits of dedicatory caches of jade and serpentine blocks, as well as axes, figurines and ornaments of these extremely hard materials drawn from distances of between 160 and 560 kilometres, some indication of the extent of territory served by the centre.

Table of main stages of Mesoamerican civilization

Periods	Dates	Cultures	Sites
Postclassic	A.D. 900–1520	Aztec	Tenochtitlán
		Toltec	Tula
Classic	A.D. 300–900	Maya	Tikal, Capán, Uaxactún
Late Formative	300 B.C.–A.D. 300	Teotihuacán	Teotihuacán I–II
Middle Formative	1000–300 B.C.	Olmec	La Venta
Early Formative	?–1000 B.C.	Ajalpán	Tehuacán

The Late Formative period witnessed the beginnings of the great Classic civilization of the valley of Mexico based on the ceremonial centre and political capital of Teotihuacán. The initial phases of this development have been revealed on the northern edge of the capital at the site of Ostoyahualco, where traces have been uncovered not only of ceremonial platform mounds, but even more significantly of an extensive but close-packed residential area.

Teotihuacán

During the full Classic period, indeed, one of the main contrasts between the civilizations of the valley of Mexico and of the Maya territories of east Mexico, Guatemala and British Honduras is that it was only in the former that the ceremonial centres were also the seats of dense urban populations; elsewhere in both the Highland and Lowland Maya territories the people lived scattered over the land in small village communities made up of thatched huts. The ruins of the city of Teotihuacán cover more than 18 square kilometres (7 square miles) including the ceremonial as well as the residential area. Ceremonial structures included one of the largest known from early America, the Pyramid of the Sun built in four steps rising on a base 210 metres square to a flat top some 64 metres high. At the northern end of the ceremonial avenue from which steps gave access to the top of the Sun Pyramid was a smaller pyramid perhaps dedicated to the Moon and south of the Sun Pyramid a rectangular court enclosing a temple and surrounded by palace buildings. Spreading out from the central area were thousands of domestic structures including some large ones having numerous rooms set round a sunken plaza, often provided with an altar. Estimates for the population living at Teotihuacán vary very greatly from something like ten thousand to a hundred thousand, due to the difficulty of knowing how much of the site was occupied at any one time. During the Early Classic period it not only formed the political as well as the religious centre of the valley of Mexico, but influenced the style of structures over a much wider zone of Mesoamerica. When the city was destroyed around A.D. 600 it was most probably at the hands of comparative barbarians from the north whose impact was to make itself felt on two more occasions of great significance before the Spanish Conquest.

Maya

Meanwhile the Maya civilization was developing, most probably first of all in the Lowland area around the highly important centres of Tikal and Uaxactún. The ceremonial centres of the Maya conformed to the basic Mesoamerican pattern, already described. Although still having an earth or rock fill, the pyramids, which rose to heights of 60 metres or more, were now in the important centres faced with dressed masonry blocks set in mortar. The buildings set on the tops of the pyramids and to which access was gained by flights of external steps were primitive in the sense that in relation to their bulk their interiors were small and dark; the only method of vaulting known to the architects was that of corbelling by oversailing courses, a technique employed by some of the megalith builders of the Old World. Yet the loftiness achieved by placing them on acutely stepped pyramids, together with their carved and stucco-sculptured ornamentation and elaborate roof-crests, must have given them an over-powering impressiveness to a population accustomed to living in small villages of humble dwellings in forest clearings. To modern observers the most striking thing about them is that they were built by people whose technology was based on stone tools, among whom copper tools only began to be imported in Late Classic times.

The explanation for the apparent discrepancy between archi-tectural scale and technical means lies, as it does in the case of Avebury, Carnac and Stonehenge, or for that matter the great medieval cathedrals of Europe, in the driving force of religion. The Maya were obsessed by the need to propitiate each of their plenitude of gods at the correct moment. They were also pre-occupied by the need to transact business of whatever description at the most auspicious time. For religious purposes they used a sacred year or tzolkin made up of thirteen twenty-day units. Since each day had its name and hieroglyph and since days were also numbered in series of thirteen, it was possible to record the precise day of the religious year on monuments. Moreover by combining religious with secular years (*haab*) of 365 days, they arrived at the concept of the calendar round of 18,980 days, in the course of which precisely 73 sacred and 52 secular years would pass. If for no other reason than that it came to be believed that the world was likely to end at the conclusion of a calendar round, the event was looked forward to with some dread and when safely passed was followed by rejoicing. The Maya were well aware that the solar year was in fact rather longer than 365 days and developed a method of correcting the discrepancy between solar and calendrical years by calculating with surprising accuracy the length of the solar year: the Maya value of 365·2420 days was in fact closer to the modern astronomical value (365·2422) than was the corrected Gregorian calendar (365·2425). They also derived an accurate lunar calendar, and calculated the intervals between eclipses of sun and moon. They were also interested in

Venus and arrived at an extremely accurate value (584 as compared with the scientifically observed 583·92 days) for the synodi-
cal revolution of the planet Venus; they were fully aware that
in approximate terms 5 Venus years = 8 solar years. There is
little doubt that the priests owed much of their power to their
control of the calendar and their ability to predict astronomical
events that might otherwise have caused some consternation. One
of their most important means of taking observations was to use
the lines of sight to distant points on the horizon obtained from
the tops of their temples. The ceremonial centres were themselves
laid out with astronomy in mind. For example the temple at
Uaxactún was laid out in such a way that an observer standing on
the steps of the opposite pyramid would see the Sun rise at the
equinox exactly over the centre of the middle temple and at
solstices over the north front corner of the north and the south
front corner of the south temple. In working out the results of
their astronomical observations and for calculating the grotesquely
long periods of time based on *Katuns* of 14,000 days, by which
they sought to assuage their anxieties about the continuity of
time, the priests employed the concept zero and used a vigesimal
system of numeration. Of no less importance for the control of
the calendar and the regulation of religious observance was the
system of hieroglyphs devised by the Maya, and so far as is known
used for no other purpose.

It is a striking fact that within less than a hundred years the
ceremonial centres passed into decline and dissolution. Many
reasons have been advanced for this, including over-rapid increase
of population bearing on a primitive basis of food-production,
adverse ecological changes resulting from excessive slash and
burn clearance, soil-exhaustion, the spread of epidemic diseases
and the dislocation of society through military incursions from
central Mexico. Whatever the cause the old theocratic civilization
in large measure broke down and there was nothing for the Spanish
conquerors to overcome but the dispersed village communities

which the old centres were designed to serve and on whose labours they ultimately rested.

Postclassic of Mesoamerica: Toltec and Aztec

During the Postclassic period the leading role in Mesoamerica was taken by the inhabitants of central Mexico. Here the abandonment or destruction of many ceremonial centres was linked with the incursion of Chichimecs, or northern barbarian tribes driven or attracted south by crop failure, population pressure or the prospect of easy loot. As so often happened in other parts of the world, the barbarians having triumphed were themselves absorbed by the traditional culture. The first group to reach prominence were the Toltecs, who built their most important ceremonial centre at Tula in the tenth century A.D. and ultimately grew to be a powerful force in Mesoamerica as a whole. Yet by c. A.D. 1160 the incursion of another wave of semi-civilized tribes from the north overwhelmed Tula and initiated another period of turmoil. Out of this the Aztecs emerged as victors. By the end of the first quarter of the fifteenth century they had made themselves undisputed masters of central Mexico. The growth of their power and authority was symbolized by the great city of Tenochtitlan, at present buried under the streets of Mexico City, but originally situated on an island in Lake Texcoco to whose shores it was linked by numerous causeways. From this base they entered on a career of warfare and imperialism. Under the reign of Ahuitzotlo (1486–1502) they expanded their empire to the shores of the Pacific and the Gulf of Mexico and from the valley of Mexico in the north to Guatemala in the south. As a people who emerged and attained success by defeating, incorporating and dominating their neighbours, the Aztecs were so to say self-selected for fierceness and cruelty. Their social structure was strongly hierarchical and was crowned by a semi-divine king. They worshipped a god Huitzilopochtli whose inordinate desire for human sacrifice could most conveniently be met by prisoners taken in war. They were a scourge to their weaker neighbours, Huaxtecs, Mixtecs, Zapotecs and the like. Ironically it was the authoritarian structure of their society that was their undoing when challenged by the Spaniards. Excessive veneration for their ruler Montezuma II made them incredulous of his seizure by Hernando Cortes and hatred of their Aztec overlords prevented the subject peoples of Mexico from rallying against the invader. Thus it was that Hernando and his followers admittedly better armed were able within the space of two or three years (1519–21) to overthrow a militaristic empire in the full pride of its power.

Early civilization in Peru

The civilization which developed in Peru was distinct from that of Mesoamerica although, as might be expected, it shared many broad features. As we have seen a good deal has been learned about the beginnings of plant cultivation especially on the Peruvian coast. Much less is known about the Formative stage in which a distinctively Peruvian civilization first developed. Recent discoveries at Haldas and Kotosh of elaborate temple structures dated by radiocarbon to the earlier half of the second millennium B.C. suggest that civilization may have begun to take shape in some parts of Peru some hundreds of years before it did in any part of Mesoamerica. If these early dates are confirmed they would drive home the point that maize was by no means the only cultivated plant of importance in the New World, since on present showing it did not contribute significantly to subsistence in Peru before the ninth century B.C., when a Mesoamerican strain was apparently introduced and appropriated by the cultivators of the Chavin culture. Other Mesoamerican elements to appear in this culture were stepped pyramids, cranial deformation, stirrup-spouted jars and elements of the Olmec style.

It has long been accepted that the Classic period in Peru, exemplified on the coast by the Mochica culture in the north and the Nazca in the south and in the southern highlands at such sites as Tiahuanaco and Pucara, opened about the same time as the Christian era, that is some three hundred years before a comparable stage in Mesoamerica. Moreover, although the ancient Peruvians never developed either hieroglyphic writing or an elaborate calendar, their technology was in some respects more advanced. For instance, whereas the Mesoamericans remained in the Stone Age, the Peruvians developed metallurgy on a considerable scale, working gold, silver, copper and their alloys and making from them not only ornaments and weapons, but in the case of copper even the blades of digging-sticks. They made excellent polychrome pottery. Their textiles, both of cotton and wool, were outstanding. Many different products, including tapestry, brocades and gauzes, were produced to high standards of fineness. This was due in part to the high standard of selection and spinning of the actual fibres and in part to exceptional dexterity in weaving for which belt looms were employed, but in which the hands themselves played the main role. The effect was heightened by the use of vegetable dyes, indigo, red and yellow to orange-brown. In general the impression of richness is enhanced by a marked regional differentiation in the decorative arts.

The immediate Postclassic age was marked by the expansion of highland and specifically Tiahuanaco influence to the coastal zone. For some centuries following this the population of the coast began to concentrate in cities. These were organized into three states, of which Chimú in the north, extending from Timbeg to the region of Lima in the south, was the largest and most powerful. The capital city, Chan-chan, covered an area of approximately 29 square kilometres (11 square miles) and comprised ten or more rectangular enclosures averaging some 400 × 200 metres, each defended by walls up to 12 metres high. Concentrations of population on this scale were made possible by combining irrigation schemes previously restricted to individual valleys, and it may well have been at this time that roads were first constructed up and down the coast.

The Incas

On the other hand in the highlands broken topography and multiple sources of water made for the development of many small states. Only one of these, the Incas of the Cuzco valley, managed by their aggressiveness and superior powers of organization to rise to dominance and then only during the century immediately before the arrival of the Spaniards. Like the Aztecs, the Incas established and enlarged their empire with great rapidity only to be cut down in full career by the Spanish conquerors. One of the reasons for their success was the exceptional ability of their rulers. Between c. 1438 and 1460 Pachacuti conquered most of the Peruvian highlands. Under his son Topa Inca (1471–93) the Incas conquered most of Ecuador, as well as the state of Chimú and later the south coastal zone of Peru, the highlands of Bolivia, northern Argentine and Chile north of the Maule river. Over this considerable empire, rounded off under Huayna Capac (1493–1527) by the rest of Ecuador, a divine ruler presided, helped by a hereditary nobility related to him by blood, by a priestly hierarchy and by an army of appointed officials, who between them controlled every aspect of the lives of the hapless people. The Incan state, indeed, with its minute regulation of economic and social life, forecast some of the worst features of modern collectivist societies: a completely regulated economy was associated with a relentless system of taxation exacted in the form of labour for agricultural works, mining, road-making and the army; marriages were arranged by appointed officials; and conquered populations were forcibly transferred to distant provinces. The empire was knit together on a material plane by an extensive system of narrow but well-built roads embracing the sometimes precipitous highlands as well as the easier coastal regions, a system equipped at intervals with rest- and store-houses and traversed by llamas and human runners; and on a spiritual one by means of a religious system administered by a priestly hierarchy. Worship of a lord of creation and of the heavenly bodies was carried on in stone temples decked with gold. Further, the religion of the day called for sacrifices, on normal occasions of such things as llamas and maize beer, but at moments of crisis, such as the illness or death of the ruler, of the lives of women and children. Yet the empire, though by far the most extensive and the best organized in the New World, was much too weak to withstand the impact of a small but resolute body of Spanish adventurers. By comparison with that of sixteenth-century Europe, the technology of the Incan civilization was miserably defective: ahead of the rest of the New World in the ability to make bronze tools and weapons, its lack of iron and gunpowder was yet decisive; again, the Incas, though possessing a decimal system of numeration, lacked any form of writing; and there were inherent weaknesses in its constitution which made the state exceptionally vulnerable on the death of a ruler—power was excessively centralized in the person of the Emperor but, the Emperor having many wives, the succession, though passing to a son, was not fixed on any particular one. As ill luck would have it the Spaniards under the leadership of Pizarro reached the country during precisely such a crisis of succession: Atahuallpa had no sooner staged a successful revolt against his half-brother, the new emperor Huascar, than he was seized by the Spanish conqueror (1532). The Incan Empire fell at the height of its vigour and glory, only local resistance surviving to remind the conquerors of their victory.

MARGINAL CULTURES

Basket-maker and Pueblo cultures of the North American south-west

Beyond the comparatively restricted zone of indigenous higher civilization in the Americas there were vast tracts over which the intruding white man encountered a varied but everywhere less advanced level of culture; indeed, there were only two regions north of Mesoamerica in which maize cultivation was practised during Pre-Columban times, namely the south-west and the east. The most clearly defined and vital focus of culture in the south-west was centred on the present-day junction of the four states of Utah, Colorado, Arizona and New Mexico. Here, in the centuries around the beginning of the Christian era, there developed from a Desert culture basis a type of settled economy that has managed to retain its essential pattern down to the present day. Within this area ethnologists distinguish three main cultures, exploiting rather different environments, laying a different emphasis on various aspects of the quest for food and displaying individual styles: at the juncture of the four states the Anasazi people, who for descriptive purposes we shall take as typical, occupied a predominantly plateau region (1200–2100 metres); by contrast, the Hohokam people to the south-west were desert-dwellers, whose economy depended to an important degree on irrigated maize-cultivation; and to the south-east the Mogollon-Mimbres people, occupying a more mountainous territory with forest and scrub, laid a greater emphasis on plant-gathering.

The Anasazi people emerged, probably in the second century A.D., from a generalized Desert culture background. They depended for food on maize, which they cultivated by digging-sticks and ground on saddle-querns, and on pumpkins, as well as on gathering wild seeds and hunting mainly small game, in which they used spears armed with stemmed and notched flint heads and propelled by atlatls. They grew tobacco which they smoked in tubular pipes. They had no domestic animals other than dogs. Although practising agriculture, the earliest Anasazi people relied for containers on bags made from vegetable fibres and on twined and coiled baskets, for which reason they are often referred to as Basket-Makers (second century A.D.–A.D. 500). They buried their dead in caves, wrapped in skin blankets and cloaks and provided with plaited sandals and with objects used in daily life. They lived in small hamlets, commonly of two or three houses, which were rounded in plan, had floors sunk below ground-level, and were provided with storage-pits for food. During the thousand years that ensued before the first intrusion of the Spaniards, the basic pattern of the Anasazi culture persisted, though subject to a number of important modifications. The so-called Modified Culture Stage (A.D. 500–700) was marked by the introduction of bean cultivation and turkey-keeping, by the substitution of the bow and arrow for the spear and atlatl, by the adoption of potting, at first moulded in baskets, later modelled by hand, by the aggregation of dwellings to form villages and by the construction of *Kivas*, the men's club-houses or ceremonial centres that played a leading part in later phases of the culture. The main trend in the Pueblo stages of the Anasazi culture (Pueblo I, 700–900; II, 900–1050; III, 1050–1300) was a progressive enlargement in the size of settlements, culminating in great cliff-house settlements and hill-top towns, compact masses of up to a thousand rooms of well-built masonry from one to four stories high. During the span of Pueblo IV (1300–1700), while the Indians were still limited by a Stone Age technology, the Spaniards appeared for the first time in New Mexico (1540) and by the end of the period European influence had spread over the whole region. Yet, although no longer free to move their settlements, the Pueblo V Indians of the present day still retain a considerable control over their affairs and the painted pottery they sell to motorists carries on recognizably an ancient tradition.

Woodland culture

Over a large part of the eastern area the Archaic was transformed into the Woodland stage, mainly during the broad period 500 B.C.– A.D. 500, under impulses from two main directions. From the north came pottery-making and mound-building, the two most prominent traits in the purely archaeological record, but the practice of maize-cultivation, which doubtless helped to sustain the elaboration of mortuary and ceremonial practices with their attendant monuments so characteristic of the Woodland stage, must have come from the south-west—most probably from Mexico. Other innovations introduced from outside included tobacco-smoking in tubular pipes and weaving. Two distinct intensifications have been noted: the Adena, centred on south Ohio, south-east Indiana, north Kentucky, north-west West Virginia and south-east Pennsylvania; and the Hopewell, which seems to have appeared somewhat later and to have been centred on the south Ohio, Illinois and Mississippi area, with extensions down to Louisiana and Florida and across from Oklahoma to New York. In both cultures the burial mounds and associated monuments testify to a pronounced degree of social stratification. Thus, whereas the ordinary Adena individual was cremated without much ado, people of higher status were given an elaborate form of burial that took quite a long time to reach completion. First the dead man was placed in a log tomb erected on the floor of his house, together with suitable grave-goods and the corpses of other people, probably retainers slaughtered for the purpose. After a while their bones were disinterred, painted and placed once again in the tomb which was now heaped over by a small mound. Finally a gigantic mound up to 21 metres high was erected to cover both the grave and the remains of the house.

Middle Mississippi culture

A final step in the development of the eastern tradition occurred somewhere around A.D. 1000 with the emergence of the Middle Mississippi culture. Centred on a track from north-central Georgia through north Alabama and Mississippi to west Tennessee, Kentucky, south Illinois and south-east Missouri, it radiated influence over a much wider area. Even so, it had not everywhere brought Woodland cultures to an end at the time of European contact: when De Soto traversed the south-east in the middle of the seventeenth century he encountered Indians with a Middle Mississippi culture, but the English colonists of Virginia and the Carolinas found the Algonquin and Siouan peoples still preserving their Woodland heritage. The Middle Mississippi culture was not marked by technical innovations of any note, but rather by an intensification of the ceremonial aspect of social life. The larger village centres were built round plazas or squares and were marked by rectangular temple mounds, frequently built in tiers as though several times reconstructed to a greater height. One of the largest—at East St Louis in Illinois—covered an area of no less than 6·5 hectares (16 acres), was 329 metres long, 217 metres broad and around 30 metres tall. Although the temples themselves were only enlarged versions of the ordinary domestic buildings, made of timber, lath and plaster and provided with a gabled roof, the whole arrangement recalls that found on a more elaborate scale in Mesoamerica. Several new art motifs executed in clay, carved stone, shell and sheet copper—winged snakes, dancing bird-men with speech-scrolls and human skulls—point in the same direction, even if it is only fair to state that no precise source has been detected. Probably we should think in terms of inspiration, perhaps through a very few individuals, rather than of any movement of ethnic significance; indeed, as we have emphasized in this section, there was a very real continuity in the cultural history of the eastern United States from Archaic and even Palaeoindian times up to the moment of European penetration.

Hunting, fishing and gathering communities

Over the rest of North America, as well as over the inhospitable regions of the extreme south, communities subsisting exclusively on hunting, fishing and gathering prevailed down to modern times and in some instances still survive. Subject to this limitation, there was scope for considerable variation according to ecological conditions and to the nature of the response made by different societies. Thus among the Indians of central and southern California a pattern of subsistence formed at latest in the Anathermal period in the sphere of the Desert culture persisted throughout the prehistoric period well into the nineteenth century. A leading part was played by wild seeds, among which the acorn was of predominating importance, and these were prepared by grinding-stones, supplemented in due course by pestles reminiscent of those used so much earlier by the Natufians of Mount Carmel. That hunting still had a certain role is shown by the occurrence at each stage of chipped flint spearheads, at first leaf-shaped or squared at one end, and later stemmed, and by the introduction towards the end of the prehistoric period of the bow. On the coast fishing and the gathering of shell-fish were often leading sources of food. The prehistoric Californians depended throughout on flint and stone and on such materials as antler and bone from which they made fish-hooks and barbed spearheads. Pottery was strictly local in occurrence and well-twined and coiled baskets served for containing food and liquid, as well as cooking.

Coastal culture of the north-west

The aboriginal culture of the north-west coastal region was first brought into effective contact with European civilization at the time of Captain Cook's visit in 1778 and has survived, though with modifications, down to the present day. To judge from the small amount of material excavated, no change of note seems to have occurred in the equipment of the coastal Indians of British Columbia during the last five or six hundred years. Subsistence was based on exploitation of the resources of rivers and the sea: sea-fish and sea-mammals, like whales, seals, sea-lions and sea-otters, were significant sources of food, but it was the plentiful harvest of salmon, easily caught on their seasonal runs upstream, that made possible the elaboration of culture exemplified for instance by the historical Nootka and Kwatuitl. Although they undertook some seasonal movements in the quest for food, the assured supply of salmon made it possible to occupy permanent villages and live in comparatively large communities. Their villages might comprise upwards of thirty houses. These were built on massive timber frames with shells of wooden planking and might be as large as 159 metres long and 18 metres broad, providing accommodation for more than 100 people. The material culture included some elements, like twined basketry containers, derived ultimately from the ancient Desert culture, but many items of specialized coastal equipment show significant agreements with analogous ones from the Aleut and Eskimo areas. On the other hand the social system was highly complex: society was organized on a hierarchical principle with noble or chiefly families, commoners and slaves; and surplus wealth was dissipated in ceremonial feasting and competitive display.

Denbigh and Dorset cultures of the Arctic

The Arctic territories of North America seem to have been settled mainly by successive migrations from west to east, movements that stemmed ultimately from Siberia, and which represent no doubt only the latest of a series, the earliest of which brought the first men into the New World. Few certain traces of the earliest migrations have yet been recognized in Alaska, and the oldest assemblage of material yet recovered there, that from the Denbigh River, relates not to the great southern migrations but to the peopling of the Arctic Zone; indeed, Denbigh material has since been traced across the Hudson's Bay region to the Sarqaq area of west Greenland. The precise age of the Denbigh finds in western Alaska is still uncertain, but there seems no good reason for doubting the radiocarbon dates of up to c. 4000 B.C. already obtained. The Denbigh people were skilled at knapping materials like flint and turned out miniature burins, delicately flaked projectile-heads and side-blades for mounting in handles, and regular micro-blades, which at Trail Creek, Seward Peninsula, were found set in slotted bone projectile-heads. The burins are in every respect similar to those made by the Advanced Palaeolithic and Mesolithic peoples in Eurasia, but also by the Sub-neolithic people of the Lena Valley of north-east Siberia; and the slotted bone projectile-points extend right across northern Eurasia to western Norway. The lithic tradition of the Denbigh culture seems to have contributed to the formation of the first well-defined culture based on the Hudson's Bay region, that named after Cape Dorset on the south-west of Baffin Island. Although possessing marked characteristics of its own, notably the delicacy with which bone and ivory were worked and the art, comprising incised geometric designs and carved animal and human figurines, the emphasis on chipped stone and the presence of burins and micro-blades both point to Denbigh influence; on the other hand ground slate tools were also used and the culture shows some affinities with the early Eskimo cultures developing further to the west.

Old Bering Sea, Thule and recent Eskimo cultures

The earliest specifically Eskimo group yet recognized is the Old Bering Sea culture of Alaska, St Lawrence Island and north-east Siberia, which on the evidence of radiocarbon analysis seems to go back to the last centuries before Christ. The people were adapted to a coastal way of life and lived in semi-subterranean houses, rectangular in plan and approached by narrow passages, a type of dwelling that goes back to Upper Palaeolithic times in Siberia. Their basic implements were made of chipped stone and ground slate and they used pottery cooking vessels and lamps. In course of time regional groups seem to have developed on this basis, for instance the Punuk culture of St Lawrence Island and the Birnik culture of Point Barrow and the Arctic coast of Alaska. The last of these is of basic importance as the immediate source of the widespread Thule culture centred on Hudson's Bay, but once covering a large part of northern Canada, including Labrador, and extending to Greenland. The Thule people, who spread east from northern Alaska, evidently came into contact both with the Dorset culture, occupying the heart of their new territories, and with the Norse settlers who had reached south-west Greenland already during the tenth century. Their basic economy and the type of houses in which they lived resembled those of their forebears in Alaska and Siberia, but their technology now depended on the iron borrowed from the Norse, rather than upon stone. In some parts of Canada the Thule culture has persisted in modified form down to the present day, but elsewhere it has been replaced by that of the existing Eskimos: there is evidence for a certain backwash of culture from the central regions to northern Alaska, and on the west coast of Greenland a distinctive Inugsuk culture grew up on the Thule basis. Since the Eskimo were the first people in the New World to encounter Europeans, and since they must always have been thinly spread—today barely 40,000 of them occupy more than 9650 kilometres of coast—their survival might at first sight seem surprising until we remember that their way of life marks one of the most effective adaptations to an environment of exceptional severity.

Yahgan, Ona and Alacaluf peoples of Tierra del Fuego

At the other end of the New World in Tierra del Fuego the Yahgan and their neighbours the Ona and Alacaluf maintained down to modern times the most southerly settlements of mankind. Isolation and an adverse environment combined to preserve a way of life that seems hardly to have differed from that revealed in the middens on the Beagle Channel which began to form perhaps some ten thousand years ago. These lowly denizens of a miserable land, as they were viewed by Charles Darwin, lived on a diet of shell-fish, supplemented by fish, birds, seals, whales, otters and wild vegetable food. Their dwellings were caves, windbreaks or primitive huts and they wore little beyond a skin mantle thrown over the shoulders in cold weather. Like many early Americans they were ignorant of pottery and used coiled baskets as containers. Their chipped stone projectile-heads, both stemmed and hollow-based, recall Palaeoindian ones in many different parts of America, and their harpoons and barbed spearheads of bone recall in a general way those of many North American groups, Archaic,

Radiocarbon dates for early man in the New World

UNITED STATES OF AMERICA

Desert culture

		B.C.
Fort Rock Cave, Oregon	C 428	7103±350
Danger Cave, Utah	Tx 85	8650±200
Gypsum Cave, Nevada	C 221	8505±340
Leonard Shelter, Nevada	C 599	9249±570
Ventana Cave, Arizona	A 203	9340±500

Folsom culture

Lubbock, Texas	C 558	7933±350
Brewster, Wyoming	I 472	8425±700
Bonfire Shelter, Texas	Tx 153	8280±160
Lindenmeier, Colorado	I 141	8900±550
Blackwater Draw no. 1,	A 379–80	8300±320
near Clovis, New Mexico	A 386	8500±900

Clovis culture

Blackwater Draw no. 1,	A 490	9090±500
	A 481	9220±360
near Clovis, New Mexico	A 491	9680±400
Dent, Colorado	I 622	9250±500
	A 40b	8950±450
	A 375	8990±100
Lehner, Arizona	K 554	9220±140
	A 42	9290±190
	M 811	9340±500
Domebo, Oklahoma	SM 695	9095±647
	SI 172	9270±500

MEXICO

Infiernillo culture

| Portales Cave | M 498 | 6250±450 |
| Ojode Agua Cave | M 500 | 6590±450 |

Santa Marta Culture

| Santa Marta Cave | M 980 | 6780±400 |

Lerma culture

| Diablo Cave, Tamaulipas | M 499 | 7320±500 |
| San Bartolo, Atepehuacan | M 776 | 7720±400 |

SOUTH AMERICA

Various

Intihausi Cave, Argentina	Y 228	6020±100
	P 345	6110±100
Palli Aike Cave, Chile	C 485	6689±450
Lagoa Santa (levels VI–VII), Brazil	P 54	7770±128
Cerro dos Chivateros, Peru	UCLA 683	8480±160
Fell's Cave, Chile	W 915	8770±300

North-western and Circumpolar. Unlike the Eskimo, who were comparatively recent intruders, the Tierra del Fuegians were survivors, in a modified and possibly even degenerate form, of the early Palaeoindians who found their way right down both the American continents. The contrast they offer to the sophisticated citizens of Mexico and Peru at the time of the Spanish conquests is a testimony to the achievements of the aboriginal Americans in Mesoamerica and on the Andean highlands.

FURTHER READING

NOTE. In compiling this list of references for further reading care has been taken to cite works in English wherever possible. References are mainly confined to books and monographs, most of which have more or less comprehensive bibliographies; communications in the periodical literature are as a rule only cited when these have not yet been assimilated in larger works.

PREFACE

A valuable summary of radiocarbon dates up till 1954 is contained in the second edition of W. F. Libby's *Radiocarbon Dating*, Chicago, 1955. Successive lists of determinations were later published in *Science*, but since 1959 they have appeared in *Radiocarbon* (vols. I–IX) supplements.

Some convenient lists with useful discussions have been published from time to time and reference may be made to the following:

Brandtner, F. J. 'More on Upper Palaeolithic Archaeology', *Current Anthropology*, II (1961), 427–54.

Bucha, V. and Neustupny, E. 'Changes of the Earth's Magnetic Field and Radiocarbon Dating', *Nature*, CCXV (15 July 1967), 261–3.

Clark, J. G. D. 'Radiocarbon Dating and the spread of Farming Economy', *Antiquity* (1965), 45–8.

Ehrich, Robert W. *Chronologies in Old World Archaeology*, Chicago, 1965.

Ghosh, A., in V. N. Misra and M. S. Mate (eds.) *Indian Prehistory: 1964*. Poona, 1965. Tables, pp. 139–40.

Haynes, C. Vance. 'Carbon-14 dates and Early Man in the New World', *Proc. 6th Int. Conf. Radiocarbon and Tritium Dating*, 145–64 (table and maps). Washington State University. Pullman, 7–11 June 1965.

Movius, H. L. 'Radiocarbon dates and Upper Palaeolithic Archaeology in Central and Western Europe', *Current Anthropology*, I (1960), 355–91.

CHAPTER I

Physical environment

Butzer, K. W. *Environment and Archaeology*. Chicago, 1964.

Deevey, E. S. 'Biogeography of the Pleistocene', *Bull. Geol. Soc. Amer.* LX (1949), 1315–416.

Flint, R. F. *Glacial Geology and the Pleistocene Epoch*. 4th reprint, New York, 1953.

Godwin, H. *The History of the British Flora*. Cambridge, 1956.

Zeuner, F. E. *The Pleistocene Period, its Climate, Chronology and Faunal Successions*. London, 1959.

Human evolution

Boule, M. and Vallois, H. V. *Les Hommes Fossiles*. 3rd ed. Paris, 1946.

Campbell, B. G. *Human Evolution: an Introduction to Man's Adaptations*, London, 1966.

Clark, W. le G. *The Fossil Evidence for Human Evolution*. 2nd ed. Chicago, 1964.

The Antecedents of Man. Edinburgh, 1959.

Howell, F. C. 'The Age of the Australopithecines of Southern Africa', *Am. J. Phys. Anthrop.* XIII (1955), 635–62.

'Upper Pleistocene Men of the Southwest Asian Mousterian', *see below under* Koenigswald, pp. 635–62.

Koenigswald, G. H. R. von (ed.) *Hundert Jahre Neanderthaler*. Wenner-Gren Foundation, New York, 1958.

Oakley, K. P. 'Swanscombe Man', *Proc. Geol. Assoc.*, LXIII (1952), 271–300.

Frameworks for Dating Fossil Man. London, 1964.

Ovey, C. D. (ed.) *The Swanscombe Skull: a Survey of Research on a Pleistocene Site*. London, 1964.

Tobias, P. V. *Olduvai Gorge, Volume II: the cranium and maxillary dentition of Australopithecus (Zinjanthropus) boisei*. Cambridge, 1967.

Weidenreich, F. 'The Skull of *Sinanthropus pekinensis*'. *Palaeontologia Sinica*, no. 127, Pekin, 1943.

CHAPTERS 2 AND 3

Bader, O. N. *La caverne Kapovaïa*. Moscow, 1965.

Balout, L. *Préhistoire de l'Afrique du Nord*. Paris, 1955.

Black, D. *et al. Fossil Man in China. Mem. Geol. Surv. China*, ser. A, II, Pekin, 1933.

Boriskovskii, P. I. *Palaeolithic of the Ukraine*, Materialy Issledovaniya po Arkheologiyi S.S.S.R. no. 40. Moscow, 1953.

Breuil, H. *Four Hundred Centuries of Cave Art*. Montignac, Dordogne, 1952.

Burkitt, M. C. *South Africa's Past in Stone and Paint*. Cambridge, 1928.

Clark, J. D. *The Prehistory of Southern Africa*. London, 1959.

'Prehistory' in R. A. Lystad (ed.), *The African World: a Survey of Social Research*. London, 1965.

Cole, S. *The Prehistory of East Africa*. London, 1964.

Coles, J. M. and Higgs, E. S. *Time, Man and Stone*. London, 1968.

Coon, C. S. *Seven Caves*. London, 1957.

De Sonneville-Bordes, D. *Le Paléolithique supérieur en Périgord*. Bordeaux, 1960.

Garrod, D. A. E. and Bate, D. M. A. *The Stone Age of Mount Carmel.* Oxford, 1937.

'The Relations between South-west Asia and Europe in the Later Palaeolithic Age', *J. World History*, I (1953), 13–37.

Golomshtok, E. A. 'The Old Stone Age in European Russia.' *Trans. Am. Phil. Soc.* N.S. XXIX, 2. Philadelphia, 1938.

Grahmann, R. 'The Lower Palaeolithic Site of Markkleeberg and other contemporary localities near Leipzig.' *Trans. Am. Phil. Soc.* N.S. XLV, 509–687. Philadelphia, 1955.

Graziosi, P. *L'Arte dell'Antica Eta della Pietra.* Florence, 1956.

Hayes, C. *The Ape in our House.* London, 1952.

Higgs, E. S. 'The Climate, Environment and Industries of Stone Age Greece', *Proc. Prehist. Soc.*, 29, XXX (1964), 199–244; XXXII (1966), 1–29; XXXIII (1967), 1–29.

Klima, B. 'Übersicht über die jüngsten paläolithischen Forschungen' in Mähren's *Quartär*, IX (1957), 85–136.

Dolní Věstonice. Prague, 1963.

Köhler, W. *The Mentality of Apes.* London, 1952.

Laming, A. *Lascaux, Paintings and Engravings.* London, 1959.

Laming-Empéraire, A. *La Signification de l'art paléolithique.* Paris, 1962.

Leakey, L. S. B. *Stone Age Africa.* Oxford, 1936.

Olduvai Gorge. Cambridge, 1951.

Adam's Ancestors. 4th ed. London, 1953.

Leroi-Gourhan, A. *Préhistoire de l'art occidental.* Paris, 1965.

McBurney, C. B. M. 'Evidence for the Distribution in Space and Time of Neanderthaloids and Allied Strains in Northern Africa', in G. H. R. von Koenigswald (ed.), *Hundert Jahre Neaderthaler*, pp. 253–64. New York, 1958.

Haua Fteah and the Stone Age of the South-east Mediterranean. Cambridge, 1967.

Movius, H. L. *The Lower Palaeolithic Cultures of Southern and Eastern Asia.* Trans. Am. Phil. Soc. N.S. XXXVIII, part 4. Philadelphia, 1948.

'Palaeolithic and Mesolithic Sites in Soviet Central Asia', *Proc. Am. Phil. Soc.* XCVII (1953), 383–421.

'The Mousterian Cave of Teshik-Tash, Southeastern Uzbekistan, Central Asia', *Amer. School of Prehist. Res. Bull.* XVII (1953), 11–71.

'Palaeolithic Archaeology in Southern and Eastern Asia, exclusive of India', *J. World History*, II (1955), 257–82, 525–53.

Oakley, K. P. *Man the Tool-maker.* 4th ed. London, 1958

Obermaier, H. *Fossil Man in Spain.* Oxford, 1925.

Okladnikov, A. P. *Palaeolithic and Neolithic in the SSSR.* Materialy i Issledovaniya po Arkheologiyi S.S.S.R. no. 59. Moscow, 1957.

Pericot y García, L. *La Cueva del Parpallo.* Madrid, 1942.

Robinson, J. T. and Mason, R. J. 'Occurrence of Stone Artefacts with *Australopithecus* at Sterkfontein', *Nature*, CLXXX (1957), 521–4.

Thorpe, W. H. *Learning and Instinct in Animals*. Cambridge, 1956.

Von Lawick-Goodall, Baroness Jane. *My Friends the Wild Chimpanzees*. Nat. Geogr. Soc., Washington, 1967.

Vértes, L. *et al. Die Höhle von Istállóskö*. Acta Arch. Hung. V. Budapest, 1955.

Washburn, S. L. *Social Life of Early Man*. London, 1962.

Yerkes, R. M. *Chimpanzees. A Laboratory Colony*. New Haven, 1943.

CHAPTER 4

Bostianci, Enver Y. 'Researches on the Mediterranean Coast of Anatolia...', *Anatolia*, IV (1959), 129–78.

Braidwood, R. V. and Howe, B. *Prehistoric Investigations in Iraqi Kurdistan*. Chicago, 1960.

Clark, J. G. D. *The Mesolithic Settlement of Northern Europe*. Cambridge, 1935.

Clark, J. G. D. *et al. Excavations at Star Carr*. Cambridge, 1954.

Coon, Carleton, S. *Cave Explorations in Iran, 1949*. Philadelphia, 1951.

Flannery, Kent V. 'The Ecology of Early Food Production in Mesopotamia', *Science*, CXLVII (1965), 1247–56.

Garrod, Dorothy A. E. 'The Natufian Culture: the Life and Economy of a Mesolithic People in the Near East', *Proc. Brit. Acad.* XLIII (1957), 211–27.

Garrod, D. A. E. and Bate, D. M. *The Stone Age of Mount Carmel*, vol. I. Oxford, 1937.

Garrod, D. A. E. and Clark, J. G. D. *Primitive Man in Egypt, Western Asia and Europe*. Cambridge, 1965.

Harlan, Jack R. and Zohary, Daniel. 'Distribution of Wild Wheats and Barley', *Science*, CLIII (1966), 1074–8.

Hole, Frank and Flannery, Kent V. 'The Prehistory of Southwestern Iran: a Preliminary Report', *Proc. Prehist. Soc.* XXXIII (1967), 147–206.

Kenyon, Kathleen M. *Digging up Jericho*. London, 1957.

Kirkbride, Diana. 'Five seasons at the Pre-pottery Neolithic Village of Beidha in Jordan', *Palestine Exploration Quarterly*, XCVIII (1966), 8–66.

Mellaart, James. *Earliest Civilizations of the Near East*. London, 1966.

Neuville, R. 'Le Paléolithique et le Mésolithique du Désert de Judée', *Arch. de l'Inst. Pal. Hum.*, no. 24. Paris, 1951.

Perrot, J. 'Le Mésolithique de Palestine...', *Antiquity and Survival*, II (1957), 90–110.

Renfrew, C., Dixon, J. E. and Cann, J. R. 'Obsidian and Early Cultural Contact in the Near East', *Proc. Prehist. Soc.* XXXII (1966), 30–72.

FURTHER READING

Solecki, Ralph S. 'Prehistory in Shanidar Valley, Northern Iraq', *Science*, (1963), 179–93.
Stekelis, M. and Yizraely, Tamar. 'Excavations at Nahal Oren. Preliminary Report', *Israel Explor. J.* XIII (1963), 1–12.

CHAPTER 5

Anatolia

Bittel, K. *Grundzüge zur Vorgeschichte Kleinasiens.* 2nd ed. Tübingen, 1950.
Blegen, C. W. *Troy.* 4 vols. Princeton, 1950. 1951, 1953, 1958.
French, D. W. 'Excavations at Can Hasan', *Anatolian Studies*, XII (1962), 27–40; XIII, 29–42; XIV, 125–34; XV, 87–94.
Garstang, J. *Prehistoric Mersin.* Oxford, 1953.
Gurney, O. R. *The Hittites.* London, 1952.
Koşay, H. Z. *Les Fouilles d'Alaca Hüyük. Rapport préliminaire 1937–9.* Ankara, 1951.
Lloyd, Seton. *Early Highland Peoples of Anatolia.* London, 1967.
Lloyd, Seton and Mellaart, J. *Beycesultan.* 2 vols. London, 1962–4.
Mellaart, J. 'Excavations at Hacilar', *Anatolian Studies*, VIII (1958), 127–56; IX, 51–66; X, 83–104; XI, 39–76.
  The Chalcolithic and Early Bronze Ages in the Near East and Anatolia. Beist, 1966.
  Çatal Hüyük. A Neolithic Town in Anatolia. London, 1967.
Mellink, M. J. 'Anatolia: Old and New Perspectives', *Proc. Am. Phil. Soc.* CX (1966), 110–29.
Ozguc, T. *Kültepe-Kanis.* Ankara, 1959.

Iran and Turkmenia

Contenau, G. and Ghirshman, R. *Fouilles de Tépé Giyan.* Paris, 1935.
Egami, N. and Masuda, S. *The Excavations at Tall-i-Bakun, 1956.* Tokyo 1962.
Ghirshman, R. *Fouilles de Sialk.* 2 vols. Paris, 1938–9.
Hole, F. and Flannery, K. 'The Prehistory of Southwestern Iran: A Preliminary Report', *Proc. Prehist. Soc.* XXXIII (1967), 147–206.
McCown, D. *The Comparative Stratigraphy of Early Iran.* Chicago, 1942.
Masson, V. M. 'The First Farmers in Turkmenia', *Antiquity*, XXXV (1961), 203–13.
Porada, Edith. *Ancient Iran. The Art of Pre-Islamic Times.* London, 1965.
Pumpelly, R. *Explorations in Turkestan, Expedition of 1904.* Washington, 1908.
Schmidt, Erich F. *Excavation at Tepe Hissar, Damghan, 1931–1933.* Pennsylvania, 1937.

Iraq

Braidwood, R. J. and L. 'The Earliest Village Communities of Southwestern Asia', *J. World History*, II (1953), 278–310.

Childe, V. G. *New Light on the Most Ancient East*. 4th ed. London, 1952.

Frankfort, H. *The Birth of Civilization in the Near East*. London, 1951.
Art and Architecture of the Ancient Orient. London, 1958.

Hall, H. R. and Woolley, L. *Ur Excavations I: al'Ubaid*. London, 1927.

Kramer, S. N. *The Sumerians*. Chicago, 1963.

Lloyd, S., Safer, F. and Braidwood, R. J. 'Tell Hassuna', *J. Near Eastern Studies*, IV (1945), 255–89.

Mallowan, M. E. L. and Rose, J. C. *Prehistoric Assyria: The Excavations at Tell Arpachiyah*. Oxford, 1935.

Mallowan, M. E. L. *Twenty-five years of Mesopotamian Discovery*. 2nd ed. London, 1959.

Perkins, A. L. *The Comparative Archaeology of Early Mesopotamia*. Chicago, 1949.

Schmidt, H. *Tell Halaf*, vol. I. Berlin, 1943.

Speiser, E. A. *Excavations at Tepe Gawra*, vol. I. Philadelphia, 1935.

Tobler, A. J. *Excavations at Tepe Gawra*, vol. II. Philadelphia, 1950.

Woolley, L. *Ur Excavations II: The Royal Cemetery*. London, 1934.
'The Prehistoric Pottery of Carchemish', *Iraq*, I (1934), 146–62.

Levant

Albright, W. F. *The Archaeology of Palestine*. 5th ed. London, 1960.

Anati, E. *Palestine before the Hebrews*. London, 1963.

Harden, Donald. *The Phoenicians*. London, 1962.

Kenyon, K. M. *Archaeology in the Holy Land*. London, 1960.
Amorites and Canaanites. London, 1965.

Schaeffer, C. F. A. *Ugaritica*, vols. I–III. Paris, 1939, 1949, 1956.

Stubbings, F. H. *Mycenaean pottery from the Levant*. Cambridge, 1951.

CHAPTERS 6 AND 7

Arnal, J. and Burnez, C. 'Die Struktur des französischen Neolithikums...', *Ber. Röm.-Germ. Komm.* (1956–7), 1–90.

Atkinson, R. J. C. *Stonehenge*. London, 1956.

Bailloud, G. and Mieg de Boofzheim, P. *Les Civilizations néolithiques de la France*. Paris, 1955.

Berciu, D. *Contributee la Problemele Neoliticului in Rominia in Lumina Noilor Cercetari*. Bucharest, 1961.

Bloch, R. *The Etruscans. Ancient Peoples and Places*. London, 1958.

Bohm, J. and de Laet, S. J. (eds.) *L'Europe à la fin de l'âge de la pierre*. Prague, 1961.

Brjussov, A. J. *Geschichte der neolithischen Stämme im europäischen Teil der USSR.* Berlin, 1952.

Brøndsted, J. *Danmarks Oldtid,* vols. I–III. Copenhagen, 1957–9.

Buttler, W. *Der Donauländische und der westische Kulturkreis der jüngeren Steinzeit.* Berlin, 1938.

Childe, V. G. 'The Final Bronze Age in the Near East and in Temperate Europe', *Proc. Prehist. Soc.* XIV (1948), 177–95.
The Dawn of European Civilization. 6th ed. London, 1957.

Clark, J. G. D. *Prehistoric Europe: the Economic Basis.* London, 1952.

Daniel, G. E. *The Megalith Builders of Western Europe.* London, 1958.

Daniel, Glyn and Evans, J. D. *The Western Mediterranean.* Camb. Anc. Hist. vols. I–II, fasc. 57. Rev. ed. Cambridge, 1967.

Déchelette, J. *Manuel d'archéologie préhistorique,* vols. I–III. Paris, 1924–7.

Dehn, W. 'Die Heuneburg beim Talhof...', *Fundber. aus Schwaben,* XIV (1957), 78–99. Stuttgart.

Dunbabin, T. J. *The Western Greeks.* Oxford, 1948.

Eggers, H. J. *Der Römische Import im Freien Germanien.* Berlin, 1951.

Evans, Sir A. *The Palace of Minos,* vols. I–IV. London, 1921–8.

Evans, J. D. 'Excavations in the Neolithic Settlement of Knossos, 1957–60: Part I', *Ann. Brit. School Arch. Athens,* LIX (1964), 132–240.

Filip, J. *Keltové ve Středni Europě.* Prague, 1957.

Fox, Sir Cyril. *Pattern and Purpose. A Survey of Early Celtic Art in Britain.* Cardiff, 1958.

Gaul, J. H. *The Neolithic Period in Bulgaria.* Am. School of Prehist. Res. Bull. XVI. Harvard, 1948.

Gimbutas, M. *The Prehistory of Eastern Europe.* Am. School of Prehist. Res. Bull. XX. Harvard, 1956.
Bronze Age Cultures in Central and Eastern Europe. The Hague, 1965.

Gjessing, G. *Norge Steinalder.* Oslo, 1945.

Guyan, W. U. (ed.) *Das Pfahlbauproblem.* Basel, 1955.

Hawkes, C. F. C. 'From Bronze Age to Iron Age: Middle Europe, Italy and the North and West', *Proc. Prehist. Soc.* XIV (1948), 196–218.

Hencken, H. *The Archaeology of Cornwall and Scilly,* chap. V. London, 1932.
Indo-European Languages and Archaeology. Am. Anthrop. Mem. (1955).
Tarquinia, Villanovans and Early Etruscans, vols. I, 2. Cambridge, Mass. 1968.

Heurtley, W. A. *Prehistoric Macedonia.* Cambridge, 1939.

Holmqvist, W. *Germanic Art.* Stockholm, 1955.

Hutchinson, R. W. *Prehistoric Crete.* London, 1962.

Jacobsthal, P. *Early Celtic Art.* Oxford, 1944.

Jazdzewski, K. *Poland. Ancient Peoples and Places.* London, 1965.

Joffroy, R. *Le Trésor de Vix.* Paris, 1954.

Karo, G. *Die Schachtgräber von Mykenai.* Munich, 1930.

Keiller, A. *Windmill Hill and Avebury*. Oxford, 1965.

Kimmig, W. 'Zur Urnenfelderkultur in Südwesteuropa', *Festschrift für Peter Goesseler*, pp. 41–107. Stuttgart, 1954.

Klindt-Jensen, Ole. *Bornholm i Folkevandringstiden*. Copenhagen, 1957.

Milojčić, V. *Chronologie der jüngeren Steinzeit Mittel- und Südosteuropas*. Berlin, 1949.

Minns, E. H. *Scythians and Greeks*. Cambridge, 1913.

The Art of the Northern Nomads. British Academy, London, 1942.

Mongait, A. *Archaeology in the U.S.S.R.* Moscow, 1959.

Muluquer de Motes, J. 'Pueblas Celtas', *Historia de España*, I, part 3, 5–194. Madrid, 1954.

Navarro, J. M. de. *A Survey of Research on an Early Phase of Celtic Culture*. British Academy, London, 1936.

Nilsson, M. P. *The Minoan–Mycenaean Religion and its Survival in Greek Religion*. 2nd ed. Lund, 1950.

Pendlebury, J. D. S. *The Archaeology of Crete*. London, 1939.

Pericot García, L. *La España primitiva*. Barcelona, 1950.

Piggott, S. *The Neolithic Cultures of the British Isles*. Cambridge, 1954.

Ancient Europe. Edinburgh, 1965.

Pittioni, R. and Preuschen, E. *Untersuchungen im Bergbaugebiete Kelchalpe bei Kitzbühel, Tirol*. Vienna, 1937 and 1949.

Urgeschichte des Österreichischen Raumes. Vienna, 1954.

Powell, T. G. E. *The Celts. Ancient Peoples and Places*. London, 1958.

Previté-Orton, C. W. *The Shorter Cambridge Medieval History*. Cambridge, 1952.

Rice, T. T. *The Scythians. Ancient Peoples and Places*. London, 1957.

Rivet, A. F. L. (ed.) *The Iron Age in Northern Britain*. Edinburgh, 1966.

Rostovtzeff, M. *Iranians and Greeks in South Russia*. Oxford, 1922.

Sandars, N. K. *Prehistoric Art in Europe*. London, 1968.

Shetelig, H., Falk, H. and Gordon, E. V. *Scandinavian Archaeology*. Oxford, 1937.

Stone, J. F. S. and Thomas, L. C. 'The Use and Distribution of Faience in the Ancient East and Prehistoric Europe', *Proc. Prehist. Soc.* XXII (1956), 37–84.

Taylour, Lord W. *Mycenaean Pottery in Italy and Adjacent Areas*. Cambridge, 1958.

The Mycenaeans. Ancient Peoples and Places. London, 1964.

Theocharis, D. P. *The Dawn of Thessalian Prehistory*. Volos, 1967.

Ventris, M. and Chadwick, J. *Documents in Mycenaean Greek*. Cambridge, 1956.

Vulpe, R., *Izvoare. Săpăturile din 1936–48*. Bucharest, 1957.

Wace, A. J. B. and Thompson, M. S. *Prehistoric Thessaly*. Cambridge, 1912.

Wace, A. J. B. *Mycenae. An Archaeological History and Guide*. Princeton, 1949.

Wace, A. J. B. and Stubbings, Frank H. *A Companion to Homer*. London, 1962.

Weinberg, S. S. *The Stone Age in the Aegean*. Camb. Anc. Hist. vols. I–II, fasc. 36. Rev. ed. Cambridge, 1965.

CHAPTER 8

Arkell, A. J. *Early Khartoum*. Oxford, 1949.
Shaheinab. Oxford, 1953.

Baumgärtel, E. *The Cultures of Prehistoric Egypt*. Oxford, 1947.

Bishop, Walter W. and Clark, J. Desmond. *Background to Evolution: N. Africa*. Chicago, 1967.

Brunton, G. and Caton-Thompson, G. *The Badarian Civilization*. London, 1928.

Caton-Thompson, G. *The Zimbabwe Culture*. Oxford, 1931.
The Desert Fayum. London, 1935.

Clark, J. D. *The Prehistory of Southern Africa*. London, 1959.
'Prehistory'; in R. R. Lystad (ed.) *The African World: a Survey of Social Research*. London, 1965.

Cole, S. *The Prehistory of East Africa*. London, 1964.

Davies, O. *West Africa before the Europeans*. London, 1967.

Delacroix, R. and Vaufrey, R. 'Le Toumbien de Guinée française', *L'Anthropologie*, XLIX (1939–40), 265–312.

Edwards, I. E. S. *The Pyramids of Egypt*. London, 1947.

Emery, W. B. *Archaic Egypt*. London, 1961.

Fagan, B. M. *Iron Age Cultures in Zambia*, vol. I. London, 1967.

Fagg, B. 'The Nok terracottas in West African art-history', *Actes du 4ᵉ Congr. Pan-African*, II, 445–50. Tervuren, 1959.

Glanville, S. R. K. (ed.) *The Legacy of Egypt*. London, 1947.

Hugo, H. J. (ed.) *Missions Berliet Ténéré-Tchad*. Paris, 1962.

Junker, H. 'Vorläufige Berichte über die Gräbung...auf der neolithischen Siedlung von Merimde-Benisalâme', *Anz. d. Akad. d. Wiss. Wien, phil.-hist. kl.* 1929, 1930, 1932 and 1940.

Leakey, M. D. and L. S. B. 'Report on the excavations at Hyrax Hill, Nakuru, Kenya Colony', *Trans. Roy. Soc. S. Afr.*, XXX (1945), 271–409.
Excavations at the Njoro River Cave. Oxford, 1950.

Lowe, C. van Riet. *The Distribution of Prehistoric Rock Engravings and Paintings in South Africa*. Pretoria, 1956.

Oliver, R. and Fage, J. D. *A Short History of Africa*. London, 1962.

Petrie, W. M. F. *The Royal Tombs of the First Dynasty*, parts I and II. London, 1900–1.

Quibell, J. E. and Green, F. W. *Hierakonpolis*, vols. I, II. London, 1900–2.

Robinson, K. R., Summers, R. and Whitty, A. *Zimbabwe Excavations 1958*)
  Nat. Mus. S. Rhodesia, Occ. Papers, vol. III, no. 23 A. Causeway, 1961.
Shaw, C. T. 'Excavations at Bosumpra Cave, Abetifi', *Proc. Prehist. Soc.* x
  (1944), 1–67.
Vaufrey, R. *L'Art rupestre nord-africain.* Paris, 1939.

CHAPTER 9

India

Alchin, F. R. *Piklihāl Excavations.* Hyderabad, 1960.
  Neolithic Cattle-keepers of South India. Cambridge, 1963.
Casal, J. M. *Fouilles d'Amri.* 2 vols. Paris 1964.
Dales, G. F. 'Recent Trends in the Pre- and Protohistoric Archaeology of
  South Asia', *Proc. Am. Phil. Soc.* CX, 2 (1966), 130–9.
'A Suggested Chronology for Afghanistan, Baluchstan and the Indus Valley',
  in Robert W. Erich (ed.), *Chronologies in Old World Archaeology*,
  pp. 257–77. Chicago, 1965.
Dani, A. H. *Prehistory and Protohistory of Eastern India.* Calcutta, 1960.
Fairservice, W. A. 'Excavations in the Quetta Valley, West Pakistan',
  Anthrop. Papers Am. Mus. of Nat. Hist. XLV, part 2. New York, 1956.
Ghosh, A. 'The Indus Civilization: its origins, authors, extent and chron-
  ology', in V. B. Misra and M. S. Mate (eds.) *Indian Prehistory: 1964*
  pp. 113–56. Poona, 1965.
Lal, B. B. 'Excavations at Hastinapura and Other Explorations in the Upper
  Ganga and Sutlej Basins, 1950–2', *Ancient India*, nos. 10–11 (1954–5),
  11–151.
Mackay, E. J. H. *Further Excavations at Mohenjo-daro.* Delhi, 1958.
Marshall, Sir John *et al. Mohenjo-daro and the Indus Civilization.* London,
  1931.
Misra, V. N. and Mate, M. S. (eds.) *Indian Prehistory: 1964.* Poona, 1965.
Piggott, Stuart. *Prehistoric India.* London, 1950.
Rao, S. R. 'Excavations at Rangpur and Other Explorations in Huzerat'
  Ancient India, 18–19 (1962–3), 5–207.
Sankalia, H. D., Deo, S. B., Ansari, Z. D., and Ehrhardt, S. *From History
  to Prehistory at Nevasa (1954–56).* Poona, 1960.
Sankalia, H. D., Subbarao, B. and Deo, S. B. *The Excavations at Maheshwar
  and Navdatoli 1952–3.* Poona, 1960.
Sankalia, H. D. *Prehistory and Protohistory in India and Pakistan.* Bombay,
  1963.
Subbarao, B. *The Personality of India.* 2nd ed. Baroda, 1958.
Vats, M. S. *Excavations at Harappa.* Delhi, 1940.
Wheeler, Sir R. E. M. *Ancient India and Pakistan*, London, 1959.
  The Indus Civilization. 3rd ed. Cambridge, 1968.

CHAPTER 10

China

Andersson, J. G. 'An Early Chinese Culture', *Bull. Geol. Soc. China*, no. 5. Peking, 1923.

Children of the Yellow Earth. London, 1934.

'Researches into the Prehistory of the Chinese', *Bull. Museum Far Eastern Antiquities*, Stockholm, no. 15 (1943).

Arne, T. J. 'Painted Stone Age Pottery from the Province of Honan, China', *Palaeontologia Sinica*, ser. D, vol. 1, fasc. 2. Peking, 1925.

Bishop, C. W. 'The Neolithic Age in Northern China', *Antiquity* (1933), pp. 389–404.

Bylin-Althin, M. 'The Sites of Chi' Chia P'ing and Lo Han T'ang in Kansu', *Bull. Museum Far Eastern Antiquities*, Stockholm, no. 18 (1946), 383–498.

Chang, Kwang-Chih, *The Archaeology of Ancient China*. New Haven, 1963.

Chêng Tê-K'un. *Archaeological Studies in Szechwan*. Cambridge, 1957.

'The Origin and Development of Shang Culture', *Asia Major*, VI (1957), 80–98.

Archaeology in China, vol. I, *Prehistoric China*. Cambridge, 1958.

New Light on Prehistoric China. Cambridge, 1966.

Childe, V. G. 'The Socketed Celt in Upper Eurasia', *Ann. Rep. Inst. Arch. Lond. Univ. 1953*, II, 25.

Creel, H. G. *The Birth of China*. London, 1936.

Finn, D. J. *Archaeological Finds on Lamma Island near Hong Kong*. Hong Kong, 1958.

Karlgren, B. 'Some Weapons and Tools of the Yin Dynasty', *Bull. Museum Far Eastern Antiquities*, Stockholm, no. 17 (1945), 101–45.

Li Chi *et al.* 'Ch'êng-tzû-yai, A report of Excavations of the Proto-historic Site at Ch'êng-tzû-yai, Li-ch'eng Hsien, Shantung', *Archaeologica Sinica*, no. 1. Nanking, 1934.

Loehr, Max. 'Zur Ur- und Vorgeschichte Chinas', *Saelum*, III (1952), 15–55.

Maglioni, R. 'Archaeology in South China', *J. East Asiatic Studies*, II (1952), 1–20.

Maringer, J. *Contribution to the Prehistory of Mongolia*. Stockholm, 1950.

Needham, J. *Science and Civilization in China*, vol. I, *Introductory Orientations*. Cambridge, 1954.

Nelson, N. C. 'The Dune Dwellers of the Gobi', *Natural History*, XXVI (1926), 246–51.

Pei Wên-Chung, 'On a Mesolithic (?) Industry in the Caves of Kwangsi', *Bull. Geol. Soc. China*, no. 14 (1935), 383–412.

Teilhard de Chardin, P. and Pei Wên-Chung. *Le Néolithique de la Chine*. Peking, 1944.

Tolstoy, P. 'Some Amerasian Pottery Traits in North Asian Prehistory', *Amer. Antiquity*, XIX (1953–4), 25–39.

Torii, R. and K. 'Etudes Archéologiques et Ethnologiques. Populations Primitives de la Mongolie Orientale', *J. Coll. Sci. Imp. Univ. Tokyo*, XXXV, art. 4 (1914), 1–100.

Watson, W. *China. Ancient Peoples and Places*. London, 1959.

Willetts, W. *Foundations of Chinese Art*. London, 1965.

Wu, G. D. *Prehistoric Pottery in China*. London, 1938.

South-east Asia, Indonesia and the Philippines

Beyer, H. O. 'Outline Review of Philippine Archaeology...', *Philippine J. Sci.* LXXVII (1947), 205–374.

Dunn, F. L. 'Excavations at Gua Kechil, Pahang', *J. Malaysian Branch Roy. Asiatic Soc.* XXXVII, part 2 (1964), 87–124.

Goloubew, V. 'L'âge du Bronze au Tonkin et dans le Nord-Annam', *Bull. de l'Ecol. Franç. d'Extrême Orient*, XXIX, 1–46.

Harrisson, T. 'The Great Cave of Niah', *Man* (1957), no. 211.

Heekeren, M. R. van. *The Stone Age of Indonesia*. The Hague, 1956.
The Bronze–Iron Age of Indonesia. The Hague, 1958.

Heine-Geldern, R. von. 'Prehistoric Research in the Netherlands Indies', in P. Honig and F. Vendoon (eds.) *Science and Scientists in the Netherlands Indies*, pp. 129–67. New York, 1945.

Mansuy, H. 'Contribution à l'étude de la préhistoire de l'Indochine. IV. Stations préhistoriques dans les carènes du massif calcaire de Bac-Son (Tonkin)', *Mém. Serv. Géologique de l'Indochine*, XI, no. 2 Hanoi, 1924.

Mansuy, H. and Colani, M. 'VIII. Néolithique inférieure (Bacsonien) et Néolithique supérieure dans le Haut-Tonkin', *op. cit.* XII, no. 2. Hanoi, 1925.

Sieveking, G. de G. 'Excavations at Gua Cha, Kelantan, 1954, Part I', *Federation Museums J.* (Malaya), I–II (1954–5), 75–138.

Solheim, W. G. 'Philippine Archaeology', *Archaeology* (1953), pp. 154–8.
'Pottery and the Malayo-Polynesians' *Current Anthropology* (December 1964), pp. 360 and 376–84.

Tweedie, M. W. F. 'The Stone Age in Malaya', *J. Malayan Branch Roy. Asiatic Soc.* XXVI, part 2 (1953), 1–90.
Prehistoric Malaya. Singapore, 1955.

Verneau, R. 'Les récentes découvertes préhistoriques en Indochine', *L'Anthropologie*, XXXV (1925), 46–62.

Japan

Befu, H. and Chard, C. S. 'Preceramic Cultures in Japan', *Amer. Anthropologist*, LXII (1960), 815–49.

Groot, G. J. *The Prehistory of Japan*, New York, 1951.

Ikawa, F. 'The Continuity of Non-Ceramic to Ceramic Cultures in Japan', *Arctic Anthropology*, II, 2 (1964), 95–119.

Kidder, J. E. *Japan. Ancient Peoples and Places*. London, 1959.

Maringer, J. 'A Core and Flake Industry of Palaeolithic Type from Central Japan', *Artibus Asiae*, XIX, part 2 (1956), 111–25.

'Some Stone Tools of Early Hoabinhian Type from Central Japan', *Man* (1957), no. 1.

Sugihara, S. *The Stone Age Remains Found at Iwajuku, Gumma Pref., Japan*. Tokyo, 1956.

North-East Asia

Chard, C. S. 'An Outline of the Prehistory of Siberia', *Southwestern J. of Anthropology*, XIV (1958), 1–33.

CHAPTER II

Australia and Tasmania

Balfour, H. 'The Status of the Tasmanians among the Stone-age Peoples', *Proc. Prehist. Soc. East Anglia*, V (1925), 1–15.

Basedow, H. *The Australian Aboriginal*. Adelaide, 1925.

Bulmer, S. and R. 'The Prehistory of the Australian New Guinea Highlands', *Amer. Anthropologist (Special Publ. New Guinea)* (1964), 39–76.

Campbell, T. D. and Noone, H. V. V. 'South Australian Microlithic Stone Implements', *Rec. S. Australian Mus.* VII (1943), 281–307.

Chappell, J. 'Stone Axe Factories in the Highlands of East New Guinea', *Proc. Prehist. Soc.* XXXII (1966), 96–121.

Davidson, D. S. *Aboriginal Australian and Tasmanian Rock Carvings and Paintings*. Mem. Am. Phil. Soc. V (1936).

Gill, E. D. 'Geological Evidence in Western Victoria Relative to the Antiquity of the Australian Aborigines', *Mem. Nat. Mus.* (Melbourne), XVII (1953), 25–92.

Hale, H. M. and Tindale, N. B. 'Notes on Some Human Remains in the Lower Murray Valley, South Australia', *Rec. S. Australian Mus.* IV (1930), 145–218.

Howells, W. H. 'Anthropometry of the Natives of Arnhem Land and the Australian Race Problem', *Papers Peabody Mus. Arch. and Ethn. Harvard Univ.* XVI (1937), 1–97.

McBryde, Isabel. 'Radiocarbon Dates for Northern New South Wales', *Antiquity* (1966), pp. 285–92.

McCarthy, F. D. 'The Lapstone Creek Excavation', *Rec. Australian Mus.* XXII (1948), 1–34.

'Stone Implements from Tandandjal Cave—An Appendix', *Oceania*, XXI (1951), 205–13.

'The Archaeology of the Capertee Valley, New South Wales', *Rec. Australian Mus.* (Sydney), XXVI (1964), 197–246.

Australian Aboriginal Stone Implements. Sydney, 1967.

Macintosh, N. W. G. 'Archaeology of Tandandjal Cave, South-west Arnhem Land', *Oceania*, XXI (1951), 178–204.

Meggitt, M. *Desert People.* Sydney, 1962.

Mitchell, S. R. *Stone-Age Craftsmen. Stone Tools and Camping-Places of the Australian Aborigines.* Melbourne, 1949.

Mountford, C. P. *Arnhem Land, Art, Myth and Symbolism.* Melbourne, 1956.

Mulvaney, D. J. 'The Stone Age of Australia', *Proc. Prehist. Soc.* XXVII (1961), 56–107.

Mulvaney, D. J. and Joyce, E. B. 'Archaeological and Geomorphological Investigations on Mt Moffatt Station, Queensland, Australia', *Proc. Prehist. Soc.* XXXI (1965), 147–212.

Noone, H. V. V. 'Some Aboriginal Stone Implements of Western Australia', *Rec. S. Australian Mus.* VII (1943), 271–80.

Pulleine, R. H. 'The Tasmanians and Their Stone Culture', *Rep. 19th Meeting Australian Assn. Adv. Science, Hobart (1929)*, pp. 294–322.

Roth, H. L. *The Aborigines of Tasmania.* London, 1890.

Spencer, B. and Gillen, F. J. *The Native Tribes of Central Australia.* London, 1899.

Thomson, D. F. *Economic Structure and the Ceremonial Exchange Cycle in Arnhem Land.* Melbourne, 1949.

'Some Wood and Stone Implements of the Bindibu Tribe of Central Western Australia', *Proc. Prehist. Soc.* XXX (1964), 400–22.

Tindale, N. B. 'Culture Succession in South Eastern Australia from Late Pleistocene to the Present', *Rec. S. Australian Mus.* XIII (1957).

The Pacific

Duff, R. *The Moa-hunter Period of Maori Culture.* Wellington, N.Z., 1956.

Freeman, J. D. and Geddes, W. R. (eds.) *Anthropology in the South Seas.* New Plymouth, N.Z., 1959.

Gifford, E. W. and Shutler, D. 'Archaeological Excavations in New Caledonia', *Univ. of California Anthrop. Records*, XVIII, 1 (1956).

Golson, J. 'Dating New Zealand's Prehistory', *J. Polynesia Soc.* LXIV (1955), 113–36.

Golson, J. and Gathercole, P. 'New Zealand Archaeology', *Antiquity* (1962), pp. 168–74 and 271–8.

Green, R. C. *A Review of the Prehistoric Sequence in the Auckland Province.* Auckland Archaeological Society, no. 1. 1963.

Groube, L. M. *Settlement Patterns in New Zealand Prehistory.* Anthropology Department, Otago Univ. no. 1, 1965.

Heyerdahl, T. and Skjölsvold, A. *Archaeological Evidence of Pre-Spanish Visits to the Galapagos Islands.* Mem. Soc. Am. Arch. no. 12 (1956).

Métraux, A. *Easter Island. A Stone-age Civilization of the Pacific.* London, 1957.

Oliver, Douglas I. *The Pacific Islands.* Harvard, 1951.

Sauer, C. O. 'Agricultural Origins and Dispersals', *Am. Geogr. Soc.* 1952.

Sharp, A. *Ancient Voyages in the Pacific.* London, 1957.

Solheim, W. G. 'Oceanian Pottery Manufacture', *J. East Asiatic Studies*, I, (1951), 1–39

Spoehr, A. 'Marianas Prehistory. Archaeological Survey and Excavations on Saipan, Tinian and Rota', *Fieldiana: Anthropology*, XLVIII (1957), 1–187.

Suggs, R. C. *The Island Civilization of Polynesia.* New York, 1960. *The Archaeology of Nuku Hiva, Marquesas Islands, French Polynesia.* New York, 1961.

Bird, J. B. *Preceramic Cultures in Chicama and Viru*, Mem. Soc. Am. Arch. no. 4 (1948), 21–8.

'Antiquity and Migrations of the Early Inhabitants of Patagonia', *Geogr. Rev.* XXVIII (1938), 250–75.

Bushnell, G. H. S. *Peru. Ancient Peoples and Places.* 2nd ed. London, 1963. *The First Americans.* London, 1968.

Coe, William R. 'Tikal', *Expedition*, VIII, no. 1 (1965), 1–56. Univ. of Pennsylvania.

Drucker, P., Heizer R. F. and Squier, R. J. *Excavations at La Venta Tabasco, 1955.* Bur. Am. Ethn. Bull. 170. Washington, 1959.

Giddings, J. Louis. 'A Flint Site in Northernmost Manitoba', *Amer. Antiquity*, XXI (1951), 255–68. *Ancient Men of the Arctic.* London, 1967.

Green, F. E. 'The Clovis Blades: an important addition to the Llano Complex', *Amer. Antiquity*, XXIX (1963), 145–65.

Griffin, J. B. *Archaeology of Eastern United States.* Chicago, 1952. *Handbook of South American Indians.* Bur. Am. Ethn. Bull. 143. Washington, 1946.

Haynes, C. Vance. 'Fluted Projectile Points: their age and dispersion', *Science* CXLV (1964), 1408–13.

Jennings, J. D. *Danger Cave.* Utah, 1957.

Krieger, A. D. 'The Earliest Cultures in the Western United States', *Amer. Antiquity*, XXVIII (1962), 138–43.

Kroeber, A. L. *Cultural and Natural Areas of Native North America.* Berkeley, 1939.

Lothrop, S. K. *The Indians of Tierra del Fuego.* New York, 1928.

MacNeish, R. S. 'Preliminary Archaeological Investigations in the Sierra de Tamaulipas, Mexico', *Trans. Am. Phil. Soc.* XLVIII, part 6 (1958).

Martin, P. S., Quimby, G. L. and Collier, D. *Indians before Columbus.* Chicago, 1946.

Mathiassen, T. *Archaeology of the Central Eskimos.* Copenhagen, 1927.

Miles, S. W. 'A Revaluation of the Old Copper Industry', *Amer. Antiquity*, XVI (1951), 240–7.

Morley, S. G. *The Ancient Maya.* Stanford, 1946.

Rex Gonzalez, A. 'Antiguo horizonte precerámico en las Sierras Centrales de la Argentina', *Runa Arch. para las Ciencias del Hombre*, V, 110–33. Buenos Aires, 1952.

Thompson, J. E. S. *The Rise and Fall of Maya Civilization.* Oklahoma, 1954.

Vaillant, G. C. *The Aztecs of Mexico.* London, 1951.

Willey, G. R. *An Introduction to American Archaeology*, vol. I, *North and Middle America.* New Jersey, 1966.

Wormington, H. M. *Ancient Man in North America.* Denver, 1957.

Wormington, H. M. and Forbis, Richard G. *An Introduction to the Archaeology of Alberta, Canada*, Denver, 1965.

INDEX